# CANNABIS CRIMINOLOGY

*Cannabis Criminology* explores the prohibition, decriminalization, and liberalization of cannabis policy through the lens of criminological and sociological theory, essential concepts, and cannabis research. It does so by focusing on five thematic areas: law, society, and social control; police and policing; race, ethnicity, and criminalization; the economics of cannabis; and cannabis use and crime. It is the first book on cannabis since President Joe Biden signed an executive order in 2022 to pardon citizens and lawful permanent residents convicted of simple cannabis possession under federal law and DC statute. Cannabis is now legal in some form in 37 US states. To understand the reform of cannabis policy and the challenges to come, we first need to understand the connections between cannabis and criminology.

The book links key areas in past and contemporary cannabis research to criminological and sociological theories, including key concepts, emergent concerns, and new directions. Based on an up-to-date review of this growing area of research, the book outlines a research program based on five essential thematic areas. Introducing cannabis as a critical case study in moral-legal renegotiation, it outlines how cannabis prohibition has influenced cannabis around the world. Five discrete chapters focus on thematic areas, including criminological and sociological theories, define essential concepts, and provide research focused on law, society, and social control (Chapter 2), police and policing cannabis (Chapter 3), race, ethnicity, and criminalization (Chapter 4), the economics of cannabis (Chapter 5), and cannabis and crime (Chapter 6). The book concludes by presenting new ways to engage prohibitionist thinking, challenging myths, embracing social media, and developing a duty of care to guide future cannabis researchers and explicitly involve people who use cannabis.

*Cannabis Criminology* will be of interest to a variety of readers, including students and scholars from a range of backgrounds studying drug use, drug policy, cannabis legalization, and other drug-related issues. It will also appeal to policymakers who want to know more about cannabis legalization and drug prohibition, those working in the criminal justice system, and social work professionals. Due to its accessible style, people involved in the cannabis industry as well as cannabis users may also find the book interesting.

**Johannes Wheeldon** has more than 20 years of experience in criminal justice, including teaching in prisons; working with those deemed at high risk to reoffend; and designing, conducting, and managing justice reform projects worldwide. He has worked with the American Bar Association, the Canadian International Development Agency, the Open Society Foundations, and the World Bank. Wheeldon has published 6 books and more than 30 peer-reviewed papers on criminal justice, restorative justice, organizational change, and evaluation. He is an adjunct professor at Acadia University. In 2022, he edited *Visual Criminology: From History and Methods to Critique and Policy*, published by Routledge.

**Jon Heidt** is an Associate Professor of Criminology at the University of the Fraser Valley in British Columbia, Canada. Dr Heidt has studied criminological theories, drug policy, and drug using behavior for over 20 years and has taught criminology courses at several different academic institutions in British Columbia. He is also an associate of the International Centre for Criminal Law Reform & Criminal Justice Policy. He has co-authored several books including *Introducing Criminological Thinking: Maps, Theories and Understanding* and *Youth Crime Prevention and Sports* (with Yvon Dandurand).

# DRUGS, CRIME AND SOCIETY

This new series will be a natural home for research on the topic of drugs and crime, bringing together original, innovative and topical books that, broadly conceived, address the role and impact of drugs and drugs policy on crime, criminality the criminal justice system and its agents. Aiming to showcase cutting edge theory and research in the area, it will serve as a focal point around which the field can continue to develop and flourish. Welcoming both research monographs and edited volumes, the series will serve as an outlet for exceptional early career researchers, established scholars and productive collaborations between those working in the field, across the globe

Series Editors: Jack Spicer and Mark Monaghan

**The Cannabis Social Club**
*Mafalda Pardal*

**Cannabis Criminology**
*Johannes Wheeldon and Jon Heidt*

**Disneyization of Drug Use**
Understanding Atypical Intoxication in Party Zones
*Tim Turner*

The idea for this book series emerged in 2019. From conversations at different conferences and with a growing awareness of a proliferation of modules and programmes across a range of different universities, it became apparent that there was no natural home for drugs-related research of monograph length. We were approached by Routledge to see if we might want to intervene, to develop a series where the latest research in the field of drugs and crime and the role and understanding of drugs in society and the responses to them could be published. Our aim, in creating this series, is to bring together original, innovative, and topical books from scholars of all career stages. The series aims to be methodologically diverse, theoretically sophisticated, and international in its outlook. With drug policy reform gathering traction, yet many drug harms intensifying now more than ever, such learning is required.

One of the enduring criminological concerns when it comes to drugs research has been the position of cannabis in society. There is a long tradition of ground-breaking, critical scholarship that has shed light on the social role and function of cannabis use, as well as challenged the myths and misconceptions about those who use and sell it. Classic work from the likes of Howard Becker and Jock Young during the 1960s and 1970s used the subterranean world of cannabis as the bedrock for developing influential concepts in the sociology of deviance. The work of the normalization theorists from the 1990s onwards captured the changing cultural position this drug has in society in line with increasing trends of use. As policy reform continues to progress internationally, work also continues to be undertaken on what an alternative legal framework that minimizes harm should look like. Without cannabis, the discipline of criminology would therefore look quite different to what it is today. Indeed, cannabis plays an important role in the first two books published in this series, from the edited collection on *Cannabis Social Clubs* led by Mafalda Pardal, which documents their existence across various countries, to the occasional reference to a joint smoked by the Ibiza revelers documented in Tim Turner's *Disneyisation of Drug Use*.

Placing cannabis front and center, *Cannabis Criminology*, by Wheeldon and Heidt, represents an ambitious project that both recognizes this important criminological legacy and sets out where the field could (and should) go next. Developing a detailed, critical review of the significant body of international literature, it links past with future by drawing on a range of sociological and criminological theory to inform its analysis and provide valuable context. It also does not shy away from grappling with the thorny moral issues bound up with the social position of cannabis, or the related role that its international prohibition has played in its history, contemporary standing, and the potential avenues that may be pursued in the coming years. Instead, it explicitly uses these as a platform to develop cannabis as a case study that invites the reader to consider wider questions about the role of law, criminalization, and social control.

The core five themes that are put forward by Wheeldon and Heidt and serve to organize this book set the parameters of cannabis criminology as a multidisciplinary field for criminologists (and their students) to study, develop, and debate. Necessarily wide ranging in scope, yet admirably cohesive, these themes cover law, society, and social control; police and policing; race, ethnicity, and criminalization; the economics of cannabis use; and cannabis use and crime. Importantly for such a project, the authors also attempt to encourage others to further their vision for cannabis criminology, providing useful suggestions not just about what future research could involve but also about how it should be done. Just as cannabis is important for criminology, Wheeldon and Heidt successfully make the case that criminology is important for cannabis. Their work represents a significant and original contribution, capable of stimulating the thoughts of the seasoned drug researcher and the imagination of the fresh-faced student. We are delighted to welcome this timely text to 'Drugs, Crime and Society'.

**Jack Spicer** – University of Bath, UK
**Mark Monaghan** – Loughborough University, UK

# CANNABIS CRIMINOLOGY

*Johannes Wheeldon and Jon Heidt*

LONDON AND NEW YORK

Cover image: Kym MacKinnon

First published 2023
by Routledge
4 Park Square, Milton Park, Abingdon, Oxon OX14 4RN

and by Routledge
605 Third Avenue, New York, NY 10158

*Routledge is an imprint of the Taylor & Francis Group, an informa business*



*British Library Cataloguing-in-Publication Data*
A catalogue record for this book is available from the British Library

*Library of Congress Cataloging-in-Publication Data*
Names: Wheeldon, Johannes, author. | Heidt, Jon, author.
Title: Cannabis criminology / Johannes Wheeldon and Jon Heidt.
Description: Abingdon, Oxon; New York, NY: Routledge, 2022. |
Series: Drugs, crime and society | Includes bibliographical references and index.
Identifiers: LCCN 2022035257 (print) | LCCN 2022035258 (ebook) |
ISBN 9781032140865 (hardback) | ISBN 9781032140858 (paperback) |
ISBN 9781003232292 (ebook)
Subjects: LCSH: Cannabis–History. | Cannabis–Social aspects. |
Cannabis–Government policy. | Cannabis–Law and legislation.
Classification: LCC HV5822.C3 W48 2022 (print) |
LCC HV5822.C3 (ebook) | DDC 362.29/509–dc23/eng/20220728
LC record available at https://lccn.loc.gov/2022035257
LC ebook record available at https://lccn.loc.gov/2022035258

ISBN: 978-1-032-14086-5 (hbk)
ISBN: 978-1-032-14085-8 (pbk)
ISBN: 978-1-003-23229-2 (ebk)

DOI: 10.4324/9781003232292

Typeset in Bembo
by Newgen Publishing UK

# CONTENTS

# FIGURES

# TABLES

# ACKNOWLEDGMENTS

*Cannabis Criminology* is years in the making, even though it has only existed in this iteration in the last year. Thank you first to our families who support us even as we once more retreat to our writing dens to wrestle with what Norwegian playwright Henrik Ibsen called the "trolls in heart and mind." This book is part of a larger project that involved reading and reviewing hundreds of papers and books. We designed and conducted qualitative research projects and developed conceptual and critical efforts. Our analysis led us toward policy models, which inform and are informed by criminological theories and criminal justice practices. Most recently, we have begun to investigate more popular accounts about the moral, legal, and cultural renegotiation currently underway, as cannabis culture, once described as "stable," is increasingly in flux. Thank you to those who have joined us in this work.

As we began submitting our work for peer review, the number of misinformed responses we received was shocking. Some reviewers remain steeped in prohibition myths, while others suggested that cannabis legalization was merely a trend that would soon recede. Depressingly, the idea that racial and ethnic disparities in policing cannabis were manufactured or overblown was common, especially in established, respected, and august criminological publications. The rot goes deep. Oddly, these comments fueled us in ways that complacent acceptance of our work never would have. So, thank you to the moral crusaders, the new prohibitionists, and the many scholars who have benefitted from funding for research designed to uncover the harms of cannabis while ignoring any benefits.

If some inspired us by their aversion to cannabis and their refusal to accept that its social construction as dangerous served colonial, racist, and economic interests, others assisted us in ways that are difficult to untangle. Thank you to David Brewster, Gale Buford, Adrienne Chan, Irwin Cohen, Yvon Dandurand, Emily Dufton,

Michele Giordano, Raegan Heidt, Peter Kraska, Kym MacKinnon, Hayli Millar, Mark Monaghan, Stan Shernock, Martin Silverstein, Jack Spicer, Liz Suiter, Alex Stevens, and many others.

*Cannabis Criminology* is a stark reminder of the power of bad ideas, how moralism and religion influence policy, and the role of paternalism in public health. If criminology must contend with what is defined as deviant, who gets targeted, and how the justice system can harm as well as help, the study of cannabis within criminology can no longer be ignored.

*Johannes Wheeldon*
*Jon Heidt*

# 1

# CANNABIS CRIMINOLOGY

## An Introduction

### Introduction

Efforts to control cannabis have caused much more harm to individuals, families, communities, and the criminal justice system's legitimacy than the damage caused by consuming it (Kaplan, 1970; Mize, 2020). This has been recognized by the United Nations (UN),[1] the US National Institute on Drug Abuse (NIDA) Director Nora Volkow,[2] and recently President Joe Biden. While some countries are moving forward with alternatives to punishment, including decriminalizing drug possession for personal use, prohibition ideas and ideals endure. This book presents cannabis as a critical case study in moral–legal renegotiation (Wheeldon & Heidt, 2022). Recent developments have provoked important criminological questions for those who study crime and society's responses to it. Some are old and established. Others are new and still emerging. This book links criminological theories, concepts, and research within five defined areas of interest.

One essential aspect of contemporary criminology is its international span. In terms of cannabis policy, there are numerous lessons to be drawn from cannabis prohibition, depenalization, decriminalization, legalization, and regulation based on the experience of countries around the world. From Washington and Colorado in the US to Canada and Uruguay, jurisdictions have established new laws and policies. Other jurisdictions have deprioritized cannabis enforcement. Seddon and Floodgate (2020) provide a detailed list. More liberal policies may be set out formally in law or informally in practice by those working within criminal justice organizations. In Argentina, Germany, and Italy, court decisions provoked legislative or policy changes. In other countries, specific laws were passed, which led to decriminalization. These include Belize, Bermuda, Chile, Colombia, Costa Rica, Croatia, Czech Republic, Ecuador, Estonia, Georgia, Jamaica, Luxembourg, Malta, Mexico, Paraguay, Peru, Poland, Slovenia, and Switzerland (Seddon & Floodgate,

DOI: 10.4324/9781003232292-1

2020: 40–43, 53–56). Enforcement changes represent a profound challenge for police, courts, and corrections. However, just as cannabis liberalization is spreading, so has the backlash.

The persistence of prohibitionist ideas related to cannabis is longstanding and deeply embedded. For example, in 2022, Snoop Dogg was photographed in Los Angeles smoking cannabis before performing at the Super Bowl Halftime Show. More than 100 million people viewed his performance, and reviews were loudly and universally complimentary. However, although the recreational use of cannabis has been legal in California for more than five years, some media presented his consumption of cannabis in negative terms.[3] It is but one example of the inebriation double standard, whereby many accept sponsorship of events by transnational alcohol-based enterprises while vilifying the use of other intoxicants. A new wave of prohibitionists has emerged against the normalization of cannabis in social and cultural terms. By weaponizing social anxieties built on nearly a century of the demonization of drugs, the New Prohibitionists seek to limit the use of cannabis often by misrepresenting past research to present risks that simply do not exist (Heidt & Wheeldon, 2022).

## This Book

In this book, we document and demonstrate, through a review of cannabis research, the lack of support for many dire cannabis-related claims that inform many views and policies surrounding cannabis. For example, we show that legalizing cannabis does not expand the number of young people who report using cannabis. It does not lead to an increase in crime rates. Nor does it result in new mental health crises, cannabis use disorders, or psychosis. It certainly does not increase the rates of violent crime. Evidence for most alarmist claims about cannabis evaporate after even cursory examination. However, recent findings have failed to disrupt the policies and practices of justice systems around the world. As criminologists begin to wrestle with the legalization of cannabis and its implications for the justice system, new ways to organize research are needed (Heidt, 2021; Heidt et al., 2018).

Cannabis, as part of drug reform analysis, is hardly new (ACDD, 1968; Becker, 1963; Bennett, 1974; Bonnie & Whitebread, 1970; Mikuriya, 1969; Schur, 1965). It has long been observed that despite the high costs of policing cannabis use, prohibition has demonstrably *failed* to reduce use (Donnelly, Hall, & Christie, 1995; Kaplan, 1970; Reinarman, 2009; Williams & Bretteville-Jensen, 2014). Recent work has attempted to imagine a cannabis-informed research program (Fischer et al., 2021). This builds on an analysis that explores cannabis in one or more jurisdictions through comparative studies focusing on one or more specific issues or outcome measures (Corva & Meisel, 2021). These efforts can provide examples of international approaches and expand mere law-based considerations.

Indeed, after decades of gradual policy liberalization in various jurisdictions around the world, scholars are turning their attention to law reform and regulation.

Such efforts must make peace with the failures of the past. Seddon and Floodgate (2020: 8) observe:

> The core failure is perhaps the most stark and obvious: very large amounts of money have been spent enforcing prohibitive cannabis laws that have not only failed to reduce or eliminate consumption but have in fact coincided with increasing use. Whichever measure or time frame or place we look at, the picture generally appears similar. For example, in 1961, when the Single Convention was introduced, the global prevalence of cannabis use was relatively low .... In 2019, after nearly 60 years of this global prohibition regime, the figure is approaching 200 million.
>
> *UNODC, 2019*

This requires additional analyses focused on the future of cannabis regulation and governance models based on the experience of attempting to regulate other inebriating substances.

In their search for lessons from the regulation of other substances, Decorte et al. (2020: 5) provide a series of "... case studies of cannabis policy reforms and the experiences of scholars from the alcohol and tobacco research fields to inform this unfolding process of cannabis reform." However, based on a recent review of literature relating to outcomes of cannabis regulatory change, Oldfield et al. (2021) suggest that cannabis studies are leading to an increasingly cluttered landscape. Perhaps, more definitional precision is required. This book establishes a means to study cannabis that is informed by criminology's multidisciplinary character. Such an effort is informed by four directives.

The first is to resist framing cannabis using strictly law-based concepts. Instead, analysis can and should be based first on criminological and sociological theories. From the stains of the stigma that allow prohibitionist ideas to persist to the tenets of rational choice theory, we explore new ways to understand how people who use cannabis and those operating within illicit markets respond to policy reform. The second is engaging in a review of research and assessing the practical realities associated with cannabis reform. We show how contemporary research is challenging many older findings regarding the risks of cannabis use and documenting the benefits of instituting more liberal approaches to cannabis policy.

Third, in criminological terms, we combine traditional areas of interest related to police, courts, and corrections with those that confront how laws are made, enforced, challenged, and ultimately reformed. We argue this explicit focus can provide essential insights into how the justice system will (or won't) adapt to legal cannabis. It also may suggest where and how formal social control, previously described as both predictable and discouraging (Heidt & Wheeldon, 2022), is likely to push against the rising tide of cannabis liberation.

Fourth and final is our international focus. Although there is a tendency to consider cannabis prohibition in North American terms, cannabis research is international in character and scope. In this book, we highlight studies from Canada

(Heidt, 2021), Norway and Sweden (Feltmann et al., 2021; Sandberg, 2008, 2012a, 2012b, 2013), Nigeria (Nelson, 2021), Mexico (Agoff et al., 2021), and Poland (Wanke et al., 2022). We highlight international organizations engaged in vital work as well as nongovernment organizations (NGOs) in numerous countries that highlight insights from people who use cannabis, the costs of criminalization, and the complexity of liberalization.

## Prohibition and the New Prohibitionists

Concerns about cannabis prohibition and the high social, economic, and human costs, directly and indirectly, attributable to criminalization are longstanding. Since 1894, governments have commissioned and published reports that claimed cannabis did not cause mental illness and was not associated with crimes other than those arising due to its legal status. The most prophetic finding was that it would cost much more than could be reasonably justified to prohibit, police, and punish its use (Kaplan, 1970). Of specific concern was that harsh laws and punitive policies would harm young Americans by alienating them from society while justifying police intrusions and the deterioration of constitutional values (Kaplan, 1970: 192–193). Ironically, it may not be the state itself that represents the biggest threat to future cannabis liberalization.

As we have documented (Heidt & Wheeldon, 2022), a new, more subtle approach to drug prohibition has emerged in the past decade. The New Prohibitionists are distinct but still related to their predecessors, the Old Prohibitionists. Like the Old Prohibitionists, who opposed drug policy reform in earlier eras, the New Prohibitionists begin with the assumption that cannabis use is dangerous, causes mental illness, and leads to violence and crime. Despite these similarities, some defining features set these New Prohibitionists apart from their Old Prohibitionist counterparts. First, the New Prohibitionists appear to be less stringent and moralistic. For example, they often claim that they have nothing against cannabis use by responsible adults:

> **Let's get one thing straight right off the bat**, before we even begin this thing: I am not concerned with casual adult marijuana use. So long as kids don't see you (and if they do, realize that it reduces their perception of risk, making them more likely to use before their brains are developed and causing them much more harm), and you are not driving (I don't think I need to make much of a case against driving under the influence), I seriously don't care if an adult chooses to consume weed.
>
> *Cort, 2017: 1, bold in original*

Some even admit to having smoked themselves:

> I'd smoked a few times in my life. I remember walking down Amsterdam Street in 1999, laughing uncontrollably, a twenty-something American cliché.

> I never took to the stuff, but I had no problem with it. If anything, I tended to be libertarian on drugs, figuring people ought to be allowed to make their own mistakes.
>
> *Berenson, 2019: xv*

These comments distance the New Prohibitionists from the abstentionist policies and ideology of old-style prohibition now widely acknowledged as failures.

The New Prohibitionists are more adept at using scientific research to support their positions. Although they commonly exaggerate and twist findings to make their case, they also tend to minimize, distort, and ignore research that challenges their presumption about the dangers of cannabis (Heidt & Wheeldon, 2022). For example, the investigative journalist Alex Berenson relies on reports from the National Academy of Science, Engineering, and Medicine's (2017) review of cannabis research to support his claim that increased cannabis use will lead to more violent crime. Specifically, he focuses on the work of a cluster of psychiatric researchers in the UK, led by Robin Murray (Murray et al., 2017) and followed by Maria Di Forti (Di Forti et al., 2019). Murray and Di Forti explicitly state that their work does not prove a *causal relationship* between cannabis and mental illness. However, these claims persist and were used as part of a highly publicized article in the *New Yorker*. Malcolm Gladwell (2019) argued that cannabis is not as safe as we think and suggested that serious risks are being overlooked amid the hype surrounding the benefits of cannabis legalization.

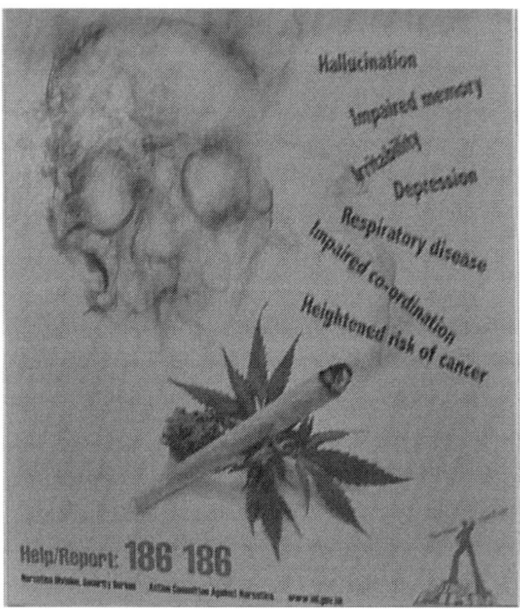


**FIGURE 1.1** Cannabis propaganda. "Cannabis Propaganda" by Mikecogh is licensed under CC BY-SA 2.0

The way the risks of cannabis have been framed continues to inform policy and public understanding in problematic ways.

Perhaps, the pushback against these misrepresentations has been muted because the New Prohibitionists often explicitly reject imprisonment and other harsh penalties for cannabis possession. Instead of relying on moralistic arguments or appeals to law, order, and deterrence, they have adjusted their tactics. Many further prohibition by using public health mantras, and some even advocate for less-punitive approaches. For example, they often espouse a firm commitment to drug treatment and mental health. These differences have allowed the New Prohibitionists to be taken more seriously by modern media outlets. They now seem like cautious progressive treatment advocates, indistinguishable from other drug policy reformers who suggest cannabis use leads to addiction (Ritter, 2021). Some view mandatory treatment programs in place of a criminal record as the pinnacle of progressive drug reform. However, replacing prison with mandated programming has the potential to be coercive and destructive.

Some New Prohibitionists may have a vested interest in maintaining cannabis prohibition for as long as possible as they profit from it. Julian Buchanan has provided a detailed list of the vested interests associated with prohibition, including drug testing and commercial drug treatment enterprises.[4] Indeed, if cannabis becomes legal and socially acceptable, some stand to lose considerable resources.[5] Others appear to be driven by a belief in abstinence of all kinds. A worrying trend is how cannabis is connected to careerist concerns (Wheeldon et al., 2014). As the number of published papers increases, some researchers fail to combat knowledge distortion by the media and others that could negatively impact social policy and result in more harm. In our previous work (Heidt & Wheeldon, 2022), we argued that countering the influence of the New Prohibitionists requires better framing the costs of maintaining prohibition to the justice system, to individuals, and for communities. Beyond leveraging these descriptions to revise and replace existing cannabis discourse, we noted that any such effort must take seriously the potential for criminal justice systems to subvert rather than embrace reform (Cohen, 1979, 1985).

## Cannabis and Criminology

Criminology is a multidisciplinary field that combines many different perspectives, including legal studies, sociology, psychology, biology, economics, political science, geography, media studies, and information technology. Cannabis prohibition is an issue that touches on criminology's multiple and numerous dimensions. For example, cannabis has been studied as part of biological and psychological efforts to understand cognition and violent crime (Niveau & Dang, 2003). In addition, it has been studied using symbolic interactionist, social learning theories, and subcultural theories (Akers & Cochran, 1985; Becker, 1963; Sandberg, 2013). Finally, cannabis use has been connected to social control (Murray, 1986) and labeling via the role of stigma (Reid, 2020).

We are not the first to imagine a cannabis-informed research program. Some provide specific parameters. For example, Fischer, Daldegan-Bueno, and Reuter (2021: 58) suggest five areas of particular interest for criminologists operating in a post-legal cannabis world. These include (1) the deterrent effect of prohibition, (2) illicit production, markets, and supply in a legalization regime, (3) use enforcement, (4) cannabis-impaired driving, and (5) cannabis and crime. Others focus on broader case studies from the US, Uruguay, Morocco, and the UK and consider emerging research areas, including governance, public health, markets and society, ecology and the environment, and culture and social change (Corva & Meisel, 2021). In their review, Oldfield et al. (2021) point to five themes emerging across the literature's breadth. These include normalization, economics, health, community, and gatekeeping. These are useful. However, in this book, we offer a different approach.

Cannabis policy and crime cannot be divorced from prohibition's historical deterrent effect. However, several tensions are emerging from cannabis research within criminology. One is between the social forces that led to cannabis legalization and the backlash, which creates a unique circumstance for criminology as a discipline. This backlash is concentrated among some groups and individuals that support the status quo of prohibition in new and different ways (Heidt & Wheeldon, 2022). In addition, another paradox is emerging. Prohibition has increased potency. Where cannabis is legal, illegal production and illicit markets persist. This is partly based on questions of cost,[6] but requires thinking about recreational cannabis as a consumer good rather than as a toxin to be restricted. In this book, we demonstrate how criminological theory can be used to uncover lessons from existing efforts to regulate cannabis.

A final tension is between the research of the past and more recent findings that challenge many assumptions about the risks and dangers of consuming cannabis. Based on our review, the evidence base should be updated in some cases and drastically reconsidered in others. This requires correcting or retracting research with limited research designs and poorly conceived variables. It means better addressing confounding factors and acknowledging research limitations. In the past, methodologically problematic research has reified racist and xenophobic attitudes about cannabis and cannabis use. Today, research continues to perpetuate myths about cannabis without acknowledging the "… false premise on which we have based this misguided policy" (Solomon, 2020: 5).

Demonizing cannabis and the people who consume it has been beneficial for politicians, the police, the military, and the media (Levine, 2003). Drug prohibition generally has been used to justify increased policing efforts based on misreading social disorganization theory (Fagan et al., 2010). Such policies often have no appreciable impact on cannabis and other drug use. They have been connected to feelings of race-based alienation, consistent with strain theories (Blau & Blau, 1982). Moreover, they have long served to undermine public faith in criminal justice (Zinberg & Robertson, 1972). Although racial and ethnic animus is unquestionably part of cannabis policy, it should be noted that cannabis has also been used to demonize other groups deemed undesirable.

The recent history of cannabis legalization provides another window to view cannabis within criminology. Past cannabis scholarship was rife with conceptual errors, methodological flaws, and practical oversights. It continues to be presented through media-savvy mechanisms that rely on old tropes and prohibitionist ideas. Antilegalization groups, who have long claimed that cannabis is dangerous and should not be legalized under any circumstances, are reemerging with unexpected allies. High-profile and otherwise "liberal" commentators like Malcolm Gladwell and Patrick Kennedy have returned to older concerns about cannabis and mental illness. This has justified renewed forms of community-based compulsory treatment, presented as criminal justice reform. Criminology's fascination with the medical model is not new. Over the past three decades, coercive treatment has been part of the expanding carceral state on five continents (Drake, 2012). This complicity was unconscious at times. Today, it demands recognition.

## *Defining Cannabis Criminology*

Cannabis criminology is an area of criminological study that focuses on how cannabis prohibition has twisted the criminological enterprise in North America and worldwide. Beyond North America, Seddon and Floodgate (2020: 8–9) summarize the international costs of cannabis prohibition. These costs include:

- Facilitating a large and untaxed income stream for groups and individuals involved in crime.
- Criminalizing millions of young people for behavior that, for most, is short-lived and causes minimal social harms.
- Enforcement activities fall most heavily on marginalized and excluded communities, undermining social justice.
- Enforcement being disproportionately targeted at minority ethnic groups, driving racial injustice.
- Incentivizing the creation of more potent and more dangerous synthetic cannabinoids.

Studying cannabis prohibition through the lens of criminology offers another way to understand these issues. The prohibition of cannabis provokes troubling questions about law creation. It has highlighted how a profoundly antiscience orientation has undermined public policy and driven the development of ever-higher strains of high-THC (tetrahydrocannabinol) cannabis infused into products around which the public and people who frequently use cannabis have little experience. Ironically, some byzantine regulatory regimes and ill-conceived taxation strategies have preserved, rather than disrupted, black and gray cannabis markets.[7] Indeed, some policies may do as much harm as simply tolerating the unregulated practices of the past.

**FIGURE 1.2** Areas of cannabis criminology

Guided by the recognition that research agendas are driven by how cannabis as an issue is constructed, we prioritize a broader description that incorporates multiple views at the risk of sacrificing staid conceptual coherence. Thus, in addition to the inevitable focus on cannabis and criminal behavior, we present cannabis criminology as an area of criminology that considers research on law and social control, the implications for policing, the racial consequences of cannabis prohibition, and economic issues surrounding cannabis use (Wheeldon & Heidt, 2022). Given the obstinate reach of prohibitionist ideologies and the social harm they have caused, we carefully consider past research and some extraordinary claims that are not based on credible evidence. We organize our analysis through five key areas.

## Criminological Theories and Key Areas of Cannabis Criminology

Cannabis prohibition is an issue that touches on criminology's multiple and sometimes contradictory dimensions. Focusing on cannabis provides a creative means to understand racism, media misrepresentations, the war on drugs, police militarization, legitimacy, mass incarceration, and numerous other issues within the criminological expanse. It is a novel way to meet the need for more imaginative explorations and analyses (Young, 2011). In place of efforts that focus merely on criminal justice considerations (Fischer et al., 2021), we argue studying cannabis as part of criminology usefully expands the scope of analysis. We identify five key research areas worthy of exploration and consonant with criminology's broad character. These include law, society, and social control; police and policing cannabis; race, ethnicity, and criminalization; the economics of cannabis; and cannabis use and crime.

## *Law, Society, and Social Control*

This first area of cannabis criminology focuses on law and social control. Research on law and society attempts to explain the formation and activities of criminal law and the criminal justice system. This area can be connected to the work of sociologist Donald Black (1976, 1984). Black (1976) argued that law attempts to organize society based on coercive notions of respectability. Social control here refers to "the normative aspect of social life, or the definition of deviant and the response to it, such as prohibitions, accusations, punishments, and compensations" (Black, 1976: 1–2). Thus, the law is viewed as a governmental form of social control. There is no better example of law as social control than the prohibition of drugs. How can the coercive ideals that have guided drug policy for a hundred years be confronted?

The criminalization of cannabis and the demonization of those who use it have impacted the criminal justice system, from the laws that govern society to the behaviors of police, prosecutors, judges, probation and correctional officers, and others associated with the criminal justice system. The prohibition of cannabis complicated law creation and contributed to increased militarized policing at home and abroad, and played on our worst tendencies around race, ethnicity, and otherness (Kraska, 2001). These include disparities in policing cannabis, coercion and control masquerading as care within diversion programs and the tendency for cannabis reforms to serve as illusory steps toward real reform. Together these expanded criminological intrusions into the lives of law-abiding people and failed to reduce use (Donnelly, Hall, & Christie, 1995; Reinarman, 2009; Williams & Bretteville-Jensen, 2014).

Three cross-cutting themes include stigma, normalization, and tolerance. These concepts inform policing, diversion, and reforms that reify prohibitionist ideas. The demonization of cannabis and the people who use it is a stark reminder of the justice system's power to harm people. This includes the history of drug regulation, the creation and maintenance of stigma, and how the media enabled prohibition and subsequently normalized its use (Parker et al., 1998; Parker, 2005). A final theme concerns how to expand tolerance to match the growing acceptance in local cultures. Issues include rethinking the influence of social forces on cannabis medicalization (Monaghan et al., 2021), the oft-reported but yet unfounded causal connection between cannabis use and mental health (Hamilton & Monaghan, 2019), and worries about the role of coercion in the cannabis treatment population (Hamilton et al., 2014). Reid's recent work (2020) on stigma, normalization, and shame extends previous research to consider how stigma operates on different explanatory levels. Such a focus is of specific interest to our examination of cannabis, law, society, and social control.

## *Police and Policing Cannabis*

Stigma is also relevant to understanding another area within cannabis criminology, specifically, police and policing cannabis. Current approaches have resulted in racially unequal outcomes, wasted resources, and eroded public trust and community relations. Police cultures rooted in the war on drugs justified aggressive police tactics that alienated communities by furthering racial divisions (Fagan et al., 2010) while allowing departments to benefit financially from its illicit status. This area considers both the history of policing cannabis, including how the search for cannabis has been connected to the growth of policing and the shift in our understanding of the role of police in society (Vitale, 2018). Tactics such as stop-and-frisk and stop-and-search policies and the militarization of police have increased police brutality, even as they make little progress in reducing street-level drug activity (Baum, 1996; Tonry, 1994).

Cannabis criminology cannot ignore how the long arm of the war on drugs has shaped contemporary practices and attitudes. Defined in various ways, Rodríguez-Gómez and Bermeo (2020: 20) offer a valuable view of the drug war. They describe it as

> the violent configuration of prohibitionist and militarized drug policies that mobilize the illicit and lucrative nature of the drug trade … [that] connects distant actors, institutions, and regulatory landscapes across the globe.

In many ways, the underlying assumptions of the drug war are still with us. Public perceptions of cannabis use are increasingly liberal. However, attitudes among law enforcement and police organizations are not. Prohibition-era myths remain part of antidrug education programs and precharge diversion programs.[8] Police have long been caught up in cultural and historical traditions that led to the strategic regulation and control of marginalized groups. Harsh criminal justice practices are connected to policing attitudes, tactics, and questions of legitimacy (Kraska, 2001; Vitale, 2018).

As criminologists begin to consider use enforcement in an era of legal cannabis, the role of police demands greater focus (Stohr et al., 2020). One area of emergent interest is how police are responding to new drug crimes. One example is the expansion of drug networks into towns and villages in the UK and the related phenomenon of "cuckooing," where drug dealers take over other people's homes. While cannabis has historically been connected to other illicit drugs in problematic and inconsistent ways, Spicer (2021) demonstrates the value of ethnographic research with police officers, the role of unintended consequences as part of drug policy, and the need to consider the dynamic relationship between law enforcement and the drug markets they police.

Policing cannabis also includes recognizing that decriminalization and the rise of international investments in cannabis represent a policy shift for law enforcement (Dandurand, 2021). Comparing and contrasting police culture in Canada, Uruguay, Portugal, and US states in Washington and Colorado, alongside policing in other American states, the UK, Australia, and beyond, is one approach. Locally, cannabis provides a specific issue that grounds general comparisons around one topic. This includes investigating the role of policing cannabis in an era of decriminalizing cannabis and how police understand and frame their role in this shifting landscape.

## *Race, Ethnicity, and Criminalization*

In our view, cannabis criminology is closely linked to discussions about race and ethnicity. Hudak (2020) explores the explicitly racist roots of cannabis policy in the US to highlight how politicians across the political divide spent much of the twentieth century using cannabis as a means of dividing America. Indeed, cannabis prohibition has exacerbated racial injustice and led to many costs that must be documented if they are to be confronted. One of the most consistent findings in the literature over decades is that the adverse effects of criminalizing cannabis disproportionately impact Black, Indigenous, and People of Color (BIPOC). Racial and ethnic minorities are more likely to be targeted by drug enforcement, less likely to be diverted, and receive harsher penalties at higher rates for the same drug offenses (Baker & Goh, 2004; Belackova et al., 2017; Hughes & Stevens, 2010; Lammy, 2017; Shiner, 2015). Differences in arrest rates cannot be explained by differences in previous nondrug and drug-offending, sociodemographic variables, or geographic location (Males & Buchen, 2014; Koch et al., 2016; Mitchell & Caudy, 2015; Mooney et al., 2018).

These findings have historical dimensions (Collins, 2021; Pembleton, 2017), and criminal justice institutions have long served as tools for controlling subjugated groups deemed threatening or disruptive to the status quo. This observation is hardly new. However, the adverse effects of criminalizing cannabis disproportionately impact people of color, their families, and their communities can be connected to recent research on the predatory nature of the criminal justice system (Page & Soss, 2021) and the racial consequences of criminalizing poverty (Mize, 2020). For Page and Soss (2021), how expanded regimes of policing and punishment produced new revenue occurred alongside the privatization of institutions of criminal justice. This was described by Haggerty (2004) as a result of the rise of neoliberal forms of governance, simplistic notions of individual responsibility, and highly symbolic public discourse about crime. Cannabis prohibition provided a pretext for predation, shifting costs from the system to individuals. This created perverse profit motives that continue to infect agencies whose nominal mission is to respect, protect, and serve citizens.

## *The Economics of Cannabis*

If the three preceding thematic areas of cannabis criminology logically follow from decades of criminological research, efforts to understand economics, choice, and cannabis use are also relevant. Such analysis can assist policymakers in rethinking and critically assessing consumer education, awareness, and marketing. Central here is understanding the role of illicit markets and the war on drugs. Robinson and Scherlen (2014) present evidence that drugs are now more available, cheaper, and more potent than at any other time. One reason that cannabis liberalization has struggled to disrupt illicit markets is that they have focused on public health first and access second. Regulations around potency, price, and advertising have limited the potential of the legal market. The economics of cannabis use means understanding illicit markets and applying economic theories (Sandberg, 2012a).

Past studies have focused on how cannabis dispensaries affect crime and public disorder in various communities and how people who use cannabis make decisions in the face of widespread and rapid liberalization of cannabis policies (Chang & Jacobsen, 2017; Contreras, 2016; Hunt, Pacula, & Weinberger, 2018). These studies have clear connections to rational choice, routine activities, and pattern theory (Brantingham & Brantingham, 1981; Cohen & Felson, 1979; Cornish & Clarke, 1986). Important questions consider whether and to what extent higher prices in the legal market stemming from overzealous regulation will ensure a role for black or gray market cannabis in different jurisdictions. Where cannabis has been legalized and regulated, applying economic theories in criminology could recalibrate the sole focus on public health.

Efforts to attract new consumers, develop innovative products, and engage new audiences to test both will lead to worries about glorifying cannabis. Finding the balance between legitimate public health concerns *while* embracing market thinking is likely to be an iterative process. However, trying to deny market realities is a mistake. As far back as 2019, there were references to companies that could become "the Amazon of cannabis."[9] An open question is how companies can adapt to online commerce. This will lead to concerns about regulating online cannabis, shipping cannabis across borders, and what this means for post-legalization cannabis and crime.

## *Cannabis Use and Crime*

The fact that cannabis prohibition has existed for a century means that for most of our lives, simply possessing cannabis meant one was engaging in criminal behavior. Challenging stigma and expanding tolerance around cannabis are two ways to confront a century of prohibition. Yet, any study of cannabis within criminology is susceptible to "law-based research programs" (Fischer et al., 2021: 65) and may fail to consider how harm reduction can serve as an antidote to the cannabis prohibition pandemic. The first harm that must be confronted has been perpetrated by governments worldwide. This is an ethical issue, as identified by Milton Friedman in 1991:

> It's a moral problem that the government is making into criminals—people, who may be doing something you and I don't approve of, but who are doing something that hurts nobody else.[10]

For many, cannabis use remains deviant, dangerous, and undesirable. It continues to be associated with criminality and criminal behavior. Where cannabis policy has been liberalized but not yet legalized, there is a growing recognition of the political unacceptability of criminal sanctions for cannabis use.

In jurisdictions where cannabis has been legalized, crimes related to cannabis still exist. This includes possessing more cannabis than the threshold limit, growing and possessing nonlegal cannabis, and consuming cannabis in public. Of specific interest is to what extent police will use the potential for nonlegal cannabis possession to justify stops, investigations, and possible arrests. One particular concern surrounds cannabis and driving. In general, there is limited research to help guide policy. While people respond differently, combining cannabis and alcohol often increases the effects of both drugs (Dubois et al., 2015; Hartman & Huestis, 2013). Reactions vary by driver, but some effects are potentially quite serious (Ramaekers et al., 2000). Since both substances affect different parts of the brain, the combination, particularly at high doses, can lead to situations that place drivers and others on the road at serious risk (Stevens et al., 2021).

Finally, persistent concerns remain around the potential for cannabis addiction (Ritter, 2021: 21). Many of these concerns do not stand up to analysis. However, prohibition myths continue to shape drug policy and practice in ways that are difficult to challenge (Ritter, 2021; Szalavitz, 2021). One area of concern relates to claims that the regular use of significant amounts of cannabis by youth (under 18) represents a danger to their physical and mental health. In Canada, legalization *has* impacted youth in one clear way. As Myran and colleagues document (2022), unintentional cannabis ingestion rose in children, increasing child cannabis-related emergency department (ED) visits in Ontario. An open question is how the justice system responds in these circumstances.

## Organization of the Book

This book is organized to present five areas of cannabis criminology. Chapter 2 focuses on law, society, and social control. We define and consider concepts of stigma, normalization, and medicalization. We also explore relevant research in jurisdictions where cannabis has been depenalized, decriminalized, and legalized. Recent research examines how stigma persists. More attention is needed on how it is furthered by compulsory and coercive treatment, which has emerged from the medicalization of cannabis. Chapter 3 considers the police and the policing of cannabis. We define and consider concepts related to the war on drugs, police militarization, and predatory police tactics to further racial divisions and alienate communities. We summarize research suggesting the value of deemphasizing cannabis for police officers, departments, and the communities they nominally serve. However, challenges to police reform include both philosophical and practical problems.

Chapter 4 examines race, ethnicity, and criminalization. Related to policing, these disparities persist within diversion programs and even where cannabis has been legalized. We present biological and psychological positivism, critical race theory, and restorative justice as important theoretical starting points. Key concepts explored in this chapter include disparities in justice system contacts, the costs of cannabis prohibition, and the potential for reconciliation. While enforcement inequities have long been observed, recent research makes clear in profound and unique ways how race and ethnicity are inextricably linked to cannabis, prohibition, and criminology. Chapter 5 focuses on the economics of cannabis. We demonstrate how rational choice theories provide insights both where cannabis remains illegal and, significantly, where cannabis has been legalized and regulated. Theoretical starting points include deterrence, routine activities theory, and rational choice. Key concepts explored include cannabis potency, accessing and differentiating cannabis markets, and cannabis as a consumer good. Emergent research focuses on the value of economic theories to understand regulatory difficulties within jurisdictions that have legalized cannabis and the general failure to dismantle and disrupt illicit markets.

Chapter 6 focuses on cannabis use, criminal behavior, and crime. We outline three main areas of interest within this domain. Recent research has complicated these associations in some cases and contradicted past findings in others. More specifically, crime has not increased where cannabis policy has been liberalized. However, new forms of potential criminality within jurisdictions that have legalized and regulated cannabis are emerging. One concern relates to cannabis and driving. Another is how to tackle illicit markets where other forms of criminality are more likely to occur. Finally, we agree with Seddon and Floodgate's (2020: 129) observation:

> That question ultimately is how can we design regulation to constitute cannabis markets that are not only rights-protecting and justice enhancing but also promote human flourishing and well-being? The sustainability of those markets, in the context of our planet's finite and depleted resources, should now also become a much higher priority in policy thinking. In the twenty-first century, we need to develop an approach to cannabis regulation that recognizes that we now live in the Anthropocene epoch.

Chapter 7 reviews key findings from our analysis of existing evidence and experience and considers critical questions based on the defined areas of cannabis criminology. We revisit and engage four significant ideas. The first is that cannabis and its prohibition have intersected with criminology in many ways. Second, the justice system has evolved in ways that allow cannabis prohibition to justify interference in the lives of Black and Brown people. The third idea is that findings from existing cannabis research and studies on adverse outcomes associated with drug use generally need to be drastically reconsidered, given research from jurisdictions where cannabis is legal. Fourth and finally, we consider how these ideas can be understood as illusory reform. This means policy reforms, although less punitive, still perpetuate the myths of the past. We believe this concept should animate the study of cannabis within criminology going forward.

## Conclusion

Scholars are increasingly turning their attention to cannabis regulation (Decorte et al., 2020; Seddon & Floodgate, 2020). In this book, we consider how past and contemporary research can guide this work. As post-prohibition research programs emerge and regulation schemes are advanced, there is a worry that the amount of commentary and opinion will limit conceptual models that can present these issues in ways that are consistent with criminology's multidisciplinary nature. By linking cannabis to defined and discrete areas of criminology, we prioritize a broad approach and incorporate multiple views (Wheeldon & Heidt, 2022). Understanding existing approaches and exploring emerging efforts to regulate cannabis requires engaging with the history of prohibition, including the religious, racist, and international dynamics that informed, propelled, and ultimately sustained prohibition.

In this chapter, we introduced cannabis criminology. We began to link criminological theory, cannabis research, and international practice on cannabis through the lenses of law, society, and social control; the implications for police and policing; the racial consequences of cannabis prohibition; economic issues surrounding cannabis use; and crime and criminal behavior. In this way, we embrace calls for efforts that expand the "criminological imagination" (Young, 2011) by rethinking the history of the discipline and reassessing cannabis use, drug policy, and contemporary research. This includes highlighting international examples. The use of cannabis is no longer uniformly viewed as a moral failing; however, those living in the era of cannabis regulation will need to learn the lessons of prohibition. In many ways, current efforts to decriminalize, legalize, and regulate cannabis seek to right the wrongs instituted a century ago. However, the history of prohibition informs the stain of stigma around cannabis use. Moreover, the trend toward normalization has been complicated by expanding carceral control in communities worldwide. Cannabis criminology provides a means to examine the moralistic underpinnings of many of our ideas about crime and justice.

The prohibition of cannabis is central to understanding criminology's past and its immediate future. The criminalization of cannabis has impacted every arm of the criminal justice system. It has led to the expansion of the military abroad and contributed to the militarization of the police in North America. In the past, criminologists have often failed to document the costs of cannabis prohibition for people within and outside the criminal justice system. Others have neglected to consider prohibition's costs to the justice system's legitimacy. Unfortunately, antiquated assumptions around drug use and methodological inaccuracies remain part of criminology's present. Future studies of cannabis, culture, and crime exploring nascent regulatory frameworks must contend with this history of harm. Broad international examples of decriminalization and specific local legalization models are emerging. Questions remain. Some cannabis reforms have dulled the worst cannabis-based carceral excesses. Recent developments in the US, and around the world, are encouraging. However, rumors of the death of cannabis prohibition have been greatly exaggerated.

## Notes

1 UNCEBC, *Summary of Deliberations* (2019), www.unsceb.org/CEBPublicFiles/CEB-2018-2-SoD.pdf [accessed June 5, 2022].
2 See https://slate.com/news-and-politics/2020/08/warrior-cop-class-dave-grossman-killology.html [accessed June 5, 2022].
3 See www.thedailybeast.com/new-york-post-dragged-for-narcing-on-snoop-doggs-weed-smoking [accessed June 5, 2022].
4 See https://julianbuchanan.wordpress.com/2015/04/02/20-benefits-from-the-war-on-drugs/ [accessed July 5, 2022].
5 See https://reason.com/2020/02/20/thc-vaping-madness-reaches-reefer-proportions/ [accessed June 5, 2022].
6 See https://munkschool.utoronto.ca/mowatcentre/wp-content/uploads/publications/169_sharing_the_costs_of_cannabis_in_canada.pdf [accessed June 5, 2022].
7 There is no universally accepted definition of the gray market. In general, black market refers to dealers or suppliers who are associated with gangs and organized crime groups that sell cannabis alongside other drugs. The gray market refers to those who grow cannabis on a smaller but still illegal scale (e.g., "Mom and Pop" grow ops, growers who divert small amounts to the illegal market) See https://cjr.ufv.ca/wp-content/uploads/2021/01/Tangled-Up-in-Green-Cannabis-Legalization-in-British-Columbia-After-One-Year.pdf [accessed July 7, 2021].
8 In the US, some examples of these myths are described in programs including the Marijuana Diversion Program (www.co.berks.pa.us/Dept/DA/Pages/Marijuana-Diversion-Program.aspx), the Misdemeanor Marijuana Diversion Program (www.centrecountypa.gov/DocumentCenter/View/17132/Description-of-Misdemeanor-Marijuana-Diversion-Program), and the Pretrial Diversion Program (www.monroeprosecutor.us/criminal-justice/pretrial-diversion-program/faq/). Some programs like the one in Texas note the problems of stigma and the limited public safety benefit from prosecuting cannabis possession. Participation in programming is still required. https://app.dao.hctx.net/video-misdemeanor-marijuana-diversion-program. In the UK, an overview with a decidedly upbeat view of diversion can be found here: https://transformdrugs.org/drug-policy/uk-drug-policy/diversion-schemes. In Australia, a useful overview of diversion and the consequences of noncompliance can be found here: https://adf.org.au/talking-about-drugs/law/decriminalisation/decriminalisation-detail/ [accessed June 5, 2022].
9 See https://mugglehead.com/this-company-is-quickly-becoming-the-amazon-of-cannabis/ [accessed June 5, 2022].
10 www.aei.org/carpe-diem/milton-friedman-interview-from-1991-on-americas-war-on-drugs/ [accessed June 5, 2022].

# 2
# LAW, SOCIETY, AND SOCIAL CONTROL

## Introduction

Within cannabis criminology, law, society, and social control focuses on norms, state responses, and stigma as related to the moral, legal, and cultural renegotiation of cannabis. Most criminological theories concentrate on explaining criminal behavior (or criminality), criminal acts, or crime rates. However, theories associated with this area also consider the development of law. This involves focusing on who has the power to define behavior as deviant and how these definitions shape those who are labeled. One key concept to consider is stigma. As Goffman (1963) described, this term refers to something more than just a negative attribute or behavior. It is best conceptualized as a process of societal reaction that can shape identity in adverse ways. Labeled individuals may begin to perceive themselves as societal outcasts or outsiders, thus freeing them to engage more fully with the more deviant aspects of their character (Lemert, 1951).

Historically, people who use cannabis were labeled evil, dangerous, and deviant. However, these negative associations started to shift in the 1960s. As conflict theories emerged, cannabis became intertwined with social movements in criminological terms. These included those associated with protesting the war in Vietnam, embracing the civil rights movement, and others connected to what is seen today as the counterculture. Since then, the use of cannabis has been increasingly normalized.

These changes in cannabis perceptions accelerated as a result of decriminalization efforts in the 1970s. This shift occurred in some US states and was furthered by the "coffeeshop" system that developed in the Netherlands. Related to cannabis, two very different concepts emerged in the 1990s: normalization and medicalization. Consistent with the "normalization thesis" (Parker, 2005), popular culture increasingly portrayed cannabis use as common, mocked its status as a Schedule I drug, and associated smoking pot with subcultures from surfing to hip hop and from skateboarding to jam bands (Heidt & Wheeldon, 2022). On the other hand,

DOI: 10.4324/9781003232292-2

people who use cannabis were increasingly pathologized. Problematic behavior, once blamed on "badness," was soon transformed. The same behavior was now seen as "sickness," needing intervention by medical professionals (Conrad et al., 1992).

In this area, cannabis research related to concepts drawn from law and society has proceeded along numerous paths. Cannabis liberalization does not appear to increase cannabis use by youth. However, even where cannabis has been legalized, stigma related to cannabis use and those who use it remains. Some recent research focuses on the incomplete process of destigmatization and racial and ethnic disparities that persist (Gagnon et al., 2020; Greer et al., 2020). Another concern is how medicalization has expanded cannabis use by justifying it as a remedy (Newhart & Dolphin, 2019). At the same time, medicalization and pathologizing cannabis use (and other drug use) has led to coercive treatment modalities drawn from different areas of the justice system (Spivakovsky et al., 2018). Medicalization and stigma provide essential starting points for studying cannabis use and policy (Newhart & Dolphin, 2019).

## Theoretical Starting Points

Law, society, and social control can be connected to the work of sociologist Donald Black (1976, 1984). Black (1976) argued that law attempts to organize society based on coercive notions of respectability. Social control here refers to "the normative aspect of social life, or the definition of deviant and the response to it, such as prohibitions, accusations, punishments, and compensations" (Black, 1976: 1–2). Thus, the law is viewed as a governmental form of social control. There is no better example of law as social control than the prohibition of drugs. However, other theories offer valuable perspectives. Specific starting points of interest are demonology, labeling perspective, and conflict theories.

### *Demonology*

An important starting place in understanding attempts to control people who use cannabis is demonology. Since the earliest days of human civilization, antisocial and criminal acts have been associated with demonic possession or other evil supernatural forces. Demonology, of course, is not a criminological theory in any meaningful sense. It is a means to pass moral judgments about right and wrong, and good and evil. As we have noted, this perspective is remarkably persistent within criminology and criminal justice studies, although increasingly hidden within assumptions about human nature (Heidt & Wheeldon, 2015). People who use cannabis have long been demonized. In the US, nativism and exclusion worked side by side, involving the one-two punch of prohibition and new, restrictive immigration laws (Moore, 2015). Interestingly, many churches have preached that foreign drug habits were both a mortal and a moral threat.

Another example is how this process was connected to "concern" with the damage that this sinful, depraved, and immoral behavior caused among these so-called inferior races. The demonization of cannabis has been connected to specific racial tropes about people of color ("Hindoos") in North America as early as 1911.[1] Duster (1970) identified the 1914 Harrison Act as creating a market in the illicit traffic of drugs and making drug use deviant, dangerous, and criminal. In 1917, an influential report from the US Treasury Department recommended cannabis be made illegal (Smith, 1917). It stated: "Mexicans and sometimes Negroes and lower-class whites smoked marijuana for pleasure." It warned of "drug-crazed" minorities that placed upper-class White women at risk (Jonnes, 1996: 128).

In the 1930s, Harry J. Anslinger, the first commissioner of the newly created Federal Bureau of Narcotics (FBN), accelerated cannabis prohibition on the federal level in the US. He was a committed alcohol prohibitionist who believed he had a mandate "to pursue any and all violations of drug laws" (Lawson, 2020: 220). Racist sentiments toward Mexicans and African Americans that predominated the US early in the twentieth century played a crucial role in the passage of the Marihuana Tax Act (Chasin, 2016). An early focus was on migrant workers from Mexico and immigrants from the West Indies. However, Anslinger shifted his focus and connected cannabis with jazz musicians, who were long viewed as a deviant subculture (Bonnie & Whitebread, 1999). For example,

> During the "reefer madness" era prior to mid-century, users were depicted as menacing, criminal, sexually deviant, and even potentially murderous or insane .... The appellation "Killer Weed" derived its claims from opiate rhetoric, erroneously suggesting that cannabis use could result in death or induce users to commit murder.
>
> *Newhart and Dolphin, 2019: 21*

Demonizing jazz and connecting this subculture with immoral and illegal behavior was part of Anslinger's efforts; however, with the rise of sociological studies of crime, a different path was taken. For example, some within the Chicago school were interested in how the transition in all aspects of social life—vocational, religious, and familial—impacted neighborhoods and crime rates. Members of the Chicago school observed that historical transformations had changed how society functioned by focusing explicitly on what researchers observed in Chicago neighborhoods. These changes also affected the prevalence of crime and societal attitudes about criminals. Social definitions of crime and how these definitions were accepted, revised, or rejected remain relevant today.

## *Labeling Theory*

The symbolic interactionist approach has been used extensively in the study of cannabis. Social psychologist, George Herbert Mead is considered by many to be "the father of symbolic interactionism" and an early pioneer in the field of social behaviorism (Akers, 1989: 24). Mead believed that the individual emerges from society and that society emerges from the individual through a dialectical process. He observed that social interactions often resulted in people altering their behavior in response to others. This near-constant process of adjustment and readjustment allowed people to acquire prosocial experiential awareness. Labeling theories can be traced to these observations.

Blumer (1969) elaborated upon Mead's ideas and defined *symbolic interactionism* based on three premises. The first is that humans act based on the meaning they attach to different things. Thus, we treat people differently when we know something about them because we attach importance to those things. The second premise is that associations arise from our social interactions with other people, such as relatives, authority figures, friends, and peers. The third and final premise states that these meanings are modified through an interpretative process, which is different for each person. All people react to events in their lives, but the implications of these events will change over time. In addition, the symbolic–interactionist approach influenced Howard Becker's (1963) and Jock Young's (1971) work on cannabis use.

During the 1960s and 1970s, criminologists began to question how those labeled as criminals were affected by this designation. Does involvement in the criminal justice system give rise to new criminal behavior? A conflict assumption of society unites this area. According to this assumption, the criminal justice establishment imposes standards of upper-class morality on everyone else. The social and economic forces that operate within societies serve to perpetuate crime. The system is designed to separate the powerful from those without power, undermining rights by using divisions including but not limited to structural factors, social hierarchies, financial differences, and gender and racial biases. These new developments eventually led to the emergence of labeling theories (Heidt & Wheeldon, 2015).

Labeling theories focus on labels and how they affect people's behavior. These theories are also known as societal reaction theories because they focus on reactions from society and the criminal justice system. By examining the social processes that give rise to crime and deviance, labeling theorists began to ask new and different questions. These include the following: What kind of behavior is considered deviant? Who believes the conduct is deviant? From what does the behavior deviate? Why is this behavior considered abnormal? (Taylor, Walton, & Young, 1973). This was applied to early explorations of drugs and society (Duster, 1970).

### *Conflict Theories*

Labeling theories emerged when the activities of the criminal justice system were under increasing scrutiny. Until the late 1960s and 1970s, socio-legal studies and legal analyses had been ignored by most mainstream criminologists (Cohen, 1974). The study of the law, the police, courts, and correctional systems from the perspective of those caught up in the justice system became an essential focus for critical and radical theorists. One direction was how criminal law, legal codes, punishment, and other forms of social control could harm those with the least power within societies.

> The shape and character of the legal system in complex societies can be understood as deriving from the conflicts inherent in the structure of these societies which are stratified economically and politically.
>
> *Chambliss & Seidman, 1971: 3*

In hindsight, cannabis policies both justified and increased the overpolicing of Black, Indigenous, and other People of Color (BIPOC).

While the 1960s are an important period, Sellin's (1938) earlier work on culture conflict theory can help shed insights into the racial dynamics associated with cannabis use and policy. Sellin proposed two forms of cultural conflict: primary and secondary. Primary conflict refers to the disconnect that arises between a recent immigrant's existing and newly adopted culture. For example, the stigma against alcohol in the US would have appeared quite strange to Eastern European immigrants who arrived in America with their own established drinking cultures. Another type of conflict, secondary conflict, arose within some groups that develop cultures of their own with values that differ from those of the broader culture. These groups could be viewed as subcultures (Williams & McShane, 2010). This confluence of stigma, prohibition, and culture relates to early efforts to prohibit cannabis.

## Key Concepts

The theories presented above help explain the shift from demonizing cannabis and those who used it to understand the role of criminal law in creating expectations about who is defined as deviant and criminal. This legacy is profound as the crime problem began to be seen through a more critical lens in the 1960s. Three key concepts inform this area of cannabis criminology. They include stigma, normalization, and medicalization. Research has provided some insights and opened the door to new and fascinating questions.

### *Stigma*

It is not difficult to see how demonization by Anslinger and others could lead people to establish negative views of those identified as immoral, dangerous, or evil. Goffman (1963) identified three types of stigma. These include physical deformities and tribal stigma associated with race, religion, and nation. This also includes character-based shortcomings like dishonesty and poor self-control, inferred from a history of mental illness, radical political beliefs, and certain types of drug addiction. The third category concerning character blemishes is most relevant to drug use generally, and cannabis use specifically. Indeed, various stereotypes about people who use cannabis have emerged and evolved during the decades of cannabis prohibition. For example, authority figures characterized them as dangerous and violent during the early years of prohibition.

Link and Phelan (2001) have attempted to expand on the definition of stigma. First, they suggest that people distinguish between and give labels to individual differences. Second, in some cases, this label may turn into a negative stereotype based on dominant cultural beliefs that characterize a society. Third, these negative labels and the stereotypes that emerge from them are used to place people into categories of "normals" and the stigmatized insiders and outsiders, or "Us" and "Them." Fourth, there is an exercise of power that involves a loss of status and discrimination. Cannabis has been a frequent target. Figure 2.1 includes numerous messages that have informed linkages between cannabis and stigma.

Despite prominent examples of stigma around drug use, there has often been pushback (Dufton, 2017). The 1960s marked a shift in the popularity of cannabis in society. The counterculture movement influenced the discourse surrounding cannabis, and musicians promoted the drug through their lyrics and their own use (Cody, 2006). Seddon and Floodgate (2020) point to the committee established by the then mayor of New York City, Fiorelli La Guardia. They continue:

**FIGURE 2.1** Weed with roots in hell. Provided by the Philadelphia Museum of Art, The William H. Helfand Collection, 1989, 1989-69-6. Used with permission

> By the late 1960s, this contestation had moved to the foreground in many Western countries, as cannabis law reform became intertwined with the emergent counterculture. The infamous full-page advertisement in *The Times* newspaper in the summer of 1967, signed (and paid for) by all four Beatles, describing cannabis laws as "immoral in principle, unworkable in practice," exemplified this new social and cultural prominence of concerns about cannabis prohibition.
>
> *Seddon and Floodgate, 2020: 7*

Surprisingly, the new countercultural movement could be viewed as the first indication of a creeping normalization of cannabis use in certain subcultural groups.

## *Normalization*

The principle of normalization originally came from studies on disability. It has since been used as an interpretive tool for understanding cannabis' growing acceptance (Newhart & Dolphin, 2019). The notion of drug use normalization first emerged in the counterculture of the 1960s. Cannabis use became increasingly common and accepted. Parker (2005) suggests that normalization refers to the notion that the nondrug-trying adolescents would be in the minority over time instead of the "normal" adolescents who had used drugs.

The 1960s were a time of social turbulence in which the "baby boomers," known as the generation born in the decade following the Second World War, challenged their parents' conservative social norms (Gerster & Bassett, 1991). During this period, cannabis use became common in communities where it had previously been unknown (Dufton, 2017). White middle-class youth began using cannabis as an act of rebellion, perhaps since it was seen as forbidden based on its racial and criminal connotations (Marqusee, 2005). As the teenagers of this era grew up, many viewed drug use as more enjoyable and less dangerous than their government and the media suggested.

The Netherlands has provided an important early example of how to liberalize cannabis policy. While formally conforming to UN treaties around drug policies, the Dutch approach to toleration and de facto decriminalization sought to avoid punishing drug use and focused on separating "soft" and "hard" drug markets. Holland's approach has resulted in one of the most developed cannabis markets globally. Since 1976, this experience has led other countries to decriminalize the use of recreational cannabis as an increasingly popular approach. In the Netherlands, where cannabis sales are regulated, cannabis possession remains officially illegal. Generally, possessing less than 5 grams of cannabis will not be prosecuted. However, charges may be filed for possessing more than 5 grams. However, only possession of more than 30 grams would usually result in prosecution. This hands-off policy to the cannabis supply chain and the toleration of sales and use amounts to de facto decriminalization.

Since 1990, the legalization of cannabis has proceeded along several paths. In recent research, Parker (2005) has suggested that normalization refers to the notion that the nondrug-trying adolescents would be in the minority over time, as opposed to the "normal" adolescents who had used drugs. Earlier, Parker and colleagues (2002) found considerable support for the five leading indicators of normalization. These included increases in availability and accessibility, increased rates of drug trying, more recent and regular use, more social accommodation for "sensible" recreational drug use (i.e., abstainers more tolerant of drugs in their environment), and broader cultural accommodation (i.e., more references in the media to drug use in television shows and by stand-up comedians).

Since the original study, Parker (2005) has identified the sixth dimension of normalization known as state response and antidrug strategies. This dimension refers to changes in state responses that reflect the normalization process. For example, it might include defining formal distinctions between problematic and nonproblematic drug use, encouraging responsible drug use, and replacing scare tactics and inflammatory rhetoric with public health and fact-based prevention strategies. Numerous studies followed Parker's (2002, 2005) ground-breaking research. For example, based on interviews of 41 adults who use cannabis in Canada, Osborne and Fogel (2017) found support for the critical aspects of cannabis normalization, including availability/access, drug trying (i.e., experimentation), and rates of use.

In support of the "normalization thesis" (Parker, 2005), some US states began legalizing medical cannabis through citizen-led ballot initiatives, even in politically conservative states. In a systematic review of trends in US attitudes toward cannabis legalization, Chiu and colleagues (2022: 1052) conclude:

> The US population has become more accepting of cannabis legalization. The attitudinal change is related to changes in the perceived risks and benefits of cannabis use, influenced by broader political and cultural changes over the study period.

Normalization is also a function of the growing recognition of the contradiction between the nature of the "crime" and the highly punitive laws targeting cannabis (Vitiello, 2021: 447–448). In 2020 an estimated 40,000 people were incarcerated in the US for cannabis offenses, even as the legal cannabis industry was booming.[2] Stigma comes in many forms. Normalization has shifted the locus of cannabis control from the justice system. Other efforts to control use have emerged.

## *Medicalization*

As late as the 1930s, the American Medical Association still endorsed the potential medical value of cannabis (Collins, 2020). Even though doctors preferred cannabis to opium due to its lack of addictive qualities and other serious adverse side effects (Booth, 2003), cannabis began to be associated with violence, insanity, and moral corruption. In 1941 the US deleted references to the medical benefits of cannabis, following Britain's decision to do the same. Newhart and Dolphin (2019: 25) connect the recently renewed medical interest in cannabis to increased public awareness stemming from a shift in its portrayal by critical media outlets such as CNN.

The therapeutic potential of cannabis for children drove the passage of limited medical laws in more than a dozen states. States like Alabama, Georgia, Kentucky, Mississippi, and Wisconsin passed laws allowing the legal use of a cannabis extract that is predominantly or exclusively cannabidiol (CBD) for treating seizure disorders. Seventeen states passed similar laws less than two years later (Newhart & Dolphin, 2019: 25). By July 2018, 46 states and the District of Columbia, and the US territories of Puerto Rico and Guam, provide for the legal therapeutic use of

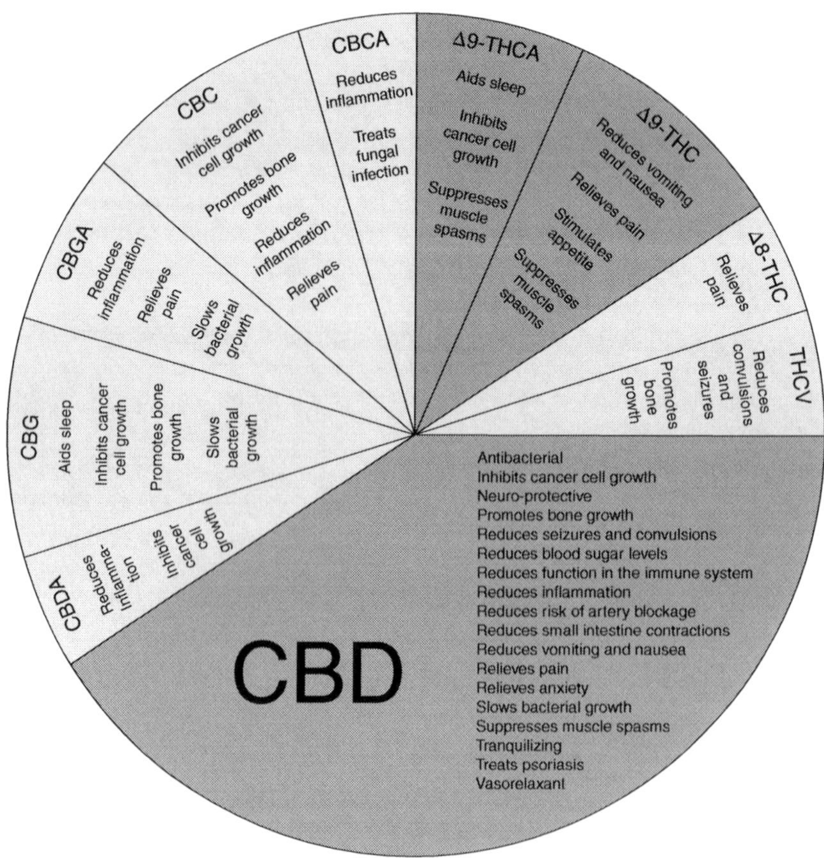


**FIGURE 2.2** Medical Cannabis by Renegade 98 is licensed under CC BY-SA 2.0

cannabis in some form. The acceptance of the medical potential of cannabis further destigmatized use among a subset of the population and increased the supply of cannabis through diversion to illegal markets (Nussbaum et al., 2015). Interest in medical cannabis is expanding (Jin et al., 2021).

Although medicalization can be seen alongside normalization in one sense, it also opened the door to the increasing "tendency [of] medical institutions to deal with non-conforming behavior" (Broom & Woodward, 1996: 358). As the influence of medical regulation in daily life replaced other institutions of social control, especially the criminal justice system, the management of deviance as explanations for human health conditions gradually changed from sin to crime, and eventually to sickness. Conrad and colleagues (1992) have suggested a five-stage sequential model of the medicalization of deviant behavior that reflects the medicalization of cannabis use. It amounts to a deliberate shift, as problematic behavior, once blamed on "badness," was transformed, Now, the same behavior was seen as "sickness." This process often unfolds through five distinct stages.

1. Definition—The conduct or behavior in question is viewed as morally deviant before the emergence of medical definitions.
2. Prospection—The medical nature of deviance is "discovered" for the first time, and this "discovery" is typically announced in a professional medical journal. It might appear as a new medical or diagnostic term or reports of medical treatment for the conduct or behavior.
3. Claims-making—Various organized interest groups aim to expand the medical territory by accentuating the size and solemnity of the problem, and such interest groups will gain profit if the new medical perspective is adopted. An example would be pharmaceutical companies.
4. Legitimacy—The proponents of the medical deviance designation make a request to the state to recognize the medical viewpoint. They seek powers of definition and management over the problem.
5. Institutionalization—The medical viewpoint is officially part of the medical or legal classification system. It is included as an official diagnosis in the medical manuals, and medical treatment for it is readily available. Moreover, institutions of social and ideological control such as government, National Institute of Health (NIH), American Psychiatric Association (APA), media, etc., support the new medical perspective financially and intellectually.

*Conrad et al., 1992: 266–271*

Once universally criminalized, changing enforcement patterns and cannabis policy have led to shifting efforts to control cannabis use using medical means. Indeed, the most prestigious of America's professional medical associations remain skeptical of cannabis' medicinal benefits. In addition, there are numerous barriers to medical research on cannabis, and "... ideology is pitted against science and the will of the public" (Newhart & Dolphin, 2019: 27).

Cannabis use disorder (CUD) is a good example. CUD is a new diagnostic term that combines two older stand-alone concepts related to cannabis abuse *and* cannabis dependence (Jutras-aswad, 2019: 2). Symptoms of CUD, according to the current *Diagnostic and Statistical Manual of Mental Disorders* (*DSM-5*),[3] include the use of cannabis for at least one year and the presence of at least two of the following symptoms, accompanied by significant impairment of functioning and distress:

- Difficulty containing use of cannabis … used in larger amounts and over a longer period than intended.
- Repeated failed efforts to discontinue or reduce the amount of cannabis that is used
- An inordinate amount of time is occupied acquiring, using, or recovering from the effects of cannabis.
- Cravings or desires to use cannabis … intrusive thoughts and images, and dreams
- Continued use of cannabis despite adverse consequences from its use, such as criminal charges, ultimatums of abandonment from spouse/partner/friends, and poor productivity.
- Other important activities in life, such as work, school, hygiene, and responsibility to family and friends are superseded by the desire to use cannabis.
- Cannabis is used in contexts that are potentially dangerous, such as operating a motor vehicle.
- Use of cannabis continues despite awareness of physical or psychological problems attributed to use—e.g., anergia, amotivation, chronic cough.
- Tolerance to Cannabis, as defined by progressively larger amounts of cannabis are needed to obtain the psychoactive effect experienced when use first commenced …
- Withdrawal, defined as the typical withdrawal syndrome associated with cannabis or cannabis or a similar substance is used to prevent withdrawal symptoms.

*APA, 2013*

The *DSM* suggests that the severity of the disorder depends on the number of symptoms. A mild case of CUD involves presenting with two or three symptoms. A moderate case involves four or five symptoms, and a severe case is present when six or more symptoms apply to someone who uses cannabis (APA, 2013). Despite the strategic redefinition of CUD, the assumption that this "disorder" represents a significant public health concern has outpaced the existing evidence (Sagar & Gruber, 2018). Indeed, rates of psychosis or other disordered behavior have not increased where cannabis has been decriminalized or legalized (Callahan et al., 2021; Frisher et al., 2009; Gabri et al., 2022; Lu et al., 2021). Recent articles posit "possible associations" between cannabis and adverse health outcomes, but apply these concerns to an ever-smaller cohort of youth, adolescents, and people with mental illness (Borodovsky & Budney, 2018; Connor et al., 2021; Leyton, 2019).

The medicalization of cannabis has normalized use in some contexts and reduced penalties for others. However, pathologizing cannabis use has complicated efforts to legalize and regulate it. By enshrining a role for the medical model of addiction, despite significant problems with this formulation, this model justifies coercive treatment models and demonstrates how the power to punish has been decentralized, reproduced, and refocused for those deemed problematic (Cracknell, 2021). Past research provides some context for understanding cannabis, stigma, normalization, and medicalization. New studies offer greater depth and detail and suggest essential and intriguing new directions.

## Cannabis and Research on Law, Society, and Social Control

Understanding the future of cannabis decriminalization and responsible regulation depends on the research undertaken and the questions that are asked. Some of these questions are comfortably situated within the area we call *law, society, and social control*. Focusing on norms, state responses, and stigma and how people understand the criminal consequences for doing so, research in this area considers societal reactions to cannabis use and the associated implications for people who engage in this behavior. Research in this area ought to start from the recognition that drug policies began by demonizing drugs and that those who use them are viewed as threats to both civil society and overall health (Reinarman & Levine, 1997). These views have aligned with racist attitudes and xenophobic fears (Solomon, 2020). Three areas of interest are normalization and cannabis use, shifts in stigma, and reinventing moral panics.

### *Normalization and Cannabis Use*

To understand the process of normalization, it is useful to consider cannabis use in the US. There are two issues of immediate interest. The first considers how people understand the consequences of cannabis use. For example, even before the widespread shift in cannabis laws in the US, MacCoun and colleagues (2009) analyzed the US National Survey on Drug Use and Health (2001–2003). They found that people who use cannabis had little knowledge of policies and overestimated statutory penalties for possession in their states. This complicates the idea that policy liberalization is an effective causal mechanism for cannabis use. It also confounds assumptions that strict laws serve as a deterrent to cannabis and other drug use.

The second considers cannabis use in jurisdictions that legalized and decriminalized cannabis. It is often presumed that liberal cannabis policies increase use. However, Grucza et al. (2018) found no increase in youth cannabis consumption rates following decriminalization based on their analysis of the Youth Risk Behavior Survey in Massachusetts, Connecticut, Rhode Island, Vermont, and Maryland. Likewise, Johnson and colleagues (2019) analyzed more than 160,000 cases drawn from the 2004–2016 Washington Healthy Youth Surveys and found that across all groups, cannabis use peaked in 2012. Ta, Greto, and Bolt (2019) reported that rates of cannabis use within the past 30 days generally stayed stable or declined. Hall and Lynskey (2020) suggested that cannabis use increased among adults but not among adolescents.

Societal responses to cannabis use are also relevant internationally. Stevens (2019) analyzed survey data from 38 countries from 2001–2002, 2005–2006, and 2009–2010. No significant association emerged between less stringent cannabis policies and increased rates of adolescent cannabis use. Cannabis use is increasingly prevalent and more widely tolerated in more and more jurisdictions. The intersection between law, societies, and cultures makes comparative work on the costs and consequences of cannabis policies an exciting area for future research. Questions of social factors such as political repression, religiosity, and informal social controls may be as important as formal methods such as fines, custodial sentences, and coercive treatment.

For example, in Poland, the disconnect between a liberal and increasingly globalized cannabis culture, on the one hand, and punitive legislation and conservative social reactions, on the other, was explored. Of some interest is how symbolic boundaries can be understood in terms of spaces to use cannabis and "...the (in) ability to control the substance and its use, and to the knowledge produced about cannabis" (Wanke et al., 2022: 9). One issue is how to understand the differences between Goffman's (1963) theoretical distinction between normalization—defined by Parker (2005) as the notion that cannabis-abstaining adolescents would be in the minority over time—and the more apt description of normification, whereby those who use cannabis internalize stigma and perform expected behaviors to meet social expectations.

## *The Stigma–Normalization Nexus*

One means to organize research in this area is to focus on jurisdictions in which cannabis was once illegal and later legalized. Before 2018, cannabis in Canada was illegal. Based on interviews with 104 people who use cannabis in Toronto, Ontario, Hathaway (2004) found that participants had specific rules or techniques for managing the stigma associated with cannabis. Some of these included keeping their use hidden from disapproving nonusers, adhering to less stigmatizing methods of use (e.g., joints and edibles), and managing the risks that accompany cannabis use and the stigma stemming from being labeled as at risk. These labels can extend to concerns beyond health.

In subsequent research by Hathway et al. (2011), in-depth interviews with 92 people who use cannabis in the Toronto area were conducted. The results suggested that although cannabis use has been normalized in the sense of it being more socially and culturally accepted, there were still threats from legal sanctions and stigma associated with its use. Interestingly, their data also revealed that over two-thirds of their sample did not fear arrest and were more concerned about informal sanctions imposed by others based on the stigma associated with cannabis use. Further, participants describe taking steps both to counter typical cultural assumptions about people who used cannabis and to present themselves as normal.

Canadian researchers found that stigma against cannabis use was confined to its immoderate and irresponsible use (Duff et al., 2012). Based on the views of 165 adults who use cannabis in Vancouver, Montreal, Toronto, and Halifax, the authors qualify their conclusions with the following statement:

> Our participants described some residual stigma, particularly in relation to the use of cannabis in certain controversial circumstances, like at work, in the company of children and the elderly, or while driving, participants routinely insisted that this stigma had more to do with the circumstances of this consumption than with the act itself.
>
> *Duff et al., 2012: 281*

Other research also suggests that the stigma remains, and societal normalization of cannabis use has not fully occurred. Instead, there is an increasing tendency in society to medicalize and pathologize drug use. This includes cannabis use.

Haines-Saah et al. (2014) analyzed nearly 2,000 Canadian newspaper reports and proposed the existence of "privileged normalization," or the notion that the normalization of cannabis is more appropriately applied to those with high levels of power and status in society. This is particularly relevant when considering to what extent minorities and people of color have experienced normalization. Although it cannot be doubted that the acceptance of cannabis has increased, society has not been able to dislodge the stubbornly persistent view that it is dangerous. For example, social concerns about cannabis use have been highly moralized in Jamaica. Negative stigma has significantly influenced the debate on establishing a legal cannabis industry or decriminalizing possession for personal use (Hanson, 2020: 379). This view has been fueled by decades of misinformation.

Although it may be true that cannabis use and some other forms of drug use have experienced destigmatization and even limited normalization in some groups and social contexts, this process has not fully taken hold on a societal level. Reid (2020: 11) suggests that

> claims of normalization may be premature. While stigmas surrounding cannabis appear to have diminished, there is little evidence that such stigmas have entirely disappeared. It is possible that sweeping claims of cannabis normalization may be symptomatic of unchecked social privileges or social distance from cannabis users.

Garland (2001) has suggested that different social transformations and the unpredictable character of modern life have led to what he has called a culture of control connected to punitive policies, like the war on drugs. Brewster (2017) has applied some of Garland's (2001) thinking by analyzing the trajectories of cannabis control in England and Wales and the Netherlands. Qualitative work in Canada can inform studies in other jurisdictions. There is much more to explore and unpack regarding how cannabis prohibition contributed to the culture of control (Garland, 2001). An important question here is how to think about moral panics and the future of cannabis policy.

## *Rethinking Moral Panics*

In the UK, recent research (Monaghan et al., 2021) examined how social forces were marshaled and led to medicinal cannabis policy reform. In 2018, laws were changed to allow cannabis-derived products to be prescribed for medicinal purposes, following focused media attention regarding two children with epilepsy. For example:

> Media stories emphasized the injustice of two extremely sick children being unable to access the medicine they apparently needed to enable them to have a "normal" childhood. Three groups of "claim-makers" were identified as important in influencing public opinion: families, high-profile individuals and campaigning groups.
>
> *Monaghan et al., 2021: 1925*

Worries about how emotive media stories can be used to manufacture scandal and drive policy change can be connected to efforts to reimagine moral panics in the social media age. Cannabis is an especially interesting example, given its social construction as both medicine and toxin (Newhart & Dolphin, 2019).

Framing cannabis policy using the concept of moral panic is not unique (Cody, 2006). It is relevant because the dramatization of evil through the process of demonization remains a feature of justice policy and cannabis laws. Moral panic research in criminology can be traced to Jock Young's (1971) study of the social meaning of drug taking and to Stanley Cohen's (1972) construction of the mods and rockers in the UK. Various critiques have since emerged, which complicate simplistic analyses (Horsley, 2017). There are several essential questions in this area. Some involve how to understand the history of cannabis moral panics and to what extent cannabis prohibition intersects with the culture of control (Garland, 2001). One place to start is historical.

In the 1930s, the themes of criminality, insanity, violence, and sexual immorality depicted in *reefer madness* are also prevalent in several other independent films produced during the same era, including *Assassin of Youth* (1938) and *Marihuana: The Weed with Roots in Hell* (1936). Cannabis propaganda efforts never really disappeared after Congress passed the Marijuana Tax Act (1937). However, these efforts reemerged in earnest in the twentieth century through varied national and international drug control initiatives. As Boyd (2010: 12) notes:

> Reefer Madness portrays innocent middle-class white, small-town youth being lured into marijuana addiction, sexual depravity, insanity, and murder. The evil drug that compels them into corruption and crime is marijuana.

These initiatives can be understood as propaganda, based on moral assumptions and not facts. Howard Becker (1963: 147) argued that law and social rules are not formed in a vacuum and are susceptible to *moral entrepreneurs* who seek to reform laws to impose a particular moralistic worldview and then try to ensure that rules are enforced by deferring to police or agents of social control when they apply laws consistent with this worldview. Cohen (1972) built on this framework by adding the notion of a moral panic (borrowed from McLuhan, 1964) and described several processes that lead to moral panics (Bennet, 2018). When events present a threat to existing societal values, the media can be used to frame this condition in a stylized and stereotypical fashion. This leads influential people, experts, and others to diagnose the problem and propose solutions to it.

This has occurred recently in the context of cannabis legalization. As we previously documented (Heidt & Wheeldon, 2022), a new, more subtle approach to drug prohibition has emerged in the past decade. As we introduced in Chapter 1, the New Prohibitionists, like the "Old Prohibitionists" (those who opposed drug policy reform in earlier eras of the 1980s, 1990s, and 2000s), believe that cannabis causes mental illness and thus leads to violence and crime. The New Prohibitionists can be described as a group of moral entrepreneurs or moral crusaders, and new approaches to prohibition have emerged (Berenson, 2019; Gladwell, 2019). The backlash sustained by prohibitionist ideas makes cannabis liberalization a potential object of moral panic.

The New Prohibitionists can be seen as employing tactics consistent with moral entrepreneurship. As Goode and Ben-Yehuda (1994: 121) explain, strengthening laws is not the only way of expressing moral panic:

> It must be emphasized that the concept of the moral entrepreneur applies not only to the definition of behavior as deviant and the creation (and enforcement) of the criminal law, but also to the moral panic as well. (And to definitions of conditions as social problems, as we shall see shortly.) That is, though strengthening society's social control apparatus through legislation is certainly one way of expressing a moral panic, there are others. Moral entrepreneurs operate on a wide range of fronts. The many efforts of moral entrepreneurs relevant to the generation and maintenance of moral panics include: attempting to influence public opinion by discussing the supposed extent of the threat in the media; forming organizations and even generating entire social movements to deal with the problems the threat presumably poses; giving talks or conducting seminars to inform the public how to counter the threat in question; attempting to get certain views approved in educational curricula; influencing legislators to allocate funds which would deal with a given threat; discrediting spokespersons who advocate alternative, opposing, or competing perspectives.

One question is whether older moral panic frameworks make sense in contemporary society.

Several critiques have emerged relating to the concept of moral panics. These include definitional imprecision, a disconnect between theory and practice, and the changing media landscape (Garland, 2008; Jewkes, 2004). Cannabis may offer one way to begin to build an updated explanation. Just as stigma and normalization help explain the criminalization and decriminalization of cannabis, the moral panic framework may help present this history in more specific ways. This could include combining Garland's (2008) expansion of moral panic indicators identified in Goode and Ben-Yehuda's (1994, 2009) work and organizing these panics as eras (Cody, 2006). Such an approach opens the door to recasting moral panic less as singular and specific, and more as interrelated with different trajectories with complex interrelationships (Bennett, 2018; Klocke & Muschert, 2010).

## New Directions

Emerging research questions in this area are based on the theoretical work of Black (1976, 1984), Cohen (1972), Garland (2001), Goffman (1963), Lemert (1951), Parker (2005), and Young, 1971) and concern phenomena such as cannabis moral panics (Cody, 2006), development of cannabis laws (Brewster, 2017; Newhart & Dolphin, 2019; Seddon & Floodgate, 2020), and normalization and levels of stigma (Hathaway, 2004; Hathaway et al., 2011; Reid, 2020; Sandberg, 2012b). Labeling theory is also relevant (Lemert, 1951). Otherwise law-abiding people, who happen to use cannabis and other drugs, might internalize a more general criminal identity after they are labeled as illegal drug users. Young (1971) and Cohen (1972) have argued that this type of labeling could eventually lead to the phenomenon known as the deviancy amplification spiral.

Medicalizing and pathologizing cannabis has led to coercive treatment modalities drawn from other areas of the justice system (Spivakovsky et al., 2018). Coercive care and cannabis are often linked through diversion programs, whereby those arrested with small amounts of cannabis can avoid criminal sanction by participating in a treatment program (Wheeldon & Heidt, 2022). Nominally educative, many appear designed to scare, shame, and stigmatize participants. Replacing criminal punishment with administrative sanctions may be a step in the right direction. However, forcing people who engage in nonproblematic cannabis use into reeducation programs is of limited clinical value and does not reduce drug use (Klag et al., 2005; Luciano et al., 2014). Even if clear evidence existed that mandating cannabis programs worked to minimize use, they would remain unethical (Stevens, 2012). More research is needed to uncover the experience of people who use cannabis in these programs and to explore how to frame the persistence of stigma where cannabis has been legalized.

Recent research offers some important context. In Canada, despite the emergence of full federal cannabis legalization, landlords and employers emphasized banning cannabis rather than adjusting to the new reality of cannabis legalization. Broad and restrictive regulations disproportionately impacted racial and ethnic minorities, those who use medical cannabis, and the poor (Gagnon et al., 2020).

Likewise, Reid (2020) complicates simple notions of stigma, normalization, and shame. This extends previous work on stigma to consider how it may operate on different explanatory levels, which is of specific interest. The macro level involves social structure or culture. These include cultural norms, state policies, and institutionalized procedures that tend to oppress and control (Livingston & Boyd, 2010). Although the stigma around cannabis use may have been diminished at the macro or structural level, further study should consider how other kinds of stigma may influence people with stigmatized identities. These include social stigmas that operate at the meso level and individual stigmas that function at the micro level.

Social stigmas (meso level) describe how organizations and groups endorse cultural messages that disadvantage stigmatized people (Livingston & Boyd, 2010). This type of stigma involves how group norms tend to influence individuals and especially how these norms are communicated through "… epithets, shunning, ostracism, discrimination, and violence" (Reid, 2020: 5). Crucial here is how cannabis use is viewed as related to social role expectations. For example:

> Parents who use cannabis may be shunned by other parents, students who use cannabis may be forced to complete a rehabilitation program, and workers who use cannabis may be fired. Even if no action is taken, the sentiment often results in heightened scrutiny towards cannabis users where any minor mistake is directly attributed to cannabis intoxication.
>
> *Reid, 2020: 5*

Finally, micro stigmas or individual stigmas refer to how judgment is experienced or internalized. These are perhaps best seen as anticipatory and preventative decisions taken to avoid suspicions that one uses cannabis. For example, Reid (2020) notes that some people who use cannabis refrain from commenting on cannabis-related issues when they arise in everyday conversations to avoid behavior that might be seen as deviant to avoid the label of "pothead" or "stoner." Such strategies can result in anxiety, compromise intimate relationships, and undermine relationships. Of interest is how these stigmas and levels interact.

## Conclusion

This chapter has explored cannabis through the lens of law, society, and social control. We considering theoretical starting points drawn from demonology, labeling, and conflict theories. These theories animate several key concepts, including the role of stigma, normalization, and medicalization. This chapter and its approach are connected to the interest in social control based on the work of sociologist Donald Black (1976, 1984). A central feature is understanding how coercive notions of respectability guided cannabis laws historically and continue to inform cannabis policy today. The connections between law, social, and social control remain relevant where cannabis has been legalized; this suggests its sustained relevance.

A central question is how the coercive ideals that have guided drug policy for a hundred years can be confronted.

Research demonstrates that while stigma has been reduced, it persists in contradictory ways. One development is the medicalization of cannabis and the shift from carceral responses to coercive care through treatment (Wheeldon & Heidt, 2022). Another is how people who use cannabis experience shame and judgment, even where cannabis has been legalized. Research on cannabis within criminology must not ignore the context under which the justice system developed, and how criminal laws were established. More work is needed to connect structural factors and attitudes to policing, race and ethnicity, and the persistence of illicit markets.

The demonization of cannabis and those who use it is a stark reminder of the justice system's power to harm people. Prohibitionist propaganda has left a lasting stigma that comes along with cannabis, and negative labeling provides a fertile seedbed for a backlash against legalization and potential moral panic. Unless criminologists retain the willingness to philosophize, question, doubt, and theorize about how those we seek to punish (including through forced treatment) serve to insulate us from taking responsibility for the elements of our own psyche, each of us will pursue punishment when we encounter things that make us uncomfortable. Reid's research (2020) examines stigma, and the ways in which it operates and interconnects on different levels is of specific interest in this regard.

## Notes

1 In fact, concerns about cannabis predate the concerns connected to Mexicans and jazz musicians in the 1930s. In 1911, Henry J. Finger, a member of California's State Board of Pharmacy wrote:

> Within the last year we in California have been getting a large influx of Hindoos and they have in turn started quite a demand for cannabis indica .... They are a very undesirable lot and the habit is growing in California very fast; the fear is now that it is not being confined to the Hindoos alone but that they are initiating our whites into this habit.

This letter and the association between Finger and Wright, who led the international delegation to the Hague, is discussed by Campos (2012) and Gieringer (1999).

2 Pinning down these statistics is difficult. See www.forbes.com/sites/joanoleck/2020/06/26/with-40000-americans-incarcerated-for-marijuana-offenses-the-cannabis-industry-needs-to-step-up-activists-said-this-week/?sh=266877a7c16f and www.celebstoner.com/news/marijuana-news/2021/03/17/forty-thousand-american-cannabis-prisoners/ for some of these issues [accessed August 15, 2021].

3 See www.psychiatry.org/psychiatrists/practice/dsm and www.theravive.com/therapedia/cannabis-use-disorder-dsm--5%2C-305.20%2C-304.30 [accessed November 16, 2021].

# 3

# POLICE AND POLICING CANNABIS

## Introduction

The prohibition of cannabis profoundly changed policing. It has been used to justify increased police contact targeting people of color, hippies, and antiwar protesters (Levine, 2003). Later, as a political cudgel, it helped align those who supported the cold war, the drug war, and the conservative Christian movement (Bentham, 1998; Bullington & Block, 1990). Problems persist. In 2016 in Arizona, an African American woman was stopped for a minor traffic violation. When the vehicle was searched, a small amount of cannabis was found. The woman was offered two options. She could either face up to two years in prison and a maximum fine of $150,000, or participate in the Marijuana Diversion Program, which would allow her to avoid prosecution altogether --if she could pay $950.[1]

In many ways, the police can't win. When political leaders require that police be the only way citizens can address their concerns, they have little choice but to respond. Thus, according to Brandon del Pozo, policing is "... like a gas, able to expand to fill any space but exerting less and less pressure as it expands."[2] By asking so much of the police, we tend to dilute their essential functions. Moving on from order policing and the emphasis on nuisance crime means focusing on public safety by solving serious violent crimes. This is what most police want to do. The idea that people joined police departments with the dream of arresting squeegee kids or harassing people smoking cannabis in the park is foolish.

Research on policing and cannabis often focuses on critical legal studies (Berger & Luckmann, 1966) and the role of systematic racism (Blau & Blau, 1982) to explore police militarization (Kraska, 2001), stop- and- frisk searches (Gelman et al., 2007), and police legitimacy (Tyler et al., 2014). Police cultures rooted in the war on drugs justified aggressive police tactics to further racial divisions and alienate communities

DOI: 10.4324/9781003232292-3

(Fagan et al., 2010). Policing cannabis has been connected to specific policies and practices that have increased police brutality, even as they make little progress in reducing street-level drug activity (Baum, 1996; Tonry, 1994). Policing cannabis also includes recognizing that decriminalization and the rise of international investments in cannabis represent a policy shift for law enforcement. What is the role of police in an era of decriminalized cannabis?

In this chapter, we explore police and policing cannabis. Three theoretical starting points include social control, strain theory, and criminal justice growth theory (Kraska, 2006). Although theories of social control justify the need for police to maintain order, strain theory suggests how unequal enforcement undermines legitimacy. An underexplored theory is criminal justice growth, in which policing tends to expand. For example, policing cannabis is connected to the militarization of the police, the drug war, and the predatory practices attributed to the justice system.

## Theoretical Starting Points

Police in a liberal democracy serve a variety of roles and functions. Under any definition, policing is an example of formal social control. Two broad approaches to studying police and policing are based on conflict and consensus. Conflict theorists often view law enforcement as a hostile outside force that seeks to impose the views of political elites on communities with less social capital. Race and ethnicity are often implicated, but more often the police are working directly in the interests of the ruling class, against the interests of everyone else. By contrast, a functionalist perspective views the police as coming from and working on behalf of the community that they police. This consensus view assumes general agreement in the community about law and order, which the police enforce. Three theories from criminology and criminal justice studies are of immediate interest.

### *Strain Theory*

Strain comes in many forms. Merton, Cohen, Cloward and Ohlin, and others have explored the disjunction between the desire to achieve the American Dream and the limits imposed by an inequitable class structure. Beyond the emphasis in American culture on materialism, wealth, and consumerism, in recent years, these theories have transformed and have shifted focus from social norms to monetary success and, finally, to a broad range of goals that people from all walks of life share. Strains and stressors may produce negative emotions, such as frustration and anger, resulting in impulsive crimes (Agnew, 2006). Crime may also result from an effort to reduce or escape from strain or seek revenge against the source of the stress and strain and other related targets.

Unnever and colleagues (2009) explored how criminology missed a vital opportunity to explore how systemic racism itself might serve as another sort of strain that leads to increased criminal behavior. By trying to demonstrate why strain theory should be relegated to the criminological dustbin, Travis Hirschi (1969) made a profound error. He inadvertently failed to recognize that his dataset contained evidence that perceived racial discrimination places African American youth at risk for engaging in crime. Unnever and colleagues (2009: 383) describe Hirschi's omission in this way:

> Hirschi's laser-like mission to falsify strain theory thus shaped his use of the questions in the Richmond Youth Project and the very specific way in which he tested whether discrimination fostered crime (i.e., in the way predicted by strain theory). This strategic approach, however, meant that Hirschi did not probe to see if other measures of racial discrimination included in the data set might contribute to delinquent involvement.

Although Cloward and Ohlin (1960: 113 - 117) had suggested delinquency was more likely when youths experience "unjust deprivation," criminologists often ignored racial discrimination as a significant risk factor for African American offending. Instead, as cannabis use increased, it was framed as a risk to young White populations, which laid the groundwork for future punitive policies. Whether the goal was to protect the morals of White people or control non-White people, the result has been the same. Policing the use of cannabis has led to profound racial injustice grounded in the fictitious narrative that drug use is especially prevalent among Black people and minority ethnic groups.

People of color are more likely to be targeted by law enforcement, less likely to be diverted, and consistently receive harsher penalties at higher rates for the same drug offenses. Consider the tactics used in two recent examples. On New Year's Eve in 2017, 70 people were arrested during a house party, 45 minutes north of Atlanta, Georgia, for allegedly possessing less than an ounce of marijuana. Of the 65 adults arrested, 50 were Black. Attendees were detained and strip-searched:

> Some as young as 17 years old, were ordered to remove all of their clothing in front of two or more deputies, bend over at the waist, spread their buttocks with their hands, and cough multiple times. Male visitors were compelled to lift their genitals.[3]

Aggressive policing of cannabis is often framed as a uniquely American phenomenon, the global prohibition of cannabis, alongside other drugs, has expansive international dimensions and profoundly negative consequences (Collins, 2021). For example, in 2020, a 15-year-old Black student in the London borough of Hackney in the UK was strip-searched by police while on her period because she was suspected of possessing cannabis. Teachers called the police because they stated she "smelt of cannabis."[4] According to a review of the incident, the student was made to bend over, spread her legs, use her hands to spread her buttocks and cough.[5] Confidence in law enforcement suffers when their activities are seen as predatory, assaultive, or fail to adhere to acceptable substantive normative benchmarks (del

Pozo, 2022). This damages the credibility of law enforcement and can lead to calls for police reform that is existential instead of incremental (Vitale, 2018).

## *Social Control*

Extreme views on drug use and cannabis have eroded over time. However, the strains that emerge based on racial disparities in policing must not be ignored. Policing cannabis has long been based on the view that any use is an immoral act. This transcends race and can be linked to the demonization and stigma of people who use cannabis, introduced in Chapter 2. Control theories originated in the work of Emile Durkheim (1938/1895, 1965/1897), who assumed that people are naturally self-interested and require external control. In line with a Durkheimian approach, past efforts defining cannabis use as a crime serve an essential social purpose by establishing moral boundaries of acceptable behavior.

In general, control theories focus on how proper socialization keeps people in line and how misbehavior can be controlled (Nye, 1958). However, external control mechanisms are required when socialization fails. Police represent the formal means by which society can maintain order. Based on a consensus view of society, some see the police as coming from and working on behalf of the community that they police. This is based on the assumed general agreement in the community about law and order. Throughout the 1950s, lawmakers and journalists seemed to have little patience or interest in making distinctions among illegal drugs. As a result, laws against possessing cannabis were strengthened, and heroin, cocaine, or cannabis were all "dope" and dangerous substances that led to addiction. In the 1950s, people

> witnessed the advent of an extremist legislative policy with respect to drugs generally and marijuana in particular. For the first time in our national history, there was public interest in narcotic drugs. Apparently there had been an increase in narcotic drug abuse in the late 40's, and the public mind was ripe for the FBN propaganda. In the paranoid atmosphere of the times, the call for harsher penalties was soothing. Unfortunately, marijuana was caught in the turbulence of this era. Although the pharmacological facts about the drug were beginning to emerge, congressional furor was aroused by the novel assertion, rejected by [FBN] Commissioner Anslinger in 1937, that use of marijuana led to use of harder drugs. This new plateau of misinformation was to provide the base for continual escalation of penalties and proliferation of offenses throughout the decade.
>
> *Bonnie and Whitebread, 1970: 1063*

From this perspective, the police were working in the interests of the ruling class and against the legitimate interests of others.

Some in law enforcement have long advocated against efforts to criminalize and try to control cannabis use. For example, Norm Stamper of the nonprofit LEAP (Law Enforcement Action Partnership) says that the criminalization of drugs has increased crime and damaged trust between communities and law enforcement.

> We've got the drug war raging since 1971 and pitting police against low-level, nonviolent drug offenders, creating natural animosity and tension between police and the community—in particular young people, poor people, and people of color.[6]

According to Christy E. Lopez, a legal scholar at Georgetown Law, "The spectrum of skill sets we are currently asking police to embody is simply not realistic."[7] This means acknowledging the uncomfortable reality that we train police to be combatants and then ask them to spend most of their time on

> disorderly crowds, domestic disputes, traffic accidents, minor disturbances, and a whole array of "unfounded" calls where the officer arrived on the scene only to discover nothing was happening.[8]

The problem, perhaps, is how we frame policing. Moving on from order policing and the emphasis on nuisance crime means focusing on public safety by solving serious violent crimes. The failure to shift mindsets may result from structural developments.

## *Criminal Justice Growth*

One underexplored explanation for aggressively policing cannabis can be derived from a theory about the growth of the criminal justice system over the past century (Kraska, 2006). The historical development of contemporary criminal justice practices has certainly been explored in the past (Black, 1976; Christie, 2000; Garland, 2001). However, the system's evolution and development in both power and size over the past 30 years requires criminologists to examine the role of non-governmental sector, the rise of paramilitary groups, the treatment industrial complex, and other increasingly involved in criminal justice functions. The level at which this scrutiny is carried out can vary from the focus on singular administrative practices to broader critiques of the system, Kraska (2006: 71) notes:

> Keeping track and making theoretical sense of trends in crime control, or the growth in size and power of the criminal justice system, is as important as it is for crime itself. Many analysts, for example, view the government's "war on drugs" as more problematic than the drug crimes themselves.

The criminal justice growth complex can explain how specific policies on cannabis persisted long after their ineffectiveness was well known. Over the past 40 years, the unprecedented expansion and intensity of policing presents a fundamental challenge to democratic societies (Vitale, 2018). This view of an ever-expanding system of control has recently been framed using provocative language. For example, Page and Soss (2021) suggest that the US criminal justice system has become "predatory" and led to the exploitation of the poor, Black, and politically unconnected populations. Just as the US war on drugs was exported internationally based on police cooperation (Braithwaite, 2021), there are reasonable fears that other predatory police practices will expand globally.

## Key Concepts

The prohibition of cannabis profoundly changed policing. Three key concepts of interest include the war on drugs, police militarization, and predatory policing.

### *The War on Drugs*

The war on drugs began as a war on drug abuse. Richard Nixon was elected US president in 1968 on a promise to restore "law and order" to a nation shaken by riots, protests, and assassinations.[9] He aggressively recruited journalists and media executives to participate in what he declared would be a *war against drug abuse*. The Nixon White House led the early developments in the war on drugs. For Nixon, smoking cannabis meant embracing the lawlessness that he saw as sweeping the country. Within the logic of "law and order," disrespect for the law seemed to be the root of many problems. Nixon stated:

> Believe me, it is true, the thing about the drug [cannabis], once people cross that line from [unintelligible] straight society to the drug society, it's a very great possibility they are going to go further .... You see, homosexuality, dope, immorality in general. These are the enemies of a strong society. That's why the communists and left-wingers are pushing the stuff, they are trying to destroy us.[10]

In a 1994 interview with *Harper's Magazine*, Nixon's counsel and assistant to the president on domestic affairs, John Ehrlichman, confirmed Nixon's intended purpose to use narcotics legislation to target his opponents. In the interview, Ehrlichman stated:

> The Nixon campaign in 1968, and the Nixon White House after that, had two enemies: the antiwar left and black people. You understand what I'm saying? We knew we couldn't make it illegal to be either against the war or black, but by getting the public to associate the hippies with marijuana and blacks with heroin, and then criminalizing both heavily, we could disrupt

> those communities. We could arrest their leaders, raid their homes, break up their meetings, and vilify them night after night on the evening news. Did we know we were lying about the drugs? Of course, we did.[11]

More recently, the war on drugs has been defined in ways that combine several features, including its international scope, the role of transnational organizations, and the moral zeal of prohibitionists into "the violent configuration" of actors and "… militarized drug policies" (Rodríguez-Gómez & Bermeo, 2020: 20).

As we introduced in Chapter 1, the war on drugs is constantly evolving. Over the past five years, "cuckooing" has become a significant concern in the UK (Spicer, 2021). Defined as drug dealers taking over vulnerable people's homes (Spicer et al., 2020), it has become an essential focus for police. While cuckooing usually occurs to further the illicit sale or short-term storage of heroin and crack cocaine, there are examples of homes being taken over as cannabis grow spaces and to store firearms and weapons. Spicer (2021) aligns "cuckooing" with "County Lines," a recent phenomenon whereby drug dealers from urban hubs set up retail networks within smaller towns. Framed in ways that span contemporary areas of policing prioritization, the exploitation of young people, and the threat of violence create public safety demands. Police forces in the UK have largely resisted overt militarization. However, tactical approaches based on crime suppression are increasingly militarized, especially in the US.

## Police Militarization

The militarization of police cannot be divorced from the war on drugs. Police forces and funding increased dramatically to support the US drug prohibition regime. Starting in the 1970s and through the wars on drugs and gangs in the 1980s and 1990s, law enforcement campaigns advanced tactical units such as "Special Weapons and Tactics" (SWAT), armored cars, tear gas, and military-grade weapons (Balko, 2014; Hinton, 2017; Murch, 2015). As a result, young men and women of color were increasingly vulnerable to these aggressive crime suppression tactics and order maintenance strategies deployed by militarized law enforcement officials (Butler, 2017; Kraska, 2001; Taylor, Buchanan, & Ayres, 2016). This continued in the 1990s. For example, between 1992 and 2008, state and local expenditures on police doubled, from $131 per capita to $260 per capita (Lynch, 2012). Federal spending increased as well (Meeks, 2006). Increased federal, state, and local funding for law enforcement translated into many more officers patrolling the streets.

Today, the development and expansion of SWAT teams, modeled on special units in the Vietnam War, exist in nearly 90% of police departments. Shockingly, they are deployed an estimated 50,000–80,000 times per year.[12] In the US, laws were passed to allow greater integration and cooperation between the Department of Defense and police forces.[13] Through these initiatives, protective vests, night-vision optics, assault rifles, bayonets, grenade launchers, and mine-resistant, ambush-protected vehicles (MRAPs) (Balko, 2014) have been transferred from Iraq and Afghanistan to main streets and suburbs in America. One consequence of cannabis prohibition has been increased drug taskforce activities such as no-knock drug raids on private residences. Such an approach needlessly increases risks and makes predatory policing more likely.[14]

### *Predatory Policing*

A significant challenge for police reform is the growing recognition of the predatory practices of the criminal justice system. This is relevant in two ways. The first relates to the suggestion that the US criminal justice system has become a financial predator, transferring "billions of dollars … from subjugated communities to governments and corporations" (Page & Soss, 2021: 291–293). The exploitation of the poor, Black, and politically unconnected populations through fines, fees, forfeitures, prison charges, and bail premiums represent significant harm. Police often receive substantial federal subsidies; sometimes, they can keep money, cars, houses, and other property that they seize. Indeed,

> while drug-related asset forfeitures have expanded police budgets, critics say the flow of money distorts law enforcement—that some cops have become more interested in seizing money than drugs.[15]

This predation has led to the overpolicing of the least well-off,[16] policing for profit in Alabama,[17] and civil asset forfeiture laws. These laws allow police and prosecutors to confiscate and retain money and property they suspect was part of a drug crime, even after all charges were dismissed.[18] Antinarcotics police can legitimately do undercover investigations almost anywhere and target nearly anyone. Government officials have used antidrug squads to conduct surveillance operations and military raids that they would not otherwise have been able to justify (Baum, 1996; Duke & Gross, 1993; Gray, 1998; McWilliams, 1992). This predation also can be seen in how criminalizing cannabis has justified police snooping, stalking, and interfering with otherwise law-abiding citizens whose only crime is ingesting dried plant matter.

## Cannabis and Research on Police and Policing Cannabis

### *War on Cannabis*

The drug war has produced profoundly unequal outcomes across racial groups, manifested through racial discrimination by law enforcement and disproportionate despair suffered by communities of color (Alexander, 2010). This is especially true for cannabis. Michelle Alexander reports a critical realization she came to over the course of her research:

> It was coming to see how the police were behaving in radically different ways in poor communities of color than they were in middle-class, white, or suburban communities. I mean, this wasn't a shock to me in any way, but the scale of it was astonishing: seeing rows of black men lined up against walls being frisked and handcuffed and arrested for extremely minor crimes, like loitering, or vagrancy, or possession of tiny amounts of marijuana, and then being hauled off to jail and saddled with criminal records that authorized legal discrimination against them for the rest of their lives. I mean, witnessing it and interviewing people one after another had its impact on me.[19]

Challenges exist for police and other law enforcement, trained in the era of the war on drugs, to adapt to the nascent regime of cannabis legalization. This may require coming to grips with the consequences of overpolicing and extreme drug sentences (Vitello, 2021). In addition, drug war policies have expanded the number of people with criminal records, have been shown to undermine employment opportunities and housing options, and prevent civic and political engagement (Pinard, 2010). Solomon (2020: 5) argues that we need to ask ourselves some tough questions:

> To move forward, we need to understand our own history, and the false premise on which we have based this misguided policy. We need to treat the cannabis policy started in 1937 the same way we treat segregated schools, miscegenation, and other race-based policy. Our inquiry needs to start with an acknowledgment of the history of racial discrimination in our drug policy.

For policing, this matters because of shifts in law enforcement (Brown & Carrabine, 2021). In some ways, police have moved from a commitment to "protect and serve" to a warning that they will impose control through "shock and awe," as visualized in Figure 3.1.

Based on the resources devoted to investigating, enforcing, and sanctioning federal policies, the war on drugs has been transformed into a campaign to combat cannabis (King & Mauer, 2006). There were approximately 750,000 marijuana arrests in 2012, 88% of which were for possession (DOJ, 2013), at the cost of nearly $4 billion to the criminal justice system (King & Mauer, 2006). Even in states that adopted cannabis decriminalization, cannabis arrests increased significantly (Logan, 2014). In Canada, historical disparities in cannabis arrests (Owusu-Bempah & Luscombe, 2021) appear to persist even after cannabis was legalized in 2018.[20]

## *Shock and Awe*

The war on drugs and the militarization of police have seeped into police culture in worrying ways. So-called warrior culture results in aggressive police tactics (Kraska, 2001). Some officers, for example, now discuss the neighborhoods they serve not as their communities but as "battlefields."[21] Many departments have readily adopted the notion that becoming a "police warrior" is good and that having a "warrior

**FIGURE 3.1** Visualizing policing missions. Image is by Egan Jimenez and is a remix of a photo by Felix Koutchinski on Unsplash (https://unsplash.com/photos/WEcl8_kqwpg) and the photo "Militarized Police" by Roscoe Myrick licensed under CC BY 2.0. Reproduced from Wheeldon (2022: 178), published by Routledge

mindset" is necessary.[22] This outlook is connected to police tactics, especially drug crackdowns designed to disrupt illicit drug markets.

Based on a review of 23 evaluations of 20 separate police crackdowns in the US and the UK, they were largely ineffective in resolving problems around drugs like abuse, dealing, and other drug-related offenses (Mazerolle et al., 2007). For example, in the five years after a crackdown in 2004 in Denmark, there were more homicides and attempted homicides than in any five years in the previous 20 years (Moeller & Hesse, 2013). Dandurand (2021: 54) concludes, based on his review:

> Crackdowns may have an impact on police-community relations. Improperly conducted, these initiatives may serve only to alienate community residents and increase criticism of the police, undermining the legitimacy of the police.

Many assumptions and beliefs about simple enforcement solutions to the drug problem need to be questioned, studied, and revised.

Police discretion with people who use drugs (PWUD) is of increasing interest. This is based on worries that the allocation of limited resources to police drugs does little except erode public trust, further racial discord, and divide communities (del Pozo et al., 2021; Fagan et al., 2010). Between 1997 and 2007, the New York Police Department (NYPD) arrested and jailed nearly 400,000 people for possessing small amounts of cannabis, a tenfold increase over the previous decade (Levine & Small, 2008). As Meeks (2006: 33) notes:

> The inner-city underclass has become socially and economically encapsulated by the urban war on crime and an increasingly militarized urban policing force waging that war, ironically, it has also become both enemy and victim in an obscure economic and social war that is sanctioned by federal, state, and local governments.

From the war on drug abuse to the war on drugs, crime, and cannabis, the combatants targeted are citizens. More research is needed to understand how perceptions of drug war goals among officers can influence police tactics and how communities respond. One area of interest considers how decriminalization and the rise of international investments in cannabis represent a policy shift for law enforcement. This necessitates understanding how cooperation between and among law enforcement agencies in countries that have liberalized cannabis policy and those that have not (Dandurand, 2021).

Another set of questions concerns how accessing military equipment reshaped some police departments. It is essential to document the extent to which these external tools shape internal attitudes (Kraska, 2001). By contrast, more research should seek examples of demilitarizing departments to assess whether this can begin to restore legitimacy in communities that have grown up facing down armed soldiers, not public servants. This might be connected to how police assess the impacts of deemphasizing cannabis arrests and to what extent they can document the value of redeploying resources once associated with cannabis enforcement. Even if cannabis decriminalization does not necessarily lead police to focus on more serious crimes, cross-national studies can help frame how best to address resistance among departments and officers to efforts to divest from the war on drugs. The first step is focusing on cannabis as a justification for pretextual stops.

## Stop and Harass

As Kraska notes (2001), the negative consequences of the war on cannabis and the role of militarized and predatory policing suggest a profound departure from most studies in criminology. Nevertheless, they must not be ignored. Recent findings on racial disparities related to cannabis enforcement generally support past research (Fagan et al., 2010). In the US, differences in cannabis arrest rates can be explicitly linked to race and ethnicity (Akins & Mosher, 2020). This is true in Canada as well. For example, Owusu-Bempah and Luscombe (2021) analyzed data on cannabis arrests in five major cities across Canada, including Vancouver, Calgary, Regina, and Ottawa, to understand how race and ethnicity influences law enforcement in Canada. Their findings reveal that Black and Indigenous people were overrepresented in cannabis arrest statistics in the cities examined before legalization. One question concerns the strain youth face from police contact (Testa et al., 2021).

One policy is stop and frisk/stop and search. In the US, close surveillance by police has long been a part of everyday life for African Americans and other minority groups (Kennedy, 1997). Just as Jim Crow responded to emancipation by rolling back many of the newly gained rights of African Americans, "... the drug war is again replicating the institutions and repressions of the plantation ..." (Boyd, 2002: 845). In the UK, one is over eight times more likely to be stopped and searched if they happen to be Black than if one is White, even though drugs are less likely to be found (Shiner et al., 2018). The focus on nuisance crimes and drug possession is rooted in a preoccupation with the moral and social control of non-White people. This has long been recognized in the form of increasing lawlessness, police corruption, lowered respect for the law, and heightened political cynicism (Zinberg & Robertson, 1972).

An underexplored finding is that abandoning the overpolicing of cannabis use benefits the police. For example, nearly 20 years ago in the UK, Lambeth police embraced a policy known as the Lambeth Cannabis Warning Scheme to replace arrest with a formal warning to free up police time and other resources to focus on more serious crimes. The pilot ran for 13 months. Adda and colleagues (2014: 1130) concluded that the policy led to significant reductions in five types of nondrug crime, allowed police to reallocate effort toward serious crime, and led to significant improvements in police effectiveness against such crimes as measured by arrest and case closure rates. Likewise, by replacing arrest with diversion, Hughes and colleagues (2014) found that such policies reduced workloads on police and the court system in Australia. In addition, this policy allowed for better use of existing resources, and subsequent research showed that these benefits endured (Hughes et al., 2019).

**FIGURE 3.2** Banksy: Stop and Search by eddiedangerous is licensed under CC BY 2.0

One question is whether and to what extent decreasing police contact related to cannabis can rebuild community views of police legitimacy. Past research shows that nearly half of the 4.4 million involuntary police stops between 2004 and 2012 in New York City were of young men. These stops often undermine public perceptions of police professionalism since only about one in ten stops resulted in an arrest or citation (Tyler et al., 2014). If discriminatory police practices result in deprivation, youth may see rules, agencies, and official norms as illegitimate. These are especially important given recent research by Testa et al. (2021) suggesting that adolescent police contact is an adverse experience that shapes their experience in profound ways. Moreover, it often serves as an important life course event that may have repercussions on later life outcomes.

## New Directions

New directions in policing cannabis must acknowledge how efforts to reform the police and deemphasize cannabis enforcement have proven difficult to sustain, especially where cannabis remains illegal. In general, police reform is difficult (Mastrofski, 2004). Some are critical of the potential for training, diversity, or tactics to confront the fundamental challenge of policing in America (Vitale, 2018). Research undertaken following the public outcry over the deaths of unarmed Black citizens in the US provides little comfort. For example, O'Guinn (2022) analyzed organizational training and accountability measures to assess whether these can reduce the likelihood of unarmed, fatal officer-involved shootings. Unfortunately, most training and accountability mechanisms were unrelated to or even, depressingly, increased the likelihood of deadly shootings. However, reform is possible.

In 2021, the Milwaukee Fire and Police Commission removed the use of no-knock search warrants from its standard operating procedures.[23] Banning no-knock search warrants has been a policy that activists, both locally and nationally, have been calling for since the death of Breonna Taylor, killed in her home by police in Louisville in 2020. In addition to banning police officers from seeking and executing no-knock search warrants, the commission expanded whistleblower protections and clarified that officers have an affirmative duty to report severe misconduct and protect the reporting officers from retaliation. They also adopted a new discipline matrix, which lays out a uniform system of disciplining officers for various violations. One approach is assessing the value of instituting external reviews of police procedures (O'Guinn, 2022).

Another question is whether state law can be used to reduce law enforcement incentives and limit the sorts of police intrusions that have divided communities and undermined their mission. An important recent contribution details how cannabis liberalization can provoke police reform (Brown, 2022). For example, legislation in New York, Oregon, and Colorado limits police authority to expand stops, conduct searches and make arrests for drug possession. The suggestion that drug decriminalization can reduce pretextual stops, militarized police, and intrusive enforcement practices doesn't mean it will. Brown (2022) offers a significant conceptual contribution. Liberalizing cannabis policy can open the door to substantive police reform. These changes can strengthen the potential for substantive police reform. However, there are legitimate questions about how successful deemphasizing cannabis enforcement can be when cannabis investigations have proven to be a lucrative means to support departmental budgets.

Combating the persistence of prohibitionist ideas also means replacing funds acquired through civil asset forfeiture, fines, fees, and other costs. In Oregon, Senate Bill 1587 would expand the quarterly transfer to the Criminal Justice Commission's Illegal Marijuana Enforcement Grant Program from $750,000 to $4 million over the next three years.[24] Possession and nonpublic use of cannabis are legal in Oregon. However, Measure 110, passed in November 2020, went further and decriminalized small amounts of street drugs. Cannabis tax revenue was directed to fund harm reduction and recovery services rather than policing. SB 1587 includes a one-time $50 million allocation from the General Fund for cities and counties to compensate for a decline in their share of cannabis tax. This marks a shift away from cannabis treatment and toward policing illicit cannabis.

A final aspect worth exploring is how police see their role in an era of increasingly legal cannabis. Law enforcement agencies are expected to confront the dangers of the illicit market in opioids and stimulants or reduce the availability of fentanyl and other opioids while supporting cannabis legalization schemes and protecting them against organized crime. Contending with varying levels of enforcement within embryonic regulatory regimes creates confusion. In 2020, police officers in Washington, where cannabis has been legal since 2012, expressed numerous concerns. These include worries about youth access and use, increases in drugged driving, prosecutorial behavior, and managing nuisance calls about cannabis usage in public (Stohr et al., 2020). The lack of police preparation for legalization is a significant issue.

Ethnographic research with police officers offers some methodological insights. This reimagined approach resituates ride-alongs, participant observation, and relationship building and allows ethnographers to probe the backstage where police and policy intersect. This includes understanding how prohibition-based drug policies are used to expand efforts to control drug use. Spicer's (2021) work in the UK applies the deviancy amplification spiral model (Young, 1971) and suggests an iterative and cyclical processes of interpretation, intensification, and magnification of social phenomena. For example:

> Drawing on a range of ethnographic data, five stages of the spiral surrounding cuckooing are outlined: (1) identifying cuckooing as a problem; (2) demonstrating a response; (3) spreading the problem; (4) making it other people's problem too and (5) the establishment of a policing priority. Shaped by the experiences of officers responding to cuckooing, the influence of wider national agendas and interactions with the practice of cuckooing itself, it is

> concluded that the spiral might be coming to a conclusion. While further developments may continue, it has become established as a policing priority, with ramifications for other organizations, communities and national policy.
>
> *Spicer, 2021: 1391*

As the model suggests, amplifying the issue leads to more policing and expands punitive approaches by recruiting other organizations to help with the police response. The multiagency response "… might actually make the situation worse" (Spicer, 2021: 1403). However, there must be more understanding of how police agencies' reactions and interactions with societal stereotypes intensify, rather than meaningfully address, the connections between and among drugs, crime, and the community.

## Conclusion

Law enforcement is always caught up in the cultural and historical traditions of the society they police. In the past, this led to the strategic regulation and control of marginalized groups through harsh criminal justice practices connected to hardline policing attitudes and law enforcement tactics. This undermined the legitimacy of the justice system. Cannabis provides an intriguing example of how police and the politics of criminal justice intersect. This chapter considered police and policing cannabis based on strain theory, social control, and criminal justice growth. Key concepts explored in this chapter include the war on drugs, the militarization of the police, and predatory practices attributed to the justice system, including stop and frisk, and stop and search. Cannabis liberalization represents a means to reform police practices going forward.

In research in this area, two findings appear again and again. The first is that differences in arrest rates cannot be explained by differences in previous nondrug and drug offending, sociodemographic variables, or geographic location (Males & Buchen, 2014; Koch et al., 2016; Mitchell & Caudy, 2017; Mooney et al., 2018). The second is net widening. It is one of the most consistent findings in research examining cannabis decriminalization and appears to impact people and communities of color disproportionately. Levine and Small (2008) report that although Whites are more prevalent among people who use cannabis, Whites were less likely than other ethnicities to be stopped, detained, investigated, and arrested.

More research is needed to bridge the gap between police practices, formal decriminalization, and the rise of international investments in commercial cannabis. This might involve trying to understand cooperation between and among law enforcement agencies in countries that have liberalized cannabis policy and those that have not (Dandurand, 2021). This also speaks to the need to understand and compare police cultures in Canada, Uruguay, Portugal, and US states in Washington and Colorado, alongside policing in other American states, the UK,

Australia, and beyond. Interest in these sorts of comparisons is not new. Cannabis provides a specific issue that grounds general comparisons around one topic. Perhaps criminologists can uncover the views that contribute to police culture and reimagine policing along the cannabis legalization–criminalization spectrum. This requires engaging questions of race, ethnicity, and racism.

## Notes

1 See www.nytimes.com/2018/08/24/us/marijuana-diversion-program-maricopa-arizona.html [accessed June 5, 2022].
2 Brendan Del Pozo (2021). See https://podcasts.apple.com/us/podcast/policing-and-democracy-with-brandon-del-pozo/id1382983397?i=1000480305083 at 51:45 [accessed June 5, 2022].
3 See www.ajc.com/news/crime/police-to-pay-cartersville-70-members-900k-to-settle-federal-lawsuit/6TOMFPFSZZHRRIDBJMNFQNS4CM/ [accessed June 5, 2022].
4 See www.standard.co.uk/news/uk/department-for-education-metropolitan-police-services-scotland-yard-hackney-b988292.html [accessed June 5, 2022].
5 See https://chscp.org.uk/wp-content/uploads/2022/03/Child-Q-PUBLISHED-14-March-22.pdf [accessed June 5, 2022].
6 See www.seattletimes.com/seattle-news/ex-police-chief-norm-stamper-takes-global-view-on-drug-crisis/ [accessed June 5, 2022].
7 See www.vox.com/2020/7/31/21334190/what-police-do-defund-abolish-police-reform-training [accessed June 5, 2022].
8 See www.vox.com/2020/7/31/21334190/what-police-do-defund-abolish-police-reform-training [accessed June 5, 2022].
9 See www.washingtonpost.com/history/2018/11/05/law-order-campaign-that-won-richard-nixon-white-house-years-ago/ [accessed September 1, 2021].
10 See https://origins-s.asc.ohio-state.edu/article/illegalization-marijuana-brief-history?language_content_entity=en [accessed October 29, 2020].
11 See https://harpers.org/archive/2016/04/legalize-it-all/ [accessed October 29, 2021].
12 See www.counterpunch.org/2021/06/11/militarized-police-a-consequence-of-the-war-on-drugs/ [accessed July 17, 2021].
13 The 1208 Program (formerly known as the 1033 Program) is explicitly connected to police militarization. See www.wired.com/story/pentagon-hand-me-downs-militarize-police-1033-program/ [accessed June 5, 2022].
14 Peter Kraska, personal communication, December 2021.
15 www.npr.org/templates/story/story.php?storyId=91490480 [accessed July 17, 2021].
16 www.thebulwark.com/policing-for-profit-targets-low-income-people-who-cant-afford-to-fight-back/ [accessed June 5, 2022].
17 https://slate.com/podcasts/what-next/2022/01/when-policing-becomes-a-towns-cash-cow [accessed June 5, 2022].
18 www.wbur.org/news/2021/08/18/civil-forfeiture-police-money-massachusetts-worcester-joseph-early [accessed June 5, 2022].
19 See www.newyorker.com/news/the-new-yorker-interview/ten-years-after-the-new-jim-crow [accessed June 5, 2022].
20 See www.vice.com/en/article/akvpe4/race-drug-arrests-canada [accessed August 15, 2022].

21 See www.npr.org/2020/07/01/885942130/militarization-of-police-means-u-s-protesters-face-weapons-designed-for-war [accessed June 5, 2022].

22 See https://harvardlawreview.org/2015/04/law-enforcements-warrior-problem/ [accessed June 5, 2022].

23 See www.jsonline.com/story/news/2021/11/18/fire-and-police-commission-bans-use-no-knock-search-warrants/8676548002/ [accessed June 5, 2022].

24 See www.kgw.com/article/money/oregon-bill-pot-taxes-police/283-ed396b87-854d-4fa6-b3ee-fb6985d75285?utm_campaign=snd-autopilot [accessed June 5, 2022].

# 4

# RACE, ETHNICITY, AND CRIMINALIZATION

## Introduction

Cannabis prohibition has exacerbated racial injustice in the US and around the world. It has led to a host of costs that must be documented if they are to be confronted. One of the most consistent findings in the literature over decades is that the adverse effects of criminalizing cannabis disproportionately impact people of color. These impacts have historical dimensions (Collins, 2022; Pembleton, 2017) and have led to unequal arrest and incarceration rates in communities of color that are not reflective of the differences in the prevalence of drug use (Alexander, 2010; Heidt & Wheeldon, 2015). Some observers argue that the net effect of the war on drugs has perpetuated White supremacy and the concomitant subordination of Blacks to Whites. The war on drugs "has become a replacement system for segregation [by] … separating out, subjugating, imprisoning, and destroying substantial portions of a population-based on skin color" (Glasser, 2000: 723).

As discussed in Chapter 3, differences in racial arrest rates cannot be explained without considering the role of race and racism (Males & Buchen, 2014; Koch et al., 2016; Mitchell & Caudy, 2017; Mooney et al., 2018). Mooney and colleagues (2018) examined California drug arrest data from 2011 to 2016 to evaluate the impact of the defelonization of drug offenses. They found that while there was an immediate drop in the numbers of arrests for people of color across the board, the Black–White relative disparity increased by 27%. Race and ethnic injustice are intimately connected with cannabis laws around the world, from Canada to the UK and Australia.

For some criminologists, this unapologetic focus on race is uncomfortable. It requires acknowledging controversial conceptions such as:

DOI: 10.4324/9781003232292-4

(a) the construction of race as biological in criminological theory
(b) the privileging of Whiteness in criminal justice practice
(c) institutional and systemic racism within criminal law and policy
(d) unspoken racist assumptions that underpin justice policies
(e) the use of coded language that supports "colorblind" rhetorical stances toward race and ethnicity in policing, prosecutions, and corrections.[1]

Beyond performative pronouncements, it is hard to seriously examine the history of cannabis policy without running into one or more of these ideas. The war on drugs has produced profoundly unequal outcomes across racial groups, manifested in racial discrimination by law enforcement and disproportionate despair suffered by communities of color (Alexander, 2010; Owusu-Bempah & Luscombe, 2021). What explains why these inequalities persist even as cannabis is decriminalized (or even legalized)? The answer involves connecting explanatory strands, including newer theories of criminal justice, with older theories originating in criminology.

This chapter considers cannabis and race, ethnicity, and criminalization. Theoretical starting points include biological and psychological positivism, critical race theory (CRT), and restorative justice. Key concepts explored in this chapter comprise disparities in justice system contacts, the costs of cannabis prohibition, and reconciliation. Research has modeled new ways to understand the racial dynamics of prohibition. Cannabis liberalization may represent an opportunity to confront historical racism and ethnic hate. One question is how cannabis liberalization can inform other efforts designed to reinvest resources in historically overpoliced and underserved communities.

## Theoretical Starting Points

To understand the role of race and ethnicity, three theories are of immediate interest. The first is biological and psychological positivism, which must be seen alongside the demonization of people who use drugs, as outlined in Chapter 2. These theories provided scientific cover for profoundly biased views based on presumed racial inferiority. Recognizing structural racism within society led to CRT, which links longstanding animus and ignorance to existing social dynamics and criminal justice policies. If these theories suggest a difficult path forward for cannabis liberalization, restorative justice may provide a mechanism for reconciliation. Confronting the disparate harms of cannabis policy and pledging to right those wrongs will require bravery, leadership, and imagination.

### *Biological and Psychological Positivism*

Biological positivist theories focus on individual characteristics that are inherited and present at birth, such as biological and mental traits. In the late nineteenth century, criminologists applied the scientific method to help identify physical stigmata, body types, and genetic differences that might help distinguish criminals from noncriminals. In 1871, Lombroso proposed his theory of an atavistic man, which was very well received, especially in the US, where it became popular. At first, his ideas competed with phrenology over which theory best explained criminality. Eventually, Lombroso's theory and approach were embraced and supported by the American Institute of Criminal Law and Criminology. This influential organization devoted more attention to his research, and his work was translated and distributed (Savitz, Turner, & Dickman, 1977).

With the benefit of hindsight, early biological positivist approaches today look like mere pseudoscience used to privilege the physical characteristics of some groups over others. Later theorists started to use psychological characteristics that can be used to identify criminals. Instead of focusing on physical traits or body types, these theories identify personality traits and mental processes that impact behavior (Heidt & Wheeldon, 2015). These theories are relevant to understanding cannabis criminology in two ways. First, biological positivism's focus on physical traits and inherited genetic predispositions was effortlessly associated with race-based conclusions about crime and criminal behavior. As Cody (2006: 19) concludes,

> the notion of race and cannabis has over the years undergone various forms of reproduction, each has nevertheless served to illustrate popularized ideological constructs through which the tradition of viewing the "other" community as a threat to the dominant culture is maintained .... "Race" as a symbol played a major role in the formation of early drug legislation and continues to do so even today where the supposed race of a drug offender is often deemed important and portrayed negatively in media reporting of the issue. However, the anti-cannabis campaign took on another symbol of the "other" beginning in the 1930s. The drug posed a new threat to society which brought ruin through its supposed ability to create criminals.

Just as this "scientific" justification for demonizing non-White populations connected unwanted behavior to sin, psychological positivism suggested a second concern. Rather than vague notions of moral insanity, emergent psychological approaches focused on how the inability to balance competing stimuli, drives, and situations could lead to crime. Central here was the early definition of psychopathy, which presented insanity as an alternative to demonic explanations for criminality (Heidt & Wheeldon, 2015).

In the US, the connection between cannabis and insanity was propagated as early as 1913. *The Salt Lake Tribune*, under the headline "Evil Mexican Plants That Drive You Insane," reported that "marijuana make(s) the smoker wilder than a wild beast" and provided anecdotal evidence of average and ordinary people who became murderers after smoking cannabis.[2] These stories and others were repeated by papers and magazines that were part of the Hearst media empire. In 1923, a Hearst paper reported that "[m]arihuana is a shortcut to the insane asylum. Smoke marihuana cigarettes for a month, and what was once your brain will be nothing but a storehouse for horrid specters."[3] In 1928, another Hearst paper reported that marijuana was known in India as the "murder drug"; it was common for a man to "catch up a knife and run through the streets, hacking, and killing everyone he [encountered]."[4] In one of the most curious claims, the article declared that one could grow enough cannabis in a window box to "drive the whole population of the United States stark, raving mad."[5]

## Critical Race Theory

Metrics used to justify policies based on presumed racial inferiority emerged in the nineteenth century. Physiognomy refers to the belief that behavior can be predicted through a person's physical appearance. Swiss scholar and theologian Johann Kaspar Lavater was one of the pioneers in this area, and his work on physiognomy received almost as much praise as Lombroso's work (Bernard, Snipes, & Gerould, 2010). The emergence of physiognomy and phrenology preceded Lombroso's work on the criminal man (Savitz, Turner, & Dickman, 1977).

Other theories of "intelligence" and "moral reasoning" based on physical attributes of race, like the shapes of skulls, soon emerged. Viennese physician Franz Joseph Gall and his student Johann Gaspar Spurzheim are considered the principal founders of this field (Rafter, 2008). Although phrenology has proved to be scientifically lacking, it grew into a well-developed field. It offered a scientific theory of criminal behavior in place of moralistic and spiritualistic explanations. However, these ideas could never escape nor replace the racist attitudes of the time. For example, in the 1830s, they "proved" that humans were made up of distinct, separate species, hierarchically ordered based on intellectual capacity. This view was used to justify slavery on scientific grounds.[6]

CRT emerged from this context and built on a framework for legal analysis, created by legal scholars Derrick Bell, Kimberle Crenshaw, Alan Freeman, and Richard Delgado. Its application in criminology is connected to the notion that the construction of cultural and psychosocial meanings is central to understanding society (Berger & Luckmann, 1966), alongside Black's (1976, 1984) view that the law exists as a governmental form of social control that both penalizes and orders social relations. This includes cultural artifacts like literature, television, and film and how these representations are rooted in legislation and laws, state policies, and individual practices.

CRT maintains that American laws, including antidiscrimination laws, are structured to maintain White privilege (Alexander, 2010; Capers, 2014; Delgado & Stefancic, 2001; Nyika & Murray-Orr, 2017). Fornili (2018: 65) notes that CRT provides a cohesive framework for examining the war on drugs:

> (a) the school-to-prison pipeline, (b) the for-profit prison system ("prison industrial complex"), (c) racialized mass incarceration, and (d) the disproportionately negative impact of the War on Drugs on families and communities of color.

An example of the enduring need for CRT is the recent effort to obscure the widespread recognition that race plays a part in the history of cannabis prohibition. For instance, Fisher writes (2021: 933):

> Race does play a role in the history of the American drug war, but not the role commonly claimed. For our earliest antidrug laws were not about the Chinese, African Americans, or Mexicans sometimes linked with opium, cocaine, and marijuana. These were laws about Whites. The lawmakers who erected America's earliest drug bans acted first and foremost to protect the morals of their own racial kin. And because the morals of most importance to White lawmakers were those of their own offspring, they acted fastest and most forcefully when a drug took White youth in its clutches.

This is a fascinating example of attempting to decouple race and cannabis prohibition. While Fisher (2021) provides examples of racial language, he argues that the lack of explicit formal examples of officials connecting race and cannabis undermines widespread findings that racial hostility led to cannabis policy. Ultimately, it is irrelevant whether these policies had their roots in moralism designed to protect White people or a desire to criminalize and control non-White people. As Tonry (1994: 27) points out, the policies adopted by the architects of the war on drugs "were foreordained disproportionately to affect disadvantaged black Americans."

### *Restorative Justice*

In criminological terms, restorative justice is often linked to reintegrative shaming (Braithwaite, 1989). However, other theories offer additional perspectives (Wheeldon, 2009). As Liz Elliott (2011) argues, too often, formal institutions ignore racism, classism, and the need for victims to play an active role in overcoming the fear, shame, and damage associated with crimes. Restorative justice seeks to address these social justice issues by making the community the primary site of social action. Although crucial principles common to restorative justice originally grew out of practice and tradition before the articulation of peacemaking criminology, these programs cannot be adequately understood without reference to theories presented after the fact. For example, harm can refer to damages suffered by victims, those responsible for causing harm, and even communities where it occurs. This expanded definition provides an essential shift in thinking about crime and an expansion in thought about how harm might be addressed (Pepinsky & Quinney, 1991).

The second principle is a desire to foster the role of the community in the neighborhood where the harm occurred. Elliott (2002) has argued that this is important in at least two ways. First, the inclusion of the community in any process to address harm acknowledges the critical role the community plays in crime commission and prevention. In addition, by explicitly including the community in the process, there is the acceptance of the notion that even those not harmed in a particular case still have an interest in its successful resolution (Elliott, 2002: 462–463). This allows restorative justice to engage community members in a process where they have a meaningful role in the outcome of decisions that matter to them. The third principle is related to the moral potential for restorative justice. By rooting morality in attending to the real needs of actual individuals through processes that reflect community values, restorative justice offers an intriguing alternative to the formal justice system.

Instead of relying on official definitions of crime that are the product of societies and cultures with problematic histories, involving people and communities in exploring the harms and coming to a collective solution is at once practical and radical. Pepinsky (1991) suggests that critical and feminist traditions inform peacemaking criminology. These are related to some of the underlying assumptions within the restorative justice movement today (Wheeldon, 2009). For example, based on critical traditions, there remains a distrust of the state as an impartial arbiter and a desire to locate justice in individual communities where residents participate in the decision-making process (Einstadter & Henry, 1995; Gibbons, 1994). From the feminist tradition, Pepinsky (1991: 310) identifies Kay Harris as an influential thinker who argued that restorative processes should allow those who have suffered harm to participate in the design of an appropriate response.

While the connection between restorative justice and peacemaking criminology has a historical pedigree, recent justifications have placed harm at the intersection of individuals, groups, and cultures. This includes thinking about state crime, including harms perpetrated by the criminal justice system itself. Restorative justice offers a means to think about cannabis and the damages done under prohibition. To what extent can new policies begin to provide redress for a century of prohibition and 50 years of the war against drugs?

## Key Concepts

### *Race as a Social Construction*

The notion that race is a social construct without biological meaning is common among scientists, despite the continued use of categorical variables like "White" and "Black" as biological determinants. The problem with using race as a biological explanation for social and cultural differences between people was first observed by W. E. B. Du Bois (1897: 53) more than a century ago. He asked:

> What, then, is race? It is a vast family of human beings, generally of common blood and language, always of common history, traditions and impulses, who are both voluntarily and involuntarily striving together for the accomplishment of certain more or less vividly conceived ideals of life.

By distinguishing the importance of history and traditions instead of blood, Du Bois' prescience has since been established by genetic research (Heidt & Wheeldon, 2015). For example, there is so much ambiguity between the races, and so much variation within them, that "… two people of European descent may be more genetically similar to a person of Asian descent than they are to each other."[7]

Another way to view the consequences of the social construction of race is to consider the racial outcomes of this approach to evolutionary theory. This involves grasping how social assumptions about race became baked into older and persistent notions about scientific methods. For example, Lombroso's theories about crime gained acceptance not because they presented new data that challenged existing assumptions. Instead, the idea that easily measurable physical characteristics could predict criminality became popular because it provided scientific cover for race-based assumptions about social groups and crime:

> When we examine the process of "'racialisation we find that our beliefs about "races" and "race relations" have more to do with the attitudes, actions, motivations and interests of powerful groups in society; and less to do with the characteristics, attitudes and actions of those who are defined as belonging to "inferior" races … we must also acknowledge that definitions, ideas and images once begun can vary and endure in ways that are complex.

This is both important and difficult for some to acknowledge. Relevant in criminal justice terms, Goff and colleagues (2014: 526) found evidence that Black boys are seen as older and less innocent than same-age White peers and predicted: "... actual racial disparities in police violence toward children." Since these attitudes, motivations, and interests persist, extra care must be taken whenever "scientific" findings appear to justify social divisions supported by administrative categorizations, policies, or laws with disparate results.

### *Race and Predation*

As introduced in Chapter 3, recent analysis has framed the operations of the American criminal justice system in provocative ways. The idea that the criminal justice system has become "predatory" and led to the exploitation of poor and politically unconnected populations through fines, fees, forfeitures, and other charges applies broadly (Page & Soss, 2021). Its impact has fallen disproportionately on Black and Brown people. This follows recent work to organize studies of racial capitalism to link market economies with racial domination. For example, Jenkins and Leroy (2021) document how Indigenous mortgage foreclosures, imperial expansion in the continental US, and the politics of banking and debt contribute to racial inequalities and intergenerational wealth. The interactions between CRT, Marxism, colonialism and unconscious racism remain difficult to untangle (Melamed, 2015).

Race-based animus within the criminal justice system can be seen in how race was historically used to control non-White populations, as documented in Chapter 2. Page and Soss (2021) argue that conceiving the potential for predation by actors within the criminal justice system offers a unique way to understand mass policing, incarceration, and other forms of racialized control. Of interest is how older work by Walter Rodney, Ida B. Wells, Manning Marable, Barbara Fields, Cedric Robinson, and W. E. B. Du Bois can be connected to more contemporary analysis that suggests criminal justice institutions serve as tools for controlling subjugated groups deemed threatening, disruptive, or unproductive in market terms (Waquant, 2009).

The notion that justice institutions could prey and feed on those caught up within the criminal justice system is both enlightening and deeply depressing. Given the overrepresentation of people of color within the justice system, the combination of the prohibition of cannabis within justice systems committed to privatization (Haggerty, 2004) has institutionalized inequality. Since the "tough on crime" rhetoric of the 1980s, costs associated with being entangled in the criminal justice system shifted from society to individuals. The expansion of policing and punishment systems produced new revenue needs that people of color in the US and beyond have been forced to pay (Page & Soss, 2021).

## *Race and the Long Shadow of Slavery*

To make sense of how predatory systems of injustice persist, it is useful to remember how the social construction of race offered a means to justify racial mistreatment on scientific grounds. The most obvious way this construction provided financial benefits to some and not others was slavery. Kenneth Stampp (1956: 7) described slavery as "America's most profound and vexatious social problem [whose] impact upon the whole country was disastrous." In many ways, Americans live in the shadow of this tragedy. The moral disquiet that accompanies the recognition of what the enslavement of human beings meant continues to disturb the foundations of society. As Erna Paris (2000: 169) noted:

> Stampp detailed abuses that were, naturally, known in the deepest recesses of many hearts—yet simultaneously "unknown," in that they were largely unacknowledged, for slavery is one of those historical episodes that provoke shame in the perpetrator, or perhaps in the children and grandchildren of the perpetrator, once the values that underscore the system have been surpassed and rejected.

Whether we have surpassed, rejected, or wrestled with the legacy of this history is debatable. Some accept the idea that racism remains a collective weight that can never quite be borne. But as with cannabis liberalization, any progress is met with fierce backlash. Indeed, in 2021 laws claiming to ban efforts to teach students about America's troubled history on race have been passed in Arkansas, Florida, Iowa, Oklahoma, Tennessee, and Texas and advanced in more than a dozen other states.[8] Beyond the inevitable constitutional challenges and near impossibility of enforcement, the idea that half the states in the US would pass laws designed to deny American history and conceal what must be confronted is, in fact, the best example of the need for students to learn this history. The long shadow of slavery and unconscious racism has long been a feature of the criminal justice system.

## Relevant Research on Race, Ethnicity, and Criminalization

It is now widely accepted that the criminal justice system perpetuates systemic biases against people of color (Alexander, 2010; Bell, 1994; Capers, 2014: Delgado & Stefancic, 2017; Fornili, 2018; Mejía & Csete, 2016; Nyika & Murray-Orr, 2017; Western & Pettit, 2010). New efforts to communicate these disparities can help uncover the consequences of past policies.

### *Cannabis, Racial Disparities, and Injustice*

Disparities arising from the enforcement of all drugs exist in the US, the UK, Australia, Canada, and several European countries with much more liberal systems (Baker & Goh, 2004; Belackova et al., 2017; Hughes & Stevens, 2010; Lammy, 2017; Shiner, 2015). People of color are more likely to be targeted by law enforcement, less likely to be diverted, and receive harsher penalties at higher rates for the same drug offenses. This holds across multiple studies and remains salient in jurisdictions with prohibition and carries over when depenalization and diversion approaches are implemented. It is especially true of cannabis prohibition.

One effort worthy of more consideration is the visual presentation of data (Burruss & Lu, 2022). Sheehan and colleagues (2021) analyzed data between 2000 and 2019 from 43 US states to compare pre-implementation and post-implementation differences in arrest rates for states with decriminalization, legalization, and no policy changes. The authors are careful not to suggest that their results categorically establish the value of either decriminalization or legalization. However, the increases in arrest rate disparities highlight how cannabis policy and racial inequality are linked in stark and obvious ways. As Figure 4.1 demonstrates, only full cannabis legalization can disrupt racial disparities in cannabis enforcement.

### *The Cost(s) of Cannabis Prohibition*

Since the 1970s, some strand of interest in the decriminalization of cannabis was based on libertarian arguments that sought to protect an adult's right to do what they wish in the privacy of their own home, rather than burdening them with a criminal record (Brecher, 1972; Kaplan, 1970). The longevity and influence of these arguments might be understood based on who is stopped, investigated, arrested, charged, and incarcerated for cannabis offenses. As we have documented, it is people of color. As people of color became the focus of the war on drugs, liberty-focused White people became less vocal.

To assess the consequences of policing cannabis, it may be worthwhile to try and calculate the direct and indirect costs to society in general but, perhaps

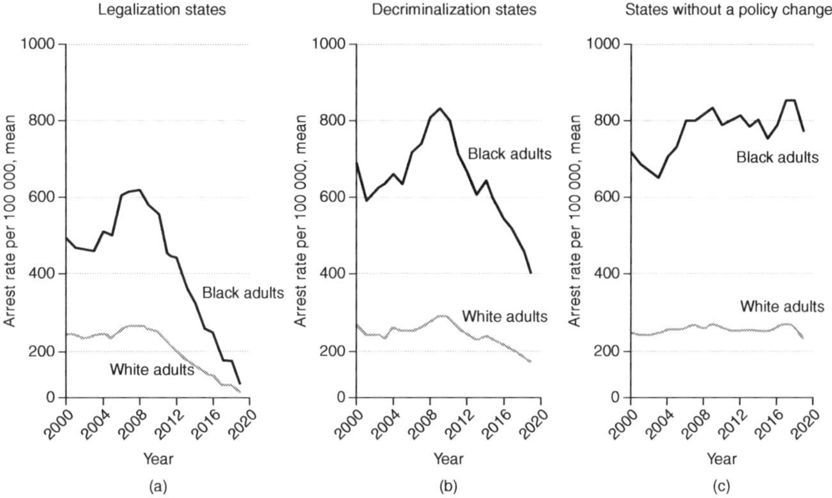


**FIGURE 4.1** Adult arrest rate trends of cannabis possession by race between legalization, decriminalization, and no policy reform states (Sheehan et al., 2021: 4)

most importantly, those entangled in the criminal justice system. Mejía and Csete (2016: 3) provide a starting place.

> The billions per year spent on incarceration of the large number of persons sentenced to at least one year in prison for drug offenses in U.S. federal and state facilities—estimated at over 304,000 in 2013—only begins to represent the cost to society and communities of mass incarceration that falls disproportionately on racial minorities and people living in poverty. In the European Union, where drug-related incarceration is much less frequent on a per-capita basis than in the United States, the member states nonetheless spend an estimated €7 billion per year (about U.S. $7.8 billion) on drug-related pretrial detention and imprisonment. None of these figures capture the high costs, including extra-judicial killings and insecurity of communities, associated with drug markets or the cost to society of corruption of state institutions with drug proceeds. A conservative estimate of the value of illicit drug markets is over U.S. $330 billion annually, resources that are in the hands of criminal networks and available for fueling corruption.

While a proper accounting of the tangible and intangible costs of the war on drugs is needed, of immediate interest are costs associated with the prohibition of cannabis. Communicating the direct and indirect costs of maintaining existing policies should be added to research on health disparities, historical and generational inequities, and damage done to the legitimacy of the criminal justice system itself. In a country consumed with costs, assigning amounts to the substantive damage done by cannabis prohibition is a strategy worthy of more attention. Some of these costs are difficult to quantify. Bruce Western and Becky Pettit (2010: 8) provide an overview.

> The influence of the penal system on social and economic disadvantage can be seen in the economic and family lives of the formerly incarcerated. The social inequality produced by mass incarceration is sizable and enduring for three main reasons: it is invisible, it is cumulative, and it is intergenerational. The inequality is invisible in the sense that institutionalized populations commonly lie outside our official accounts of economic well-being. Prisoners, though drawn from the lowest rungs in society, appear in no measures of poverty or unemployment. As a result, the full extent of the disadvantage of groups with high incarceration rates is underestimated. The inequality is cumulative because the social and economic penalties that flow from incarceration are accrued by those who already have the weakest economic opportunities. Mass incarceration thus deepens disadvantage and forecloses mobility for the most marginal in society. Finally, carceral inequalities are intergenerational, affecting not just those who go to prison and jail but their families and children, too.

These costs and the adverse spillover associated with policing and the history of laws allowing police to stop and harass citizens provide a new means to understand race, ethnicity, and injustice (Kerrison & Sewell, 2020; Sewell et al., 2021; Sewell, 2020). We discuss this idea in more detail below.

## *Race and Reconciliation*

Reconciliation requires addressing concerns about pervasive unequal and punitive criminal justice responses to cannabis use. This will involve taking steps to confront and attempt to reduce the damage done by the system itself (Quinney, 1970). This approach can be seen alongside efforts to expand restorative justice by employing a variety of programs and practices that focus on resolving conflicts through the active participation of those involved, including victims, offenders, and the broader community. Cannabis prohibition has exacerbated racial injustice and led to a host of costs that must be documented if they are to be confronted. This is underway but far from complete. It must continue.

Recall the examples in Chapter 3, which focused on strip searches conducted as part of policing cannabis in the US and the UK. Near Georgia, 44 members of the so-called Cartersville 70 were awarded a $900,000 settlement in a federal civil rights lawsuit, based on allegations that police tactics were racially motivated.[9] Following an unconstitutional search, those detained were subject to invasive strip searches, denied medical services, and had their privacy violated when their booking photos were illegally shared online.[10] The shocking strip search by London metropolitan police officers took place at a Hackney school near London. It occurred without parental consent and without another adult present. An official review found that "racism (whether deliberate or not) was likely to have been an influencing factor in the decision to undertake a strip search."[11] No drugs were found. Whatever financial settlement is forthcoming, the damage to this young person is significant. According to a review of the incident, the student is now in therapy and self-harming.[12]

These examples suggest the long and persistent role of racism and cannabis policy. Financial remuneration for past abuses is, of course, a reactive approach. More proactive and systematic efforts are emerging. One recent example is US President Joe Biden's 2022 executive order, pardoning those convicted of cannabis possession at the federal level and calling for a number of other reforms both federally and at the state level. For example, a

> number of US states, in particular New York and Massachusetts, have paved the way for a social and racial justice model of cannabis reform. Release present guiding principles in preparation for the eventual legal regulation of cannabis in the UK. These principles are designed to ensure that the same people who are locked up by punitive drug policies are not locked out of the legal market, and that cannabis reform is an opportunity to repair history.[13]

This appears to be a clear reference to an effort to reduce further harms associated with the politics of the past.

In addition to President Biden's recent efforts, this is explicitly part of The Marijuana Opportunity Reinvestment and Expungement Act (MORE Act) in the US. In 2020, the House of Representatives took an important step by voting in favor of removing cannabis from the federal Controlled Substances Act. The bill would also create pathways for ownership opportunities in the emerging industry, allow veterans to obtain medical cannabis recommendations from Veteran Affairs doctors, and establish funding sources to reinvest in communities disproportionately affected by the war on drugs.[14] If passed and signed into law, the MORE Act would decriminalize cannabis and expunge nonviolent federal marijuana convictions. In addition, it would create the Office of Cannabis Justice to oversee the financial and social reinvestment in communities disproportionately affected by the war on drugs.[15] This application of restorative justice principles is instructive.

The value of restorative justice in criminology is no longer questioned (Sherman & Strang, 2007; Strang et al., 2013). It can better support victims of harm, promote community solidarity, and offer a place for difficult conversations to occur (Wheeldon, 2009). One challenge here is how to adapt evidence on the value of various restorative programs to broader processes of community engagement and reconciliation. Kathy Fox's work (2012, 2013, 2015) suggests some important insights. Applying the lessons of restorative justice can mitigate exclusion and isolation, embrace destigmatization, and create relationships based on mutual respect and shared obligation. However, research that assesses efforts to promote reconciliation after systematic injustice suffers from few examples.

One important experience comes from South Africa. Gibson (2004), writing in the context of the Truth and Reconciliation Commission (TRC) in South Africa, suggested truth and reconciliation are connected. Moreover, for groups within

South Africa, a commitment to telling the truth seems to have led to reconciliation. Erna Paris (2000: 307–309) reports that Mary Burton, a TRC commissioner, established a national "register" of reconciliation to give voice to ordinary South Africans. "The register [is] in response to a deep wish for reconciliation in the hearts of many South Africans … who want to demonstrate in some symbolic way their commitment to a new kind of future," Burton said. People were invited to write to the TRC, and several hundreds of them turned to the internet, including many who had left their homeland. One note by Dr. Merle Friedman stands out. He wrote:

> It is with deep regret that I reflect on my past. It is with deep sorrow that I acknowledge my complicity as a white South African. And it is with immeasurable guilt that I assume responsibility for my role in our shameful past. I cannot say "I did not know." I can only say I chose not to know. I chose the safety of my own family over my moral duty to my compatriots …. I raised and educated my children with privilege, whilst those around me were deprived. I am so deeply sorry! And the opportunity to express this regret and offer apology does not unburden me … [but] allows me to reach even further into my soul to express the remorse that I feel. It impels me to continue to seek in my own small way to help repair the damage to our people and our land caused not only by "perpetrators" but also by us, the bystanders, in the tragedy of our past.[16]

The potential for these moments to help people acknowledge their shame is powerful, as the ferocious backlash demonstrated by recent laws that try to limit the teaching of America's racial history.[17]

The MORE Act does not create the conditions for reconciliation, as described by Paris (2000) or as detailed by Gibson (2004). It may begin the process, however, by recognizing and attempting to rectify the consequences of the political and economic predation associated with cannabis prohibition. This includes those who actively preyed on people ensnared by the criminal justice system and others who, as silent bystanders, perpetuated prohibitionist policies, even when they knew these policies disproportionately and adversely impacted people of color. This is more than performative and self-serving pronouncements. Indeed, coming to grips with how cannabis prohibition deepened racial injustice and continues to maintain institutions of White supremacy is essential.

## New Directions

There are four new directions of immediate interest. The first concerns to what extent racially disproportionate policing can be justified based on their public safety value. In other words, do tactics that result in racially unequal outcomes improve public safety? The second is looking at the additional or spillover costs of disproportionate policing on racial and ethnic minorities. Third, we consider how to promote police accountability. This involves better engaging those who are unjustly policed and evaluating administrative and economic efforts to change the culture of policing. Finally, we consider how racism continues to inform cannabis research.

Can racially disproportionate policing be justified on the grounds of public safety? Recent research demonstrates that it cannot (Chohlas-Wood et al., 2022). This work focuses on evaluating empirical strategies for identifying unnecessary and discriminatory policing that disproportionately burdens Black individuals without any clear gains in public safety. They define coercive strategies as "forms of policing that are not just unnecessary but discriminatory in the sense that they impose greater costs on racial minorities" (Chohlas-Wood et al., 2022: 444). They conclude, for example, that Black and Hispanic individuals detained under New York's and Chicago's stop-and-frisk programs were frisked more often than comparably risky White individuals. While highlighting the unnecessary costs borne by racial minorities, this approach demonstrates how data analysis can isolate policing tactics that are discriminatory in effect.

Another approach considers the costs of these practices. In a series of articles, the illness spillovers associated with policing and the history of ethno-racial profiling are accounted for, providing a new means to understand race, ethnicity, and injustice (Kerrison & Sewell, 2020; Sewell et al., 2021; Sewell, 2020). In just one example, the use of pedestrian stops to search for cannabis in New York City resulted in 2.2 million stops and arrests carried out from 2004 to 2008. It should come as no surprise that significant racial disparities in the implementation of cannabis enforcement have been observed (Geller & Fagan, 2010). In a separate analysis of the same phenomenon, Sewell and Jefferson (2016: 42) concluded:

> Results reveal that living in neighborhoods where pedestrian stops are more likely to become invasive is associated with worse health .... More limited deleterious effects can be attributed to living in neighborhoods where stops are more likely to involve use of force .... Living in neighborhoods where stops are more likely to result in frisking show the most consistent negative associations.

Assessing the cost and consequences involves rethinking policy from the perspective of who is policed. This requires promoting police accountability with the specific goal of challenging a long history of structural racism, police brutality, and the lack of liability that has devastated public trust. Although it may be tempting to view financial sanctions, lawsuits, or civilian payouts as a possible means to ensure that police improve their conduct, there is little evidence of their effectiveness (Schwartz, 2015). One challenge is that officers are typically protected from the financial impacts of these payouts.

What is clear is that decriminalizing cannabis does not reduce the racial disparities in the enforcement of cannabis laws (Sheehan et al., 2021). Instead, addressing racial and ethnic inequities means engaging law enforcement institutions, as well as individual police officers. In Chapter 3, we cited Spicer's (2021) work focused on the perspectives and priorities of the police. However, understanding cannabis, race, ethnicity, and criminalization requires considering the views of people who use cannabis, especially people of color, based on their interactions with police. Research suggests that the role of middle management and sergeants is essential to instill and maintain police accountability (Davenport et al., 2018; del Pozo et al., 2021). Policies designed to ensure all police provide their name, badge number, and a card with instructions for filing a complaint to the civilian oversight structure as part of every cannabis-involved investigation should be assessed. Of some interest is the idea that cannabis legalization can provoke other sorts of justice reform (Brown, 2022).

For police officers and departments that refuse to adapt, the administrative obligations on individual officers should be increased, creating additional layers of accountability. When departments cannot control their officers, cities, and states could require citizen oversight boards with a specific mandate to monitor ethnic and racial net widening and to issue public reports naming individual officers who continue the overpolicing of cannabis by targeting people of color. Questions remain about how to establish, structure, staff, manage, and train the police and civilians. This does not mean that reforming internal affairs/professional standards or external civilian oversight bodies as accountability mechanisms is unimportant or ineffective.[18]

A final means to transform the culture around policing cannabis is to make it easier for citizens to sue police departments for false arrest, discrimination, or harassment. Limited to cannabis possession, these reforms might be tied to efforts to reduce the standard for qualified immunity and to restructure civilian payouts by moving them from taxpayer money to police department insurance policies.[19] This would not make officers personally responsible financially for malfeasance. A political nonstarter for years, interest in shifting the responsibility for misconduct is growing. For example, instead of placing taxpayers on the hook for wrongdoing by police, the New York state lawmakers have proposed that individual police officers carry liability insurance.[20] Other jurisdictions may choose this approach to protect public dollars and return the responsibility for specific policing decisions to the individual officers who make them.

Changing police culture means engaging the history of drug control. The Obama White House tried. Under President Obama, federal prosecution was discouraged, and Congress adopted an amendment prohibiting federal enforcement of cannabis restrictions in states where medical use was legal. As Paris (2000) suggested, confronting the injustices of today means acknowledging the long shadow of history. Recent work connects cannabis and drug policy to colonialism (Daniels et al., 2021). The "colonization of drug control" means that the use of drug control by states in Europe and America through colonial rule sustained the systematic exploitation of people, land, and resources and ingrained racialized hierarchies. Undoing these systems requires rebuilding drug policy in a way that supports health, dignity, and human rights. Practically, this includes liberalizing drug policy, ending the mass

**FIGURE 4.2** Yes, we cannabis. "Haught Street Obama 'Yes We Cannabis' Poster" by Tony Fischer. Photography is licensed under CC BY 2.0

incarceration of people who use drugs, and investing in health and social programs and away from ineffective and punitive drug control that disproportionality targets "Black, Brown and Indigenous peoples ... for drug law enforcement and face discrimination across the criminal system" (Daniels et al., 2021: para 1). This means wrestling with how images challenge and even reinforce social norms, as presented in Figure 4.2.

This is also relevant to a fourth and final consideration about how the role of race continues to complicate meaningful reform: the racial history of cannabis prohibition and the associated harms that have resulted from exclusionary research. As we noted in Chapter 3, unless policymakers focus on racial disparities within evidence-based research, "... we will remain the willing victims of our own racist history" (Solomon, 2020: 4). Recent work by the Urban Institute provides some clarification of how to confront structural racism in research and engage more diverse communities through the research cycle.[21] Challenges remain. The noted psychologist Carl Hart describes a very questionable interaction with a Canadian official below (2021: 26–27):

> I travel extensively but dread having to go through customs in some countries because invariably I am grilled about whether I'm carrying drugs. I recall

> once travelling through Toronto airport and being taken to a back room for further questioning, supposedly about my visit. I explained that I was headed to Thunder Bay to give a public lecture. But that wasn't good enough. More interrogation followed, along with an examination of the contents on my computer. After what seemed to be an inordinately long period of time, I grew impatient and said, "Look, I'm a scientist … and a professor … and an author …. Here's a copy of one of my books." The incredulous look and impish grin plastered across the face of this customs officer told me she wasn't impressed. "Just because you wrote a book," she said, "doesn't mean you aren't a drug dealer." Being a black man traveling from one country to another was enough for me to be a suspected drug dealer, no matter that all the evidence I presented was consistent with who I claimed to be.

Addressing the exclusion and marginalization of Black voices in cannabis research and policymaking requires rethinking the intersection of public health, paternalism, and race. This has been, and remains, central to cannabis control.

## Conclusions

In this chapter, we considered cannabis and race, ethnicity, and criminalization. It bears repeating that one of the most consistent international findings over decades is that the adverse effects of criminalizing cannabis disproportionately impact people of color. As Tonry (1994: 63) noted,

> at a time when civil rights and welfare policies aimed at improving opportunities and living standards for black Americans, drug and crime policies worsened them …. [M]odern wars on drugs and crime have operated in the same ways as slavery and "Jim Crow" legalized discrimination did in earlier periods to destabilize Black communities and disadvantage Black Americans, especially Black American men.

Coming to grips with this history of division means confronting the long shadow of slavery in the US, colonialism in Europe, and how the simplistic social construction of race persists, based on neo-colonial assumptions.

Connecting biological and psychological positivism offers a new means to understand scientific racism. The foolishness of basing policy on "evidence" without considering the quality of research must be confronted. If biological and psychological positivism created racial myths, CRT has exploded them. One question is to what extent restorative justice offers a means to promote reconciliation, especially, but not exclusively, in the US. This requires conceding uncomfortable empirical realities, including the racial disparities in justice system contacts and the costs of cannabis prohibition. Resistance to such acknowledgments remains stubborn.

If protecting the civil rights of non-White people cannot prompt reform, calculating the personal costs of cannabis policies to individuals and their families may offer another means to do so. As Beckett and Herbert (2008) observed, a complete accounting of the costs of cannabis prohibition requires the consideration of tangible and intangible costs both for those who were forced into these foolish arrangements and, most importantly, for people of color who have been targeted for cannabis violations by the criminal justice system. More recent efforts operationalize costs, define institutional inequities, and better explicate systemic racism. For example, the illness spillovers associated with policing and the history of ethnoracial profiling require more exploration (Kerrison & Sewell, 2020; Sewell et al., 2021; Sewell, 2020).

Research has modeled new ways to understand the racial dynamics of prohibition. These are especially important given research by Testa et al. (2021) suggesting that young people experience negative outcomes over the life course following police contact. Cannabis liberalization may represent an opportunity to confront racism in new ways and inform other efforts to reinvest resources in historically overpoliced and underserved communities (Brown, 2022). Acknowledging the long shadow of slavery and colonialism is as elusive as ever. Bringing the known, but often unacknowledged, legacy of racism to the forefront of popular culture is difficult. Cannabis reform links police, policing, race, ethnicity, and criminalization in ways that can no longer be denied.

## Notes

1 For an interesting discussion of CRT in general, see https://owl.purdue.edu/owl/subject_specific_writing/writing_in_literature/literary_theory_and_schools_of_criticism/critical_race_theory.html [accessed July 7, 2021].

2 See "Marijuana, Mormon Racists, Mexican Bandidos, and Crazy Queen Carlotta," https://www.dailykos.com/stories/2007/11/29/415310/- [accessed October 29, 2020].

3 See the twisted marijuana history and why it's illegal. https://businessmirror.com.ph/2016/06/02/the-twisted-marijuana-history-and-why-its-illegal/ [accessed October 10, 2021].

4 See Meet the man responsible for marijuana prohibition. www.massroots.com/learn/the-man-responsible-for-marijuana-prohibition/ [accessed October 29, 2020]

5 Ibid.

6 For more on this history, see www.theatlantic.com/health/archive/2014/06/how-bad-neuroscience-reinforces-racist-drug-policy/371378/ [accessed November 12, 2021].

7 See https://genderedinnovations.stanford.edu/terms/race.html [accessed June 5, 2022].

8 See www.theguardian.com/commentisfree/2021/jun/17/critical-race-theory-republicans-moira-donegan [accessed June 5, 2022].

9 See www.ajc.com/news/crime/police-to-pay-cartersville-70-members-900k-to-settle-federal-lawsuit/6TOMFPFSZZHRRIDBJMNFQNS4CM/ [accessed June 5, 2022].

10 See www.vox.com/identities/2019/3/15/18267260/cartersville-70-lawsuit-georgia-arrests-searches-detention-marijuana [accessed June 5, 2022].

11 See https://chscp.org.uk/wp-content/uploads/2022/03/Child-Q-PUBLISHED-14-March-22.pdf [accessed June 5, 2022].

12 See https://chscp.org.uk/wp-content/uploads/2022/03/Child-Q-PUBLISHED-14-March-22.pdf [accessed June 5, 2022].

13 See www.release.org.uk/publications/cannabis-regulating-right?fbclid=IwAR2r1Qn7RvKbt_rHPDOsuRXBXI_3EaD_9gUAfOWED3VvMLbDJ_fgrG0_N-E [accessed June 5, 2022].

14 Other provisions of the MORE Act include: Ending the criminalization of cannabis at the federal level going forward, and it would also be retroactive. Cannabis arrests, charges, and convictions would be automatically expunged at no cost to the individual. Imposing a 5% tax on the retail sales of cannabis to go to the Opportunity Trust Fund. The measure was amended to start at 5% and increase the tax to 8% over three years. The MORE Act would create the Office of Cannabis Justice to oversee the social equity provisions in the law. The bill would ensure the federal government could not discriminate against people who use cannabis, including earned benefits or immigrants at risk of deportation. The measure would open the door to research, better banking, and tax laws and help fuel economic growth as states are looking for financial resources. See www.congress.gov/bill/117th-congress/house-bill/3617 [accessed June 5, 2022].

15 See www.congress.gov/bill/117th-congress/house-bill/3617 [accessed June 5, 2022].

16 See www.justice.gov.za/trc/ror/page01.htm [accessed June 5, 2022].

17 See https://www.brookings.edu/blog/fixgov/2021/07/02/why-are-states-banning-critical-race-theory/[accessed June 5, 2022].

18 See www.usaid.gov/sites/default/files/documents/Police_Accountability_Mechanisms_8.5.2020.pdf [accessed June 5, 2022].

19 See https://www.brookings.edu/blog/how-we-rise/2020/06/26/why-police-department-insurances-are-the-key-to-progress-on-police-reform/ [accessed June 8, 2022].

20 See www.brookings.edu/policy2020/votervital/how-can-we-enhance-police-accountability-in-the-united-states/ [accessed July 5, 2022].

21 See www.urban.org/sites/default/files/publication/99852/confronting_structural_racism_in_research_and_policy_analysis_0.pdf [accessed June 8, 2022].

# 5

# THE ECONOMICS OF CANNABIS

## Introduction

Economic models of human behavior have greatly influenced the rational choice tradition in criminology. These models gave rise to a group of theories known by various names, including deterrence theories, neoclassical theories, environmental criminology, the criminal event perspective, and situational choice theory (Heidt & Wheeldon, 2015). While the assumptions underlying the rational choice perspectives have long been the dominant means of understanding illicit exchanges, various critiques have emerged (Childs et al., 2020). Although applying rational choice theories to cannabis use is not without problems (Sandberg, 2012a), logical approaches to reduce, prevent, and control crime can be used to understand how illicit markets operate and how consumers are responding to legal cannabis.

In general, obtaining illegal (or unregulated) substances in large quantities often requires assistance from organized crime groups. This results in several adverse outcomes. First, profits of sales go to these groups. Second, cannabis consumers are exposed to more dangerous substances (e.g., cocaine, heroin, meth, and fentanyl) through their interactions with dealers who do not exclusively deal in cannabis. Third, customers interact with drug-dealing criminal subcultures and may then commit crimes beyond buying unregulated cannabis (e.g., drug delivery). Within jurisdictions that have legalized cannabis, other problems exist. For instance, emphasizing public health goals ahead of market conditions has limited access to legal cannabis in some areas and stunted its growth as an industry overall. Together, these developments suggest a role for economic theories within cannabis criminology.

This chapter considers the economics of cannabis. Key concepts explored include the Alchian–Allen theorem, the complexity of cannabis markets, and the cost/benefit analysis associated with cannabis use. Emergent research focuses on the

DOI: 10.4324/9781003232292-5

value of economic theories to understand prohibition and potency, accessing and differentiating between and among cannabis markets, regulatory difficulties within jurisdictions that have legalized cannabis, and the general failure to dismantle and disrupt illicit markets. One question is how legal cannabis can compete with illegal markets without explicitly embracing commercial imperatives.

## Theoretical Starting Points

Economic theories in criminology all adhere to the basic logic of the classical school. In short, people use a hedonistic calculus to make decisions and act to maximize pleasure and minimize pain. These theories assume that people are rational decision-makers who exercise control over their behavior and apply logic to criminal decision-making. There are three theoretical starting points of immediate interest. These include deterrence theory, routine activities theory, and rational choice theory.

### *Deterrence*

Gary Becker's (1976) economic deterrence theory of crime uses the expected utility principle from economics to understand crime. This theory suggests that offenders will maximize their interests based on rational calculation. Through this application, Becker attempted to clarify how severity, celerity (or swiftness), and certainty of punishment contribute to deterrence. Deterrence theories attempt to assess optimal punishment in multiple contexts to specify how offenders respond to the costs of crime imposed by the criminal justice system.

In his book *Thinking about Crime*, J. Q. Wilson (1975) took an approach that had much in common with Becker (1976). Wilson (1975) advocated a return to classical school and deterrence principles by arguing that the criminal justice system must make crime more costly by increasing the length of some punishments. However, he was careful to caution against imposing overly severe sentences. The underlying theme in Wilson's work is that our efforts to change people, either by providing them opportunities or by rehabilitating them, are likely ineffective. He suggests that the only way to reduce the crime rate is to incapacitate repeat offenders by increasing the amount of time they serve.

One problem with deterrence theory is historical. As the war on drugs increased penalties for people who used or sold drugs, actual use did not decrease. This suggests that illicit drug interactions are not entirely "rational" or that people who use drugs engage in a cost/benefit analysis through which they determine that there is a low probability of being observed, arrested, or ultimately penalized. The failure of deterrence theory to reduce cannabis use by increasing penalties suggests that its value as part of a criminological explanation for the economics of cannabis is limited. However, as we will explore below, deterrence did impact cannabis, just not in ways predicted by the theory.

### *Routine Activities Theory*

Another theory in the rational choice tradition is Cohen and Felson's (1979) routine activities theory (RAT). Connected to environmental criminology in which the question of the "place" of criminal events is central, this approach builds on the idea that criminal events occur where opportunities for crime exist. These might include where people congregate, such as work, school, home, and in transit between these places (Brantingham & Brantingham, 1981). The theory can be linked to work by Hawley (1950), who suggested that large-scale changes to people's everyday routines were essential to understanding human behavior. Cohen and Felson (1979) linked historical data, social and technological, and other structural factors to explain the rising crime rates after the 1950s. RAT is based upon three principles. The first principle comes directly from classical school logic; the other two are drawn from social ecology and sociology.

Cohen and Felson (1979) define a criminal "opportunity" by arguing that three components must be present for a crime to occur. The first component, a motivated or likely offender, is a person who commits a crime based on a rational actor model of maximizing human advantage. The second component, a suitable target, is connected to the accessibility of the target and the ability to repel the attack. The last component, an absence of a capable guardian, refers to the lack of a person or thing that can prevent a crime from occurring. A guardian may be formal – a police officer or citizen witness – or informal – a video camera, streetlights, or simply an ordinary citizen going about their daily lives (Clarke & Felson, 1993). One value of RAT is that it reminds us of older ideas about how crime, space, and individuals interact (Jacobs, 1961).

Initially, based on this framework, Cohen and Felson (1979) argued that the rising crime rates during the 1960s and 1970s could be attributed to societal shifts that impacted the routine activities of ordinary people after the Second World War. The idea that social factors could change the environmental susceptibility of certain areas to crime can be applied to cannabis markets in a couple of ways. The first connects spatial relationships and timing of cannabis transactions and suggested one way that ecological features of illicit cannabis markets operate (Moeller, 2016). The second involves thinking about how different cannabis markets are organized and coexist despite different cannabis cultures (Sandberg, 2012a). This may be relevant as criminology turns toward assessing decision-making with legal cannabis regimes. The potential for RAT as a framework to understand cannabis markets is connected to its flexibility. For example, the definition of actors, guardians, and targets may change depending on the jurisdiction.

Understanding how these shifts connect the legal status of cannabis within different jurisdictions may shape justice policy. Consider cannabis sellers. For example, where cannabis remains illegal, cannabis dealers represent both motivated offenders and suitable targets—based on their possession of cannabis and money. However, cannabis sellers could also be seen as guardians for those seeking high-quality cannabis when they take sensible precautions to avoid criminal justice actors' intrusion and potential predation. Where cannabis is decriminalized, those roles may shift again. Since the risks associated with possessing cannabis have been reduced, so too are the dangers of seeking out those who sell cannabis. Competition will likely increase because more dealers (i.e., motivated offenders) will emerge when penalties are minimal, enforced inconsistently, or not at all. Where cannabis is legal, those seeking to acquire cannabis may be suitable targets. Police in these jurisdictions serve as guardians and are obliged to protect cannabis consumers from predation from motivated actors.

## *Rational Choice Theory*

Clarke and Cornish's (1985) rational choice theory is another formulation in this tradition. This theory emphasizes the similarities between offenders and nonoffenders and suggests that other criminological theories tend to "overpathologize" crime. Essentially, this is a criticism of the medical model or the idea that criminality is something that needs treatment to be cured. It is also a critique of the sociological theories that attribute crime to poor social conditions and poverty. Like the other theories in this area, economic decision-making models provide the basis for Clarke and Cornish's (1985) formulation. Some are critical of the applicability of rational choice to drug use (Sandberg, 2012a), so this view may need some qualification when considering jurisdictions in which cannabis is legal.

Rational choice theory is a branch of criminological theory devoted to understanding criminal decision-making (Lilly, Cullen, & Ball, 2015). These theories were initially derived from the writings of classical school scholars such as Cesare Beccaria and Jeremy Bentham and were extended by Gary Becker and James Q. Wilson (Heidt & Wheeldon, 2015). These theories all agree that "... crime is broadly the result of rational choices based on analyses of anticipated costs and benefits" (Cornish & Clarke, 1986: vi). However, rational choice theorists acknowledge that most criminals operate with bounded or limited rationality due to cognitive limitations and emotional arousal that can affect decision-making. Interestingly, rational choice theorists have explicitly rejected relying on stigma to control crime. As Felson explains:

> Stigmas are a poor substitute for environmental cues, which remind *everyone* not to try an illegal act. Stigmas encourage the community to build a wall against those they think are a criminal race or group while letting the others do whatever they want ... In short, careless stigmas interfere with crime control by misleading about who is the problem
>
> *2002: 44, italics in original*

This line of thought is especially interesting when juxtaposed against the stigma associated with drug use and addiction.

Some propositions in rational choice theory (Cornish & Clarke, 2002) are derived from classical school thought. Others deviate from earlier theories in this tradition. For example, this theory assumes different crimes fulfill different needs, and different decision-making models are required to understand different types of crime (Clarke & Cornish, 1985). This logic implies that different drugs and patterns of use vary and may require separate models. This observation seems important when crafting post-prohibition drug policies. In addition, background factors, current life circumstances, and situational variables also affect decisions to participate in criminal activity. However, in an era of legal cannabis, the various incarnations of rational choice theory may provide a basis to consider decision-making around cannabis based on its status as a consumer good.

## Key Concepts

Understanding the economics of cannabis use requires applying deterrence, routine activities, and rational choice theories to cannabis policy. This involves applying concepts like the Alchian-Allen theorem and cost-benefit analysis in criminological terms. This can provide insights into the complexity of evolving drug markets and the dynamics around cannabis as a consumer good.

### *Alchian–Allen Theorem*

After a century of prohibition, deterrence has had one clear impact. Cannabis has consistently increased in potency since this policy came into effect. This increase is not surprising if one is familiar with the Alchian–Allen theorem. This economic theory predicts that when fixed per-unit amounts increase the prices of substitute goods, the consumption of higher-grade products will increase because of costs associated with transportation, storage, and other factors. This phenomenon occurs because higher-grade products with fixed per-unit amounts will retain their value over comparable lower-grade products. Cowan (1986) applied this theorem to explain how drug policy might affect supply and posited an "Iron Law of Prohibition," which suggests that there is a tendency for drugs to become more potent and more dangerous when prohibited. In short, prohibition leads to increases in drug potency. With a fixed penalty and probability of getting caught, the more potent substance is now relatively cheaper. Beletsky and Davis (2017: 157) explain how this happened during alcohol prohibition:

> Imposing substantial barriers and costs to the illicit drug supply chain create direct pressure to minimize volume while maximizing profit. More bulky products become more expensive relative to less bulky ones, incentivizing increases in potency. Indeed, relative to products with lower alcohol content like beer (Prohibition-era cost increase: over 700%), the price of spirits rose much more slowly (Prohibition-era cost increase: 270%).

Lawson and Nesbit (2013) found that the relative price of medium- and high-quality cannabis, consistent with the Alchian–Allen theorem, was higher in states with stricter law enforcement.

### Complexity and Cannabis Markets

One concept rooted in routine activities theory is how cannabis transactions operate once cannabis is legalized. For example, many assume dispensaries would be at an increased risk for property crimes, such as burglary. According to this view, employees of the dispensaries were at risk because they had access to both the cannabis and cash on site. One idea is that geography, siting, and buffers around cannabis dispensaries and retail stores may shift criminogenic opportunities because of changes in routine activities in the neighborhood more generally. However, research does not support the thesis that dispensaries inevitably lead to more criminal activity. By comparing crime data for violent and nonviolent crime patterns before and after the opening of medical marijuana dispensaries in Washington, DC, crime generally decreased or remained constant in geographical areas following the opening of a dispensary (Zakrzewski et al., 2020).

In New England, several states have a legal cannabis market. The problem is the lack of legal dispensaries with "good" products. Some estimate that 80% of the cannabis market is still underground. In 2019, Steve Hoffman of the Massachusetts Cannabis Commission stated: "It's probably premature to say that we've [made] a big dent in the illicit market … I don't think we're ever completely going to eliminate the illicit market; I think that's probably unrealistic."[1] Hoffman's work at the state's independent commission created to monitor the licensed cannabis market provides him with a unique view. It may be that illicit cannabis markets won't dry up until cannabis is fully legalized federally, and perhaps not even then. In the meantime, cannabis businesses need the ability to engage in routine financial arrangements and activities to rival existing criminal networks and protect their products. These include relying on state-supported infrastructure, legal banking arrangements, and access to startup funds and loans, which influence how new cannabis businesses assess the costs and benefits associated with entering the legal cannabis market.

### Cannabis and Cost/Benefit Analysis

A final concept of interest is cost/benefit analysis. This involves assessing the risks of dealing illegal drugs and the benefits of the potential profit to be realized through this activity. For example, Becker (1968) claimed that people generally do not vary in their motivation to commit crime, but instead, they vary in how they perceive the costs and benefits of committing a crime. Offenders, then, respond to the costs of crime imposed by the criminal justice system in various ways. Decision-making viewed through a cost/benefit model is a common feature of rational choice theorists (Clarke & Cornish, 1985). Farrington (1992) updated this calculus to account for mental states and argued that if offenders are intoxicated, angry, bored, or frustrated, they will also be more prone to crime.

For some, illicit drug interactions are not "rational" because the costs of criminal sanctions outweigh the benefit of acquiring and consuming cannabis. Another view suggests that people who use cannabis *do weigh* the risks and rewards. They choose to seek out and purchase cannabis under prohibition based on their determination that there is a low probability of being observed, arrested, or ultimately penalized. Lifting cannabis prohibition has changed opportunity structures and behavior patterns for people both buying and selling unregulated cannabis.[2] This shift raises questions about the role of regulation. As Miron (2017: para 11–12) notes:

> If regulation is instead strict, it promotes continuation of the black market … Thus legalization without excessive regulation or taxation is the only way to eliminate the black market.

Developing responsible regulation regimes requires a clear understanding of typical behavior patterns among people who use cannabis and how these patterns relate to the overall cannabis economy. As Dandurand (2021: 19) points out, cannabis presents a unique international example. The partial decriminalization of cannabis has occurred within a global environment where the production and sale of that drug continue to be heavily criminalized. In addition, the growing influence of and investment in the cannabis industry by large corporations has led to competition between and among actors inside and outside the illicit market. Cost/benefit analysis related to cannabis considers how decriminalization and regulation influence the conceptualization of cannabis as a legal product.

## Relevant Research on the Economics of Cannabis

Rational choice theorists suggest that logical approaches can reduce, prevent, and control crime (Cornish & Clarke, 1986). Many of these principles can be used to understand how both illicit markets and consumers have responded to cannabis legalization. They can also be used to understand the economics of cannabis. Research in this area focuses on potency, cannabis markets, and cannabis as a consumer good.

### *Prohibition and Potency*

Former US Representative Patrick Kennedy, a noted New Prohibitionist, argues that "the commercialization of pot will have devastating consequences for public health."[3] However, the prohibition of cannabis has led growers to engineer plants to produce higher levels of THC, leading people who use cannabis to change their methods of ingestion. In contrast to the logic of deterrence theory, increasing penalties for possessing cannabis has not led to declining use. Instead, it has resulted in more potent cannabis being ingested in shorter periods through vaping, dabbing, and consumption of edibles. The Alchian–Allen theorem helps explain this increase in cannabis potency. However, more research is needed to understand these developments. One problem is that there is no good analogy for cannabis, given that there are few substances criminalized for a century that are now legal. However, a few comparisons can be made to alcohol prohibition.

Following the 18th Amendment to the US Constitution in 1919, the manufacture, transport, use, and sale of alcoholic beverages was prohibited. Alcohol use did initially decline in the early years of prohibition. However, it began to increase after 1921 (Hall, 2010). Although there is some disagreement about the level of increase, many agree that alcohol use returned to at least 70% of pre-prohibition levels following repeal (Hall, 2010; Miron & Zwiebel, 1991: 242). Empirical work suggests that potent alcohol became more widespread during alcohol prohibition (Thornton, 1998). More recently, based on a review of cannabis prices by state, the relative cost of both medium- and high-quality cannabis has been found to be greater in states with stricter law enforcement. This suggests an increase in demand for more potent cannabis products (Lawson & Nesbit, 2013; see Reinarman, 2009 for a similar finding).

Consider the preferences of people who sell or buy prohibited substances. Lifting cannabis prohibitions changes cost/benefit calculations made by those who buy or sell drugs in sufficient quantities to attract the attention of law enforcement. Since dealers are trying to maximize their profits, a large percentage will likely be dealing in other more dangerous, illegal substances as these are far more profitable and less bulky than cannabis. On the one hand, those who consume drugs need less of the more potent substance to get high and can more easily conceal their use. On the other hand, suppliers will make revenue faster and efficiently store a more potent product. This trend can be seen in cannabis use: strains have become increasingly strong, and high THC products, like butane hash oil and concentrates (e.g., shatter and wax), have become widespread. More potent drugs provide "more bang for the buck" (Cowan, 1986). For example:

> Prohibition has had a similar impact on cannabis. Today, marijuana is stronger than it was in the past. Like alcohol, the prohibition on marijuana has resulted in a change of the product that is available to consumers on the black market. According to a study by the National Institute for Health, marijuana in 1995 contained about 4% THC, whereas that level was closer to 12% in 2014. During that same period, CBD has fallen from 0.28% to 0.15%. So, while the drug has gotten stronger with higher THC levels, the CBD that helps potentially offset the risks has fallen. In 1995, there was 14 times more THC than CBD in cannabis, and today that ratio is 80 times .... More bluntly, prohibition has made marijuana stronger.[4]

## *Accessing and Differentiating Cannabis Markets*

Cannabis has rapidly gained mainstream acceptance from consumers. However, the current regulatory environment enshrined differentiated cannabis markets, even within the same country. In the US, every state enforces different regulations, and products cannot be moved across states even if cannabis has been legalized in states that border one another. This situation creates peculiar scenarios whereby people travel to see family in one state and buy cannabis legally but can be arrested and sentenced to prison terms if they bring it home to a state where possessing cannabis remains illegal. The connections between people, places, and activities cannot be ignored. Yet, the implications of these scenarios are rarely considered. Understanding how accessing and differentiating between and among cannabis markets is essential if the concepts linked within economic theories in criminology are to offer insights into a changing cannabis marketplace.

Researchers have examined the nature of the relationship between spaces, actors, and interactions suggested by RAT. By engaging in covert surveillance of Scandinavia's principal open-air cannabis market, an area known as Christiania in Copenhagen, Denmark, Moeller (2016) explored the tempo, rhythm, and timing of cannabis transactions. These varied by time of day and day of the week. They were associated with socioeconomic developments among buyers and sellers. Police disruption of a local illicit drug market can affect the structure and organization of that market (Coomber & Moyle, 2018; May & Hough, 2001). This disruption can also facilitate market access for new cannabis sellers who could not previously compete with the more established marketplaces (Moeller, 2016).

Disruptive policies sometimes come with unintended consequences. For example, an earlier analysis by Moeller and Hesse (2013) in Denmark demonstrated disruptions within established hierarchies among criminal groups following police crackdowns in this cannabis market. In the five years after the crackdown in 2004, there were more homicides and attempted homicides than in any five years in the previous 20 years. The intergang competition that increased following police crackdowns and disruptions in the cannabis market resulted from the need to establish, defend, and attempt to expand their territory. In hindsight, the violence that followed space-based disruptions of illicit drug markets should not be a surprise. That is was speaks to the need to better understand drug markets.

Sandberg's work in Norway (2012a) suggests the importance of defining illicit markets. Based on interviews with 60 people who use cannabis and those who sold it, he found the illicit cannabis "market" could be divided into three sectors: public, semi-public, and private, each of which operated in different ways. Understanding the nature of cannabis markets may assist in efforts to expand the legal market where cannabis has been legalized. Indeed, since the repeal of prohibition in some jurisdictions, researchers have documented the flexibility, adaptability, and inherent instability that emerge within illicit drug markets. However, to date, legal and regulated cannabis has been unable to outperform existing black and gray markets. For example:

> Though each state has its own issues, the problems have similar outlines: Underfunded law enforcement officers and slow-moving regulators are having trouble building a legal regime fast enough to contain a high-demand product that already has a large existing criminal network to supply it. And at the national level, advocates also point to another, even bigger structural issue: Problems are inevitable in a nation where legalization is so piecemeal.[5]

One solution may require reconsidering cannabis as a consumer good. Viewing cannabis in this way is a relatively new phenomenon. It emerged first in the Netherlands as part of coffeeshop culture and later in the U.S. following the 2012 legalization of cannabis in Washington and Colorado. While the cannabis industry is rapidly advancing with new cannabis-related products, services, and experiences, profound questions remain about how to establish markets, confront stigma, and balance regulation. Since 2018, provinces in Canada have explored tentative approaches to commercial cannabis. These efforts are complicated by the outsized and underacknowledged long shadow of cannabis prohibition (Heidt & Wheeldon, 2022).

## *Cannabis as a Consumer Good: Competing on Price and Quality*

Applying cost/benefit analysis to cannabis involves assessing how decriminalization and regulation influence the conceptualization of cannabis as a consumer good. Spicer (2018) argues that subcultural theorists have long stressed that explanations of deviance, including drug use, predicated solely on the desire for material gain are limited. Moreover, these approaches tend to ignore the roles of status, meaning, and personal narratives (Bourgois, 2003; Cohen, 1955), which are also crucial to understanding cannabis culture (Sandberg, 2013). However, as cannabis is increasingly legalized and regulated, more traditional economic theories that frame behavior through the lens of profit maximization ought to be revisited. Two central issues for legal cannabis are potency and pricing.

In a recent study on the impact of cannabis legalization in Canada, Mahamad and colleagues (2020) found that the value of illegal cannabis decreased, and THC levels were higher than those found in the cannabis available in legal outlets. They argue that this is a function of the overregulation of cannabis, resulting in a resilient illicit market in many areas of Canada, with more potent cannabis in British Columbia and Nova Scotia (Mahamad et al., 2020). Moeller's (2016) work, based on the surveillance of a large cannabis market, was designed to assist in deploying police resources. However, this work demonstrated other valuable details as cannabis enforcement is replaced with regulation. For example, Moeller (2016: 37) observed that "buyers prefer lower price over a wider selection and that sellers adapt their opening hours according to temporal patterns in transaction frequency."

Another issue is around price. Statistics Canada reports that most cannabis sales across Canada during the fourth quarter of 2019 occurred on the black market (Ligaya, 2019). This can be traced to the uneasy truce in Canada between a desire to confront illicit markets while guaranteeing public health goals are met:

> Provincial governments embedded these goals in their own legislation, regulations, and the mandates they provided to their newly formed cannabis agencies. In turn, these bodies internalized the policy objectives through their own values statements and operational guidelines that had already emphasized

> "responsible consumption" over aggressive sales and marketing. For instance, Alberta Liquor, Gaming, and Cannabis (AGLC) lists demarketing among specific segments in its guiding values: "We're committed to keeping cannabis out of the hands of children and youth, protecting public health, promoting safety and limiting the illegal cannabis market. By adhering to these principles, we will continue to offer choices Albertans can trust."
>
> *Wesley and Murray, 2021: 1081*

Although emphasizing responsible consumption should not be faulted, especially in the early days of cannabis legalization, these contributed to cannabis overregulation. This creates a situation in which more people are accessing cannabis through the illicit market dealers resulting in a higher likelihood of youth accessing more dangerous illegal drugs.

Osborne and Fogel (2017) found that confidence in the government regulation of cannabis was relatively low, and many people who were established cannabis users expected to stay in the illicit market after legalization. In their study of 41 Canadians who use cannabis, several participants raised concerns (somewhat prophetically) over the government's approach to regulation and the involvement of large corporations in the cannabis trade. More specifically, some predicted that the quality of cannabis would decrease while the price would increase because of overregulation and high taxes. This is the case for some products (e.g., flower and edibles), and legalization has not undercut illicit markets in many jurisdictions (e.g., California, British Columbia, and Nova Scotia).

Suppose both new and veteran cannabis consumers engage in a cost/benefit analysis to determine whether they will access the illicit market. In this case, the final decision will likely be based on several considerations (i.e., How close is the store? What is the price of their cannabis? Is the cannabis of high quality? Do they have the strains and products that I am looking for?). Suppose they cannot access high-quality, fresh cannabis at a reasonable price at a relatively close location. In this situation, consumers will continue to rely on illicit markets to obtain their products. The reluctance to grant licenses, burdensome regulations and zoning restrictions, and excessive prices have allowed drug dealers to remain secure within the illicit marketplace.

## New Directions

Some new directions include how to disrupt illicit markets, engaging people who use cannabis and the subcultures where it is prevalent, attracting new consumers, and making sense of global shifts in cannabis markets. The first considers illicit markets. Decriminalization does not do much to disrupt illicit markets. Even legal cannabis regimes in Uruguay and Canada can claim only marginal successes in this regard. This may be because legalization and regulation have focused on public health first and access second. In Canada, currently the largest legal cannabis market, the federal government emphasized a public health approach to cannabis. While politically expedient, this approach has ensured that provincial government retailers would position themselves not as "sellers" of the previously illicit product but as "… protective 'providers' of cannabis in a highly regulated consumer environment" (Wesley & Murray, 2021: 1099). The desire to control the cannabis market via overly aggressive regulation results in the black market retaining greater control over the market.

In Uruguay, a recent analysis identified several similar problems (Queirolo, 2020). One is related to legal cannabis access through pharmacies. First, there are too few pharmacies to meet demand, and many pharmacies do not want to sell cannabis. Second, the amount of cannabis distributed to pharmacies is not enough to meet the demand. Third, heavy regulation caused cultivators to fall behind in production, contributing to the shortage of cannabis in pharmacies that had agreed to sell it. Finally, regulations around potency, price, and advertising have limited the potential of the legal market in both countries. Legal cannabis in Canada does not adequately address the lower cost, convenience, and established routines associated with obtaining cannabis access via illicit drug markets (Thies, 2012).

This is especially true in a province like British Columbia, which has a long history of growing cannabis illegally. The original strategy in Canada was to keep taxes low to discourage black market competition. However, the federal government delayed licensing small-scale growing operations (Spriggs, 2018). According to the Arcview Market Research Group, after almost five years of legalization, the black and gray markets currently supply roughly 27% of cannabis in Colorado, so one should not expect unregulated markets to vanish instantly. In 2014, black and gray markets maintained 59% of the overall market, meaning that the legal market has enticed over 30% of consumers away from the unregulated market (Dayton & Adams, 2017).

These challenges have led to a fascinating experiment in British Columbia, where the government is reported to have "convinced many illegal cannabis growers to begin selling legally in an effort to squeeze out illicit marijuana from the marketplace."[6] However, this initiative will require the government to engage in some controversial conversations. It might be that sustaining the legal market requires listening to stakeholders like the Cannabis Council of Canada (C3), which represents more than 700 licensed producers and processors of cannabis. In 2021, the group recommended reducing excise tax regulatory fees, limiting provincial markups, and better regulating online sales of illicit cannabis.[7] However, it is also worth considering how people who use cannabis and other cannabis subcultural insiders can offer important insights to guide policy.

Two studies from British Columbia (Heidt, 2021; Heidt et al., 2018) explored some of these issues. The authors noted that people with substantial knowledge of cannabis were ignored, resulting in many missed economic opportunities. This example provides a powerful lesson for policymakers and practitioners when deciding who should be involved in policymaking. There is a tendency on the part of governments to exclude otherwise law-abiding citizens who were known to have participated in the cannabis trade when it was criminalized. There are a minority of cases where this exclusion may be warranted; however, it seems like many have been left behind for no good reason. In general, failing to include those with experience and expertise when defining policies is foolhardy.

The value of engaging insiders is evident based on our reanalysis of past research. The quotes below from anonymous studies (Heidt, 2021; Heidt et al., 2018) provide useful context. Over regulation and taxation were cited frequently as reasons why the illicit markets would persist. The most apparent cause of this is taxes; the black market will continue to thrive if taxes are too high. Interestingly, this point was made by two people from often oppositional groups. For example, a police officer noted:

> In Washington State, the pricing was originally incredibly expensive for 1 gram of cannabis. We saw this when cigarettes got so expensive. There was a large black market for cigarettes. So, if we see that the government is going to price it over $10, that probably won't work. We think the sweet spot is the $7–8 range. If it gets much more expensive than that, people will go to the black market.

An unlicensed dispensary owner said something almost identical:

> The legitimate, legal cannabis needs to be cheaper and higher quality than the black market. Look at a regular weed smoker. Why would they buy from a dispensary that is charging $12 or 14 per gram when they can get it from a buddy down the road for $10? They need to create a regulatory framework that will allow producers to produce a price point where they can profit.

The above two quotes have proven to be prophetic. As discussed, British Columbia has been perhaps the least successful at instituting cannabis regulation primarily because of its well-established cannabis subculture and history of high-quality illicit cannabis growing operations.

A third development considers how to attract existing cannabis consumers to regulated markets. If the legal market emphasizes public health concerns over access, it is unlikely to be able to compete on cost or quality. Ironically, the emphasis on public health combined with lack of access also creates a situation in which cannabis consumers are motivated to interact with illicit markets resulting in more public issues and other complex problems (e.g., the temptation to do other more dangerous illicit drugs and opportunities to become involved in the criminal subculture). Policymakers may need to rethink and critically assess their views on consumer education, awareness, and marketing. The worry about glorifying cannabis might require that education include public health messages alongside more traditional advertising efforts. This needs to be done carefully. Warning people of the possible dangers of using a legal substance is sensible. However, this approach to messaging risks prioritizing public health over all other messages.

Another effort involves identifying new markets. This is essential if legal cannabis markets are to be sustained by replacing illicit markets and reducing the hazards associated with unregulated cannabis commerce. Developing and providing more specialized strains of cannabis with more balanced THC content is one direction. This might involve advertising cannabis strains to promote creativity, energy, or relaxation. Another is to consider who is using cannabis and why. The opposite of ever-higher THC strains would be to consider how to market low THC cannabis. Dad Grass is a company that embraces nostalgia and older sensibilities around cannabis by referring to a "clean buzz without the fuss … [and] easy and dependable, never fancy or complicated."[8]

Fourth and finally, fundamental changes to the illegal cannabis market present new complexities for the economics of cannabis. As discussed in this chapter, some challenges concerning regulation were predicted (Decorte & Potter, 2015). However, other trends have emerged over time. One development is "glocalization." This refers to the confluence of local developments within global contexts (Featherstone et al., 1995), which both "universalize and particularize tendencies in contemporary social, political, and economic systems."[9] Some connected it to postcolonialism and "interpenetration" of the global and local spheres (Ritzer & Stepnisky, 2017: 229). In terms of cannabis, this might refer to how local production of new cannabis strains enhances the quality of domestically grown cannabis and shapes international forces. For example, according to an analysis by the Wilson Center, Uruguay is poised to become a regional cannabis exporter. To do so,

> producers in Uruguay have a first mover advantage to gain a niche in export markets, and generate revenue and employment for the country. Though his party opposed legalization, President Luis Lacalle Pou now sees the potential for an economic windfall for the country, which relies heavily on exports of meat, soy and wood. Mr. Lacalle Pou, elected in 2019, has already signed two executive orders to encourage medicinal marijuana and hemp exports.[10]

As Figure 5.1 suggests, local conditions can allow the infrastructure to grow cannabis and develop in ways that allow Uruguay to make the most of international trends. The opposite is also true.

Import substitution occurs when imported cannabis products are replaced by those grown inside a country or region's borders. For example, in the Netherlands, new cultivation techniques and the cross-breeding of cannabis varieties allowed "local cannabis cultivation to boom at the expense of bulk-imported foreign cannabis" (Decorte, 2010: 271). This has occurred in the US, Canada, New Zealand, and even the UK, which is surprisingly one of the world's largest producers of

**FIGURE 5.1** Uruguay: Ahead of the cannabis curve

legal cannabis.[11] The global cannabis market has been estimated at US$ 20 billion in 2021 and is projected to reach US$ 128 billion by 2030.[12] A partial list of new cannabis products includes edibles, tinctures, creams, toothpaste, sprays, and even body butter. Cannabis drinks, as outlined in Figure 5.2, are increasingly popular. In Canada and the US, national advocacy groups seek reforms to ensure the cannabis industry is sustainable.[13]

Global cannabis culture is growing even in jurisdictions guided by punitive cannabis legislation, such as Poland (Wanke et al., 2022). As cannabis is increasingly democratized, new noncommercial models are emerging. Cannabis social clubs (CSCs) in Belgium and Spain offer an intriguing example of the interplay between cannabis decriminalization in law and policy within countries that adopt more conservative social policies. For instance, cannabis decriminalization in Spain led to the emergence of CSCs. CSCs may operate in Spain, provided they meet specific criteria and follow legal precedents (Seddon & Floodgate, 2020).[14] Similar clubs are also present in Belgium, Malta, and Uruguay. They represent an underexplored model (Pardal, 2022). These clubs allow for nonprofit associations of adults who use cannabis, as well as those who produce and distribute cannabis. These models present another example of how the economics of cannabis use is developing in various ways.

**FIGURE 5.2** Cannabis energy drink. "Cannabis Energy Drink" by JeepersMedia is licensed under CC BY 2.0

## Conclusion

Critics skeptical about simplistic applications of rational choice theories to cannabis accurately note how the cultural dimension to cannabis may supersede mere profit maximization or self-interested decision-making (Sandberg, 2012a; Spicer, 2021). However, we have argued that there is a case for revisiting economic theories within cannabis criminology. Revisiting deterrence theory, RAT, and rational choice in the context of cannabis provides insights into the failures of prohibition. This applies, on the one hand, to how cannabis became increasingly potent and, on the other, to how markets are differentiated and shape access. Moreover, once cannabis has been legalized, it transforms from an illicit substance to a consumer good. In such circumstances, we have suggested that more traditional interpretations of rational choice theories point to elements that are likely to influence those seeking to enter the cannabis market and replace their illicit arrangements with legal purchases.

One challenge for the economics of cannabis is how cannabis prohibition has influenced potency, increased prices, and shaped cannabis markets. Based on the principles drawn from deterrence theory, the Alchian–Allen theorem, and RAT, criminalizing cannabis benefited organized crime groups, furthered and funded other criminal activities, and expanded the range of routine criminal activities associated with criminal subcultures. As prohibition has given way to legalization, another set of principles is relevant. Rational choice theory suggests several challenges for legal cannabis. For example, applying cost/benefit analyses to cannabis as a consumer good implies that the legal market will struggle to overcome its illicit counterparts without rethinking cannabis access and embracing a more market-oriented approach.

There is some irony in the idea that for justice-related outcomes of cannabis liberalization to take root, there is a need to expand products, reduce costs, and increase the accessibility of cannabis. Engaging in this sort of market analysis will be uncomfortable for some and will lead to questions about getting the regulatory requirements right. For example, moving from illegal to legal cannabis creates new management issues. These include workers' rights (Bennett, 2021), health and safety, and working conditions (August, 2013; Krissman, 2016; Schirmann, 2016. Following efforts to establish cannabis certifications in the US, soil, energy, and water standards are emerging.[15] An open question is whether and to what extent the next phase of cannabis legalization considers sustainability, labor practices, and other social and environmental issues (Corva & Meisel, 2021).

## Notes

1 See www.politico.com/magazine/story/2019/07/21/legal-marijuana-black-market-227414/ [accessed July 17, 2021].

2 In this context, it becomes clear as to why legalization and regulation are preferable to simple decriminalization. Lifting criminal penalties without providing access to a safe and legal supply of cannabis ensures that demand for cannabis will be high but supply will be limited. This will result in expensive cannabis and a lucrative share of the illicit market for organized crime groups [accessed June 5, 2022].

3 See www.chicagotribune.com/news/breaking/ct-met-patrick-kennedy-opposes-marijuana-legalization-in-illinois-20190419-story.html [accessed June 5, 2022].

4 See www.forbes.com/sites/jordanwaldrep/2018/10/22/how-cannabis-prohibition-has-made-marijuana-more-dangerous/?sh=544c6cac474e [accessed July 27, 2021].

5 See www.politico.com/magazine/story/2019/07/21/legal-marijuana-black-market-227414/ [accessed July 17, 2021].

6 See www.canadianevergreen.com/news/b-c-pushes-for-black-market-cannabis-to-go-legal-faces-criticism-from-craft-growers/?utm_source=dlvr.it&utm_medium=twitter&fbclid=IwAR2IngKoCDVcmZ3DYbw6O6NAlocvquqL9rz3VXh3Ej6qV50pUEpHoNYRmMw [accessed June 5, 2022].

7 See www.cbc.ca/news/politics/cannabis-changed-canada-1.6219493 [accessed June 5, 2022].

8 See https://dadgrass.com/ [accessed June 5, 2022].

9 See www.britannica.com/topic/glocalization [accessed June 5, 2022].

10 See www.wilsoncenter.org/blog-post/marijuana-made-uruguay [accessed June 5, 2022].

11 See https://inews.co.uk/news/long-reads/inside-britain-biggest-legal-cannabis-farm-explained-medicinal-marijuana-769414 [accessed June 5, 2022].

12 See www.globenewswire.com/news-release/2021/12/28/2358365/0/en/Cannabis-Market-Size-to-Reach-128-92-Billion-by-2028-Genetic-Development-and-Modification-of-the-Cannabis-Boost-the-Market-Demand-States-Vantage-Market-Research-VMR.html [accessed June 5, 2022].

13 See https://thecannabisindustry.org/about-us/mission-values/ [accessed June 5, 2022].

14 Some judicial decisions have introduced uncertainty. In 2015, the Spanish Supreme Court's decision suggested that "organised, institutionalised and persistent cultivation and distribution of cannabis among an association open to new members is considered drug trafficking." See www.emcdda.europa.eu/publications/topic-overviews/cannabis-policy/html_en [accessed March 29, 2022].

15 See https://thecannabisindustry.org/wp-content/uploads/2020/11/NCIA-Environmental-Policy-BMP-October-17-final.pdf [accessed June 5, 2022].

# 6

# CANNABIS USE AND CRIME

## Introduction

As we have observed, for most of our lives, simply possessing cannabis meant one could be charged with a crime (Wheeldon & Heidt, 2022). A central paradox is that cannabis policy has created criminals from otherwise law-abiding people. Beyond the legal status of cannabis, however, the connections between cannabis and crime are tenuous. Decriminalization and legalization of cannabis have not led to an increase in crime rates. Although credible reviews of cannabis research demonstrate little support for many dire cannabis-related claims, punitive policies for cannabis and people who use it remain. This is based on the mistaken belief that using cannabis causes mental illness and that people with mental illness are more violent and more likely to be involved with crime (Heidt & Wheeldon, 2015). In fact, most people with mental illness are not violent and are less likely to reoffend than others (Pozzulo et al., 2015; Serin et al., 2011).[1]

Despite some extraordinary claims (Berenson, 2019), legalizing cannabis has not increased the number of young people who report using cannabis. It does not result in new mental health crises, increased cases of cannabis use disorder (CUD), or psychoses. It certainly does not increase the rates of violent crime. While evidence for these claims falls away after even cursory examination of the literature, these findings have failed to disrupt the policies and practices of justice systems around the world.

As we have argued, there are numerous dimensions to the study of cannabis within criminology. However, the focus on cannabis and crime through law-based paradigms is likely to remain popular. For example, Fischer and colleagues (2021: 58) suggest five areas of particular interest for criminologists operating in a post-legal cannabis world. These include (1) the deterrent effect of prohibition,

DOI: 10.4324/9781003232292-6

(2) illicit production, markets, and supply in a legalization regime, (3) use enforcement, (4) cannabis-impaired driving, and (5) cannabis and crime. These will remain of interest.

This chapter considers cannabis use and crime using theoretical starting points, including social learning theories, biosocial theories of criminality, and psychological theories of crime. We explore essential concepts, including youth crime, the Brain Disease Model of Addiction (BDMA), and psychosis. Areas of interest related to cannabis and crime include studies on brain imaging techniques and those associated with development and life course criminology. Research has challenged past assumptions about the relationship between cannabis use and crime. However, the potential for misuse of research in this area requires more caution than previously observed (Meier et al., 2012; Schoeler et al., 2016). Today, new criminological questions are emerging. One issue surrounds cannabis and impaired driving.

## Theoretical Starting Points

Theories from several criminological research programs can be used to frame research on cannabis and crime. Social learning theories, biosocial theories of crime, and psychological positivism offer unique and related frameworks of understanding.

### *Social Learning Theories*

In criminology, social learning theories seek to describe the process of criminal and delinquent socialization and specifically focus on how criminal behavior is observed, learned, executed, and maintained over time. One finding is the importance that peers play in influencing delinquent behavior. For social learning theorists, a renewed focus on the role of modeling and interacting with others has led to a more developed theory of learning. Often applied to a variety of social interactions to explain how people learn the values, attitudes, techniques, and motives for criminal behavior, social learning theory remains one of the most tested and supported theories in criminology. It has significant practical implications for social and justice policy (Heidt & Wheeldon, 2015).

Whereas researchers in other disciplines continued to view drug use and "abuse" as symptoms of individual pathology or maladjustment, micronormative researchers in the sociology of deviance looked instead to the social environment—relationships with family and friends—for answers to the question, "Why do people use illegal drugs?" Consequently, sociological research on drug-related deviance has provided strong support for social learning theories, such as Akers' (1998) social structure/social learning theory. In addition, some research suggests support for Sutherland's position that intimate, personal relationships are the primary source of learned techniques, definitions, and motives for behavior of all kinds (Akers, 1998). This can be connected to viewing cannabis as connected to subcultures and fears that cannabis liberalization will inevitably lead to increased cannabis use by youth.

### *Biosocial Theories*

Biological antecedents have long been connected to criminal behavior (Raine, 1993). More recent incarnations of biological theories have attempted to incorporate findings from numerous disciplines and subfields in the life sciences, including developmental biology, psychiatry, cognitive neuroscience, behavioral ecology, and endocrinology (Heidt & Wheeldon, 2015). Most of these theories focus on explaining persistent forms of criminality and antisocial behavior (Fishbein, 2001; Raine, 1993). Wilson and Herrnstein (1985: 23) define criminality as "stable differences across individuals in propensity to commit criminal (or equivalent) acts." Fishbein (2001: 13) advocates an approach that is similar but specifies that criminological theorists should focus on "the measurable dimensions (phenotypes) of antisocial behavior that increase risk for criminal activity and stigmatization." This indicates a clear emphasis on how individual differences lead to criminality (Bernard & Snipes, 1996).

Recent biosocial theories attempt to explain criminal behavior by focusing on the interactions between biological (e.g., genetics, hormones, physiology, brain structure/functioning) and environmental factors. They have expanded in scope and focus to explain many different types of criminality (Rafter, 2008: 240–241; see also Robinson, 2004). Biosocial theorists also tend to focus more on victimful crimes than victimless ones. However, they caution against using criminal law to define the object of study because crime is a socio-legal concept and not a valid behavioral construct (Eysenck & Gudjonsson, 1989; Ellis & Hoffman, 1990; Fishbein, 2001).

While we know genes play a role in violent criminal behavior, Raine and associates (1993) found that a tendency to commit nonviolent crimes seems more heritable than violent crimes. Current biosocial theories of crime generally fail to account for most political, white collar, and corporate crime (for some exceptions, see Ellis, 2005; and Robinson & Beaver, 2008). Most biosocial theories consider drug use (especially maternal drug use) a risk factor for several adverse social outcomes associated with crime. Some have considered how these ideas might be used to inform treatment for cannabis users (Gullo et al., 2021; Papinczak et al., 2019; Walsh & Beaver, 2009).

Other research focuses on drug use, psychosis, and violent crime (Di Forti et al., 2019; Murray et al., 2017). As we documented in Chapter 2, the connections between medicine and cannabis are more than a century old. The medical model emerged regarding cannabis in earnest in the 1980s (Newhart & Dolphin, 2019). One early contribution was work that predicted the expansion of enforced therapeutic approaches as a dominant means of social control (Kittrie, 1971). Connecting deviance with sickness may serve to threaten cultural pluralism, diversity, and difference.

This threat is significant given the emergence of medicalization and the intersection of medical professionals, patients, and the government. As Newhart and Dolphin (2019: 32) point out, "… in the case of cannabis, medicalization is also tied to its relationship with other institutions—most importantly, its criminalization within the legal system." Cannabis use has long been related to concerns about mental illness. The challenges for this view and the medical–juridical discourse that has emerged are myriad. Whether people who use drugs are seen as sick because of an addiction or because they are brain-damaged criminals unable to control their violent outbursts, the addiction/dependence discourse is another feature of cannabis prohibition.

## *Psychological Theories of Crime*

For those who study cannabis, psychological theories provide a basis for links for those pursuing a link between cannabis use and mental health concerns. Psychological positivist theories have much in common with biological positivist theories discussed in earlier chapters. Both approaches emphasize individual-level factors and how these might be used to understand and control criminal behavior. The impact of psychological positivism in criminology can be traced to three key influences: early work on moral insanity (Rafter, 2008), research on intelligence and feeblemindedness, and Freud's (1920, 1923) psychoanalytical approach. All identify a specific criminal type with characteristics of remorselessness, impulsivity, and limited moral development.

One Freudian explanation of criminality focuses on deviant self-identification. In this case, a person may develop a positive relationship with someone who commits a crime, excuse this behavior, or even partake in similar activities. This process resembles those described in the social learning theory and labeling perspective. The difference is how behaviors are psychologically redefined as positive by the observer. In this case, identity may become intertwined with deviant behaviors (Andrews & Bonta, 2003; Serin et al., 2011). Given that many people who use cannabis (and other drugs) connect their use to aspects of their personal identity, one can see how this might be relevant. How does criminalizing cannabis lead to changes in deviant self-identification, and does this increase the likelihood of further criminal behavior?

## Key Concepts

As introduced in Chapter 1, the New Prohibitionists have emerged as a backlash to the widespread efforts to decriminalize, destigmatize, and legalize cannabis (Heidt & Wheeldon, 2021). Like older prohibitionists of the past, they believe that cannabis causes mental illness and thus leads to violence and crime. This has led them to make claims about cannabis, addiction, and crime that require linking different concepts through an overarching narrative that sees cannabis as a dangerous drug with a harmful subculture, which leads people who use drugs into "heavier" use, addiction, and eventually psychosis and crime.

### Cannabis as Subculture

One of the most significant scholars on cannabis found the subject by serendipity. Howard Becker, known for several canonical works in sociology and who influenced many criminologists, spent his career as a professional jazz pianist. Becker's groundbreaking work on deviance emerged from his experiences working in jazz clubs (Abastillas et al., 2020). During the 1950s, he published articles on being a jazz musician and on cannabis use (Becker, 1951, 1953, 1955), drawing heavily on the symbolic–interactionist approach developed by earlier members of the Chicago school (e.g., Blumer, 1969; Mead, 1934). As Becker notes, reflecting on that work, "Instead of talking about drug abuse, I talked about drug *use*" (Gopnik, 2015). Figure 6.1 is a photograph of Howard Becker.

One of Becker's contributions was his social worlds model. This model contrasts with those developed by researchers who focused on understanding large-scale interactions and generally ignored individuals. In Becker's model, social interactions matter "on a much more micro level … individuals were inhabitants of many, complex and overlapping social worlds each with varying entrance and exit barriers" (Ackerman & Lutters, 1996: 5). A Beckerian analysis of a social "world" asks how someone comes to be called an insider in any culture or subculture while someone else gets pushed outside. Sanders (2013: 219) notes that "… [r]ather than asking the less than fruitful question of why people break rules, Becker came to focus on how people go through an identifiable process to *choose* to break rules." Recent research in Poland applies the concept of social worlds to connect the boundaries between people who use cannabis and the conservative, punitive, and sometimes regressive anticannabis culture (Wanke et al., 2022).

**FIGURE 6.1** Howard Becker, Chicago, 1950. Used with permission

In one of the earliest and most important sociological studies of drug use, Becker (1953) interviewed dozens of people who use cannabis about their initial experiences with the drug. He found that most of these people could not get "high" until they had gone through a three-stage social learning process. That is, through social interaction with more experienced users, new users (1) learned the proper technique for smoking marijuana, (2) learned to perceive the effects associated with the "high," and (3) learned to enjoy these effects—to experience the "high" as pleasurable. Becker's work set the tone for subsequent sociological research by portraying cannabis use and other drug-related deviance as an expected outcome of "normal" social learning processes. A consistent concern is that liberalizing cannabis would increase use by youth, influenced by these learning processes.

### *The Brain Disease Model of Addiction (BDMA)*

Once depicted as "Killer Weed" and the "Dropout Drug" (Olmo, 1991) because it could induce laziness, some suggested that consuming cannabis caused "amotivational syndrome" and led to the deterioration of one's personality, including the loss of energy and drive to work (Johns, 2001). In the 1990s, the view that drug use inevitably led to addiction was linked with the notion that drug addiction is a brain disease. This marriage of convenience has become known as the BDMA. In 1997, Alan Leshner published an influential editorial in *Science* titled "Addiction Is a Brain Disease, and It Matters." He wrote:

> Scientific advances over the past 20 years have shown that drug addiction is a chronic, relapsing disease that results from the prolonged effects of drugs on the brain. As with many other brain diseases, addiction has embedded behavioral and social-context aspects that are important parts of the disorder itself. Therefore, the most effective treatment approaches will include biological, behavioral, and social-context components. Recognizing addiction as a chronic, relapsing brain disorder characterized by compulsive drug seeking and use can impact society's overall health and social policy strategies and help diminish the health and social costs associated with drug abuse and addiction.
>
> *1997: 45*

Recent incarnations of biological theories have attempted to incorporate findings from numerous disciplines and subfields in the life sciences, including developmental biology, psychiatry, cognitive neuroscience, behavioral ecology, and endocrinology (Heidt & Wheeldon, 2015). Broadening biosocial perspectives brings both potential and complications. The BDMA is a good example of the difficulties associated with explaining criminal behavior by focusing exclusively on brain structure and functioning.

BDMA inaccurately portrays addiction and perpetuates the central fallacies at the heart of prohibition. More research is needed to define, demonstrate, and explain why we continue to see addiction in simplistic, decontextualized, and unscientific ways. Some suggest that addiction should be viewed as a broad set of personal factors, experiences, and social dynamics that precede actual drug use (Hart, 2017). Considering addiction in more expansive terms disrupts the tendency to think of use disorders or substance misuse merely as a process of counting how many times one has used illegal drugs. Smith (2011: 903) argues:

> Recognition of addiction as a disease has also destigmatized addicts' perception of themselves as "bad" or "weak" people and has made it more acceptable for them to seek treatment at earlier stages of their disease. Families and the medical community react less judgmentally, though the disease model does encourage addicts to take responsibility for their disease and to deal with the consequences of their addiction. Since 100 percent of addicts and alcoholics will at some time surface in the medical system, medicalization greatly improves identification, early intervention, and referral to appropriate treatment.

The quest for less stigmatizing and more clinically accurate language means referring to "use" rather than "abuse," a person with "substance use disorder" rather than an "addict," and "cannabis as medicine" rather than "medical marijuana" (see Saitz et al., 2020; Wogen & Restrepo, 2020). Clinicians and scientists are now encouraged to avoid terms like "drug abuser," "drug user," and "addict" because they are reductionist, vague, and otherwise inaccurate. However, this recent recognition has not yet supplanted past approaches. This definitional inaccuracy is also relevant to the framing of other concepts connected to cannabis.

## Cannabis Psychosis

Older research suggests that cannabis may cause neuropsychological changes to the brain, leading to psychological issues that increase the risk of criminal activity. As we introduced in Chapter 2, Harry J. Anslinger clearly played a role in promoting to the public the connection between psychosis and cannabis. He often did so in troubling ways. For example, he repeatedly referred to the case of a Florida man, Victor Licata, who murdered his parents and three siblings in 1933 after smoking cannabis. Anslinger used this violent and graphic case to illustrate the connections between cannabis use and psychosis even though medical records indicated that Licata had a family history of mental illness and had struggled for many years (Earlywine, 2002).

There is still significant interest in exploring whether cannabis use may lead to brain impairments that increase the likelihood of psychosis and violent crime (Schoeler et al., 2016). Claims that increased cannabis use will lead to more violent crime are based on a report from the National Academy of Science, Engineering, and Medicine's (NASEM) (2017) review of cannabis research and the work of a cluster of psychiatric researchers in the UK, led by Robin Murray (Murray et al., 2017) and Marta Di Forti (Di Forti et al., 2019). Important here is the terminology that is used and its questionable precision. For example, in the past, the inconsistent and ever shifting association between cannabis and psychosis in clinical psychiatric practice and scientific literature was common. This has resulted in diagnostic inaccuracy and a research base of questionable validity. This has led to the findings of numerous studies being conflated, even as persistent critiques of the validity of the underlying concepts have gone unanswered (Gage et al., 2016; Ksir & Hart, 2016). For example, Johns (2001: 116–117) summarizes some common methodological failings:

> (a) studies fail to adequately separate organic from functional psychotic reactions to cannabis; (b) they have insufficiently discriminated between psychotic symptoms and syndromes of a psychosis, and (c) they have not balanced the weight of evidence for and against the category of cannabis psychosis.

While distinctions between organic and functional reactions and symptoms and syndromes related to cannabis use are worthy of further exploration, there is an inherent "fuzziness" in current formulations (Pearson & Berry, 2019). As discussed below, recent research suggests the value of older observations. Gage and colleagues (2013) state that residual confounding variables could be providing false positives. They note that drug use, in general, is often associated with other risk factors such as certain personality types, early-life trauma, and family adversity. This notion of "shared vulnerability" (Ksir & Hart, 2016) appears to be a promising way to consider the role of these confounding variables.

## Relevant Research

The value of past cannabis research is undermined by inconsistent cannabis access, poor designs, and a persistent failure to acknowledge fundamental research limitations (Heidt & Wheeldon, 2022). One essential problem is cannabis supply. Schwabe and colleagues (2019) argue that in the US, most federally funded cannabis research relies on research-grade cannabis. This is unlike other commercial or illicit cannabis. In no other study on a substance that is reported to impact "psychiatric disorders and learning and memory impairments ... neurological consequences, including cerebrovascular events" (Kroon et al., 2020: 559), would nonstandardized use and imprecise doses of the substance in question be viewed as acceptable. These issues alone should cast doubt on much of the research undertaken to date.

### *Increased Youth Cannabis Use and Crime*

Since the use of cannabis, where legal, is limited to adults, youth who buy, possess, or use it may be committing a criminal offense. A consistent concern by policymakers is that liberalizing cannabis use would increase use by youth. Research by Akers and Cochran (1985) suggested that the principles of social learning theory were linked to adolescent drug use. Later research combined elements from social learning theory with Becker's (1963) early work on cannabis use. For example, Orcutt (1987) sought to predict cannabis use in college students, given certain motivational and associational conditions. Students with positive, neutral, and negative definitions of cannabis use were asked to estimate how many of their four closest friends smoked at least once a month.

These results were in line with Sutherland's contention that a person will engage in an illegal act if they are exposed to an excess of definitions favorable to violating a law or social rule. This research suggested that increased cannabis use by friends would lead to increases in cannabis use overall. The importance of social learning was replicated a year later in research focused on continued cannabis use among youth (Johnson, 1988). In an international and comparative study, social learning theory emerged as the leading theoretical explanation for cannabis use in the US and Bolivia (Meneses & Akers, 2011).

Other research relevant to understanding cannabis use involves examining criminal and deviant behavior over the life course (Blumstein, Cohen, & Farrington, 1988; Moffitt, 1993; Sampson & Laub, 1993; Thornberry, 1989). Some suggest that youth who use cannabis 20 times or more have 1.5 times the risk of being arrested for a property crime and 1.8 times the risk of self-reported property crime by midlife compared to light/nonusers (Green et al., 2010). Pedersen and Skardhamar (2010) suggest that cannabis use at ages 15 and 20 years predicts subsequent offending. Others suggested that "cannabis use predicts subsequent violent offending, suggesting a possible causal effect ..." (Schoeler et al., 2016: 1663). Heavy adolescent cannabis use has been associated with an increased risk of being poor, unmarried, and experiencing heightened anxiety in midlife. Heavy use is presented as a specific risk for "Black urban youth" and sets them "... on a long-term trajectory of disadvantage that persists into midlife" (Green et al., 2010: 567).

There are two major problems associated with these types of research studies. First, there is an assumption that cannabis use, especially at a young age, is associated with adverse mental health outcomes. Some people then jump to the conclusion that increased access to cannabis will result in more mental issues and inevitably lead to more crime. The logical problem with this conclusion is evident if one considers the experience of states and provinces that liberalized cannabis policy. There is little to no indication that legalizing cannabis in Massachusetts, Connecticut, Rhode Island, Vermont, Maryland, and Washington increased its use among youth (Gruczaet al., 2018; Johnson et al., 2019; Ta et al., 2019).

Several studies provide insights into how legalization impacts cannabis use among youth and young adults. Hall and Lynskey (2020) suggest that while cannabis use increased among adults, adolescent use did not. This suggests that cannabis is more difficult to get when it is regulated. Other research has focused exclusively on youth and adolescent use. Research by Stevens (2019) analyzed survey data from 38 countries from 2001–2002, 2005–2006, and 2009–2010 to examine if policy liberalization increased the likelihood of adolescent cannabis use. No significant association emerged between less stringent cannabis policies and increased rates of adolescent cannabis use.

The second issue concerns crime specifically. Studies have repeatedly concluded that cannabis liberalization policies are associated either with no impact on crime or reductions in crime and public disorder (Dragone et al., 2017; Huber III, Newman, & LaFave, 2016; Hunt et al., 2018; Kepple & Freisthler, 2012; Males & Buchen, 2014; Morris, 2018). Lu and colleagues (2021) used a quasi-experimental, multigroup-interrupted time-series design to determine if and how Uniform Crime Reports (UCR) crime rates in Colorado and Washington were influenced by legalization. They concluded that cannabis legalization and sales have had minimal to no effect on violent or property crimes in Colorado and Washington. In Canada, the implementation of the Cannabis Act (2018) is associated with a *decrease* of 55–65% in cannabis-related crimes among male and female youth (Callaghan et al., 2021). Critics might suggest that crime drops are a function of decriminalization and the reclassification of cannabis, not because communities are safer. However, this raises an important question. If changing the legal status of cannabis does not result in more harm, why would we continue to criminalize it?

## *Cannabis and Addiction*

The BDMA asserts that addiction is a brain disease, and research explores how cannabis use results in biological and neuropsychological changes to the brain. Introduced above, a recently initiated $300-million study will compare drug use and academic achievement. The Adolescent Brain Cognitive Development Study[2] seeks to gather neuroimaging data to understand adolescent drug use and addiction. Researchers will follow more than 10,000 people between the ages of 9 and 10 for a decade, collecting their genetic information and assessing their drug use and academic achievement using longitudinal data. Hart (2017: 1) has identified several problems with studies such as these. This research lacks consideration of critical social factors such as parental income, racial discrimination, neighborhood characteristics, or the consequences of decades of policing of drug use (see also Levy, 2013). Instead, this research focuses on the "diseased brain."

This view suggests that drug addiction is like Huntington's or Parkinson's disease and that drug use irrevocably damages brain structures. There is little evidence that this is so (Lewis, 2015). It has never been shown that accurate predictions about the condition involved or their symptoms are possible by looking at the brains of affected individuals. Instead, negative assumptions about drug use push research dollars toward unfounded connections between drug use and addiction. Bizarrely, few consider why the overwhelming majority of people who use drugs never become addicted, and most people who become addicted stop using drugs on their own without the aid of treatment and counseling (Hart, 2017; Heyman, 2013; Lewis, 2015). Continuing to frame all drug use as addictive behavior perpetuates stigma against people who use drugs. Research demonstrates how stigma leads to more punitive approaches (Kelly et al., 2010; Kelly & Westerhoff, 2010; Van Boekel et al., 2013).

In 2020, 6.2 million Canadians reported using cannabis.[3] If the BDMA was accurate and relevant for people who use cannabis, one might expect a considerable number of severe cases of cannabis addiction. There is no evidence to support this expectation. One measure that can assist our understanding is treatment admissions for CUD for young people. Using data from the 2002–2019 National Survey on Drug Use and Health, 43,307 individuals who met past-year *DSM-5*-proxy CUD criteria were identified. According to Askari and colleagues (2021), between 2002 and 2019, 6.1% of people reported using a CUD treatment. However, treatment use decreased by more than 50% during this time. Although CUD treatment is decreasing in general, adults are far less likely to rely on treatment than adolescents, who presumably have less agency.

Based on the data from 2004 to 2012, researchers found no increase in treatment admissions for problem cannabis use in states with liberal cannabis policies (Philbin et al., 2019). This finding mirrors Mennis and Stahler's study (2020) that found no increase in treatment admissions for adolescent substance use disorder in Washington and Colorado. Concerns that recreational cannabis legalization increased CUD among youth due to increased access to cannabis appear unfounded. However, Mennis (2020: para 4) warns readers against the current "... period of increasing permissiveness, decreasing perception of harm, and increasing adult use, regarding marijuana." In a subsequent paper, Mennis and colleagues (2021) admit that increased access to cannabis does not lead to increases in treatment admissions for cannabis use. However, the authors fuel fears that normalization is a ticking time bomb destined to explode.

> In 38 out of 50 states, including seven out of the eight states legalizing recreational cannabis during the study period, as young adult cannabis use increased, treatment admissions declined .... We speculate that increasing social acceptance of cannabis use, and declining perception of harm, may influence treatment seeking behavior, potentially resulting in growing unmet need for CUD treatment among young adults.
>
> *Mennis et al., 2021: para 3*

Recently, even those who have been funded for decades to uncover the harms of cannabis use now concede the relative safety of cannabis. They have belatedly admitted that its use is neither necessary nor sufficient to cause psychosis (D'Souza et al., 2022). While the dangers of increasing social acceptance of cannabis may appear one day, stoking these fears in the absence of evidence is inconsistent with responsible research. Unfortunately, this practice is part and parcel of many pieces of cannabis research.

## *Cannabis and Violence*

As mentioned previously, findings of the NASEM (2017) report and psychiatric work on the impact of cannabis use from UK researchers Robin Murray and Marta Di Forti (Murray et al., 2017) suggest that cannabis use is associated with an increased risk of psychosis. This research has been seized upon by those we have referred to as the "New Prohibitionists" (Heidt & Wheeldon, 2022). Some even claim that violent crime rates are rising in areas that have legalized cannabis use (Berenson, 2019).

Although there is evidence that cannabis use may contribute to psychotic disorders in certain circumstances and among certain people, these connections are complex. They are often misinterpreted by the media and journalists who lack research expertise. The evidence for cannabis acting as a causal factor for schizophrenia has not been established (Hamilton & Monaghan, 2019). One general problem is that most studies fail to consider potency, amount, or type of cannabis consumed and do not attempt to measure the level of impairment. Other confounding variables have been identified. These include the abstinence period (Kroon et al., 2021), early alcohol use, early sexual activity, poor school performance, abuse, and trauma (Ksir & Hart, 2016). Some researchers have gone so far as to posit a causal relationship between tobacco use and disorders on the schizophrenia spectrum (Scott et al., 2018). Since some people who use cannabis also smoke tobacco, these relationships are particularly difficult to untangle (Ksir & Hart, 2016). When neither the substance(s) under study nor the people who use cannabis can be accurately described, research findings must be treated with skepticism (Best, 2001).

Another consistent problem is how to define people who use cannabis. Heavy cannabis users can refer to people who report cannabis use in various ways. Table 6.1 provides some examples. These inconsistent definitions present serious challenges when interpreting and comparing research studies.

**TABLE 6.1** Twenty-five years of varying definitions of heavy cannabis use

| *Heavy use is defined as using cannabis:* | *Citation* |
|---|---|
| Five or more days per week, two or more times per day when used for at least one year | Pope and Yurgelun-Todd (1996) |
| Daily for at least two years | Degenhardt et al. (2003: 1495) |
| By smoking more than five joints per day | Yücel et al. (2008) |
| On at least ten occasions per month | Cousijn et al. (2011: 1667) |
| For ten or more days during the last month, at least 240 days during the last two years, without seeking treatment or having a treatment history for problematic cannabis use | Cousijn et al. (2012: 3846) |
| For more than 20 years of smoking one joint per day | Gracie and Hancox (2020) |
| (Nearly) daily | Kroon et al. (2020: 559) |

Perhaps the most prominent problem for those who link cannabis to psychosis and criminal behavior is that crime rates have not increased where cannabis has been decriminalized or legalized. As previously explained, cannabis liberalization does not seem to increase use among youth or young adults in most jurisdictions in North America (Gabri et al., 2022). Legalization has not been associated with significant changes in cannabis-induced psychosis or ED visits for schizophrenia (Mennis & Stahler, 2020). It has little to no effect on crime (Lu et al., 2021). Despite these findings, noted drug policy experts persist in alarmist claims. For example, Ritter (2021: 21) cites Hasin et al. (2015) and Wagner and Anthony (2002) to conclude that "… between 10% and 30% of people who consume cannabis will develop a cannabis use disorder."

According to a recent Statistics Canada report, 6.2 million Canadians 15 and older reported using cannabis by the end of 2020. This suggests that between 600,000 and nearly 2 million Canadians have a CUD, which would make the legalization of cannabis a major public health failure in Canada. The problem with this claim and others like it is that research suggests lower CUD prevalence among people who use cannabis in states with a more liberal cannabis policy (Philbin et al., 2019). Developing evidence-based policy is undermined by the influence of prohibitionist thinking. The fact that some will continue to propagate unproven myths does not mean that there are no issues in this area for future research.

Links between cannabis and crime seem to be strongest within illegal markets under prohibition. In his tripartite model of drug-related crime, Goldstein (1985) argues that drugs and violence are seen as being related in three possible ways: the psychopharmacological, the economically compulsive, and the systemic. According to this view, illegal markets are characterized by systemic violence (e.g., territorial disputes, failure to pay drug debts, selling phony drugs, informing authorities, and punishment for subcultural norm violations). Ironically, these violent activities are often byproducts or are related to drug criminalization itself.

## New Directions

One finding connects cannabis and crime based on the nature of regulation and administrative frameworks associated with cannabis liberalization. Legalization may displace crime and criminals (Zakrzewski et al., 2020); however, administrative issues around banking, zoning and other regulatory issues influence crime around cannabis dispensaries (Contreras, 2017; Hughes et al., 2019; Subica et al., 2018). For example, a recent study based on data from Oregon (Wu, Wen, & Wilson, 2020) suggested that cannabis legalization may increase crime based on specific conditions, such as inefficient regulation and the involvement of organized crime groups. One area of interest is how to promote the safe use and storage of cannabis (Myran et al. 2022). In general, especially in North America, cannabis is emerging as an issue that is increasingly normalized and remains stubbornly stigmatized.

Another emergent issue is around driving. While, in general, the connections between cannabis and crime are tenuous, impaired driving resulting from cannabis

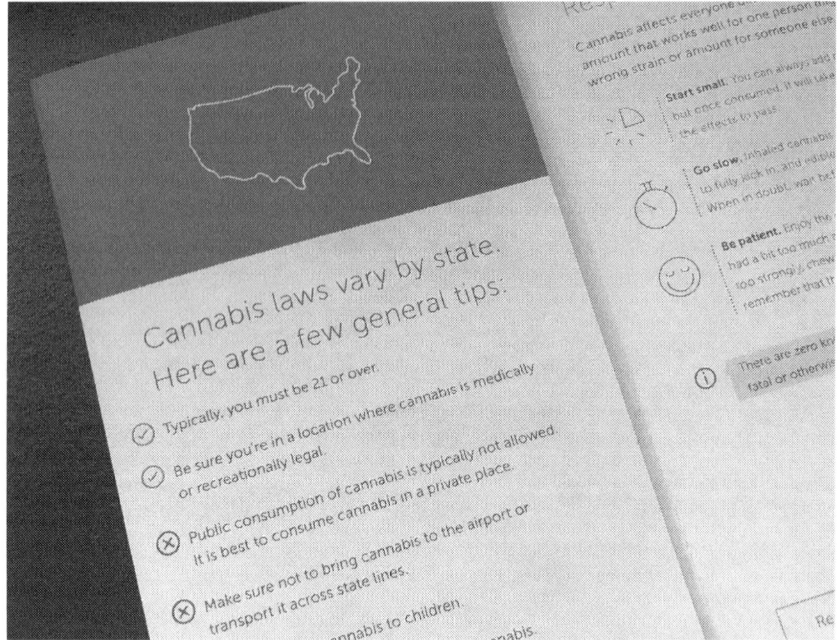


**FIGURE 6.2** Cannabis laws. "Cannabis Laws" by stockcatalog is licensed under CC BY 2.0

use is a crime and a threat to public safety. Increased dangerous driving based on cannabis impairment is routinely mentioned as a risk for cannabis policy reform. This fear goes something like this: if access to cannabis is increased, more people will use it. If more people operate vehicles under the influence of the drug, this will result in increased dangerous driving, traffic accidents, and senseless deaths and injuries. Much of this concern is fueled by the Rocky Mountain High-Intensity Drug Trafficking Area (RMHDA). Since 2014, a federally funded antilegalization group composed of law enforcement officials that have published yearly reports about road safety changes after legalization. Its annual reports suggest that cannabis legalization causes numerous traffic accidents in areas that have liberalized cannabis policy.[4] However, an analysis of the methods used reveals many methodological problems. Once again, the reality is that the picture is not quite as disastrous as the RMHDA suggests.

It is common to find elevated THC levels in motorists involved in accidents after legalization. Some research suggests that driver injuries were more severe when they tested positive for cannabis (Hamzeie et al., 2017). However, this does not necessarily mean that cannabis use is causing these accidents or that cannabis legalization significantly increases the likelihood and frequency of accidents (for detailed critiques, see Sullum, 2015, 2016). Part of the problem with the RMHDA reports is that they are overly reliant on one type of data. A more accurate way to examine the effect of cannabis on road safety would be to find data that allow for comparisons between states that have legalized cannabis versus those states where it remains illegal.

A recent study using this approach based on the fatal accident reporting system (FARS) data revealed that, compared to the eight control states that did not legalize cannabis, the rates of motor crash fatalities did not increase in states that legalized cannabis. This study arrived at these conclusions by using a different dataset. Rather than looking at the rates of driver impairment, these researchers also examined studies on overall traffic injuries and fatalities using the FARS data (Lake et al., 2018). Several other studies using the FARS data found that after the legalization of medical cannabis, there were significant reductions in motor vehicle fatalities, especially among young adults (Anderson et al., 2013; Santaella-Tenorio et al., 2017).

To understand the impact of legalization on traffic safety, Aydelotte and colleagues (2017) compared the crash fatality rates in Washington, Colorado, and eight other control states with cannabis prohibition. Using data from 2009 to 2015, they found no differences in crash fatality rates that could be attributed to cannabis legalization. In Canada, based on the data from British Columbia, Brubacher and colleagues (2019) found no increased risk of crash responsibility in drivers with 2–5 ng/ml of THC in their blood. These researchers also found more significant increases in the likelihood of crash involvement when alcohol was present in a driver's system compared to cannabis. While changing cannabis policies requires care, the negative impacts of cannabis on road safety appear overblown (Compton, 2017).

In their study comparing cannabis and alcohol impairment, Sewell and colleagues (2009) found that the detrimental effects of cannabis were more noticeable in tasks involving highly automatic driving functions (e.g., reaction time, maintaining a consistent speed), although alcohol was more likely to affect complex tasks requiring concentration and focus. Further, the researchers found that people who use cannabis tend to better compensate for their deficiencies using various behavioral strategies (e.g., driving slowly and often under the speed limit). To complicate matters further, the study also indicated that the effects of cannabis vary between individuals compared to alcohol use because of individual differences in tolerance level, differences in smoking technique and devices, and differences in absorption levels of THC—these differences are not as readily apparent when examining alcohol use.

Perhaps the biggest worry is failing to appreciate the catalytic effects of mixing alcohol and cannabis. Recent research suggests that this risk is significant (Lira et al., 2021). Unfortunately, there is limited research to help guide policy in this area. However, it does seem likely that while people respond differently, combining cannabis and alcohol often increases the effects of both drugs (Dubois et al., 2015; Hartman & Huestis, 2013). Reactions include sedation, alterations in judgment, perceptual effects that include time distortions, and physical effects such as slowed reflexes and decreased motor coordination that can present serious risks when driving or operating heavy machinery (Sewell et al., 2009; Ramaekers et al., 2000).

Since cannabis and alcohol affect different parts of the brain, their combination, particularly at high doses, can place people at increased risk.

In a recent review on driving and cannabis, Pearlson, Stevens, and D'Souza (2021) distinguish between areas where research has provided clear answers to the above questions and areas that remain unclear. They acknowledge that cannabis-impaired driving is a risk. However, they note that skewed, agenda-driven reporting has undermined this area of inquiry. They advocate more rigorous studies to address the ideological risks when "… science finds itself bumping up against public policy, with legislators and others needing to be more current/topical about the existing research, so that they can make the best, most informed, policy decisions."

Rather than relying on blood THC levels to gauge impairment or on unproven roadside sobriety tests, Pearlson and colleagues (2021) suggest expanding public health campaigns. This might mean treating cannabis-impaired driving as problematic when this impairment is demonstrable and articulable. As White and Burns (2022: 1) point out, many studies of cannabis-based impairments fail to demonstrate any impairment at all for people who regularly use cannabis due to their tolerance. They argue that selective reporting by researchers, amplified by the media, has created the "false impression that the evidence for cannabis-induced impairment is strong and consistent." As Gina Vumbaca[5] of Harm Reduction Australia points out, laws to control impaired driving can hinder the use of legally prescribed medical cannabis by patients.[6]

None of these concerns should be read as a justification for continuing to criminalize cannabis, prohibit its use, or stigmatize people who consume it. Alcohol use represents much more of a threat to road safety than cannabis use. It should not go unnoticed that a century of nonsense-based policy has left people profoundly uninformed about the uses and potential misuse of cannabis. Many readers may recall instances of people at a party "trying" cannabis after drinking alcohol. It generally does not go well. Ironically, prohibition and the myths it has perpetuated have made cannabis consumption riskier. Perhaps people have been negatively impacted because they are unprepared to manage their cannabis use. In the future, public safety can be improved by ensuring people are aware of how cannabis can enhance some experiences and diminish others. In general, consumers need to be better informed about the specific risks of the co-consumption of alcohol and cannabis.

## Conclusion

By exploring theoretical starting points, including social learning theory, biosocial theories of criminality, and psychological theories of crime, this chapter explored youth crime, the BDMA, and psychosis. Research has challenged many of the past assumptions about the relationship between cannabis use and crime. Cannabis legalization does not increase use by youth. Neither addiction nor use disorders increase where cannabis is legalized, and the always tenuous link between cannabis and violence and other crime now appears especially nonsensical. Even those engaged in public safety models of cannabis control acknowledge that cannabis is generally less likely to lead to most types of crime since

> it reduces, rather than instills aggression, thus not generating the interpersonal violence commonly associated with alcohol or psycho-stimulants ... nor is a cannabis habit so expensive to generate economic compulsive crime. Yet a variety of trajectory frameworks for cannabis-related crime have been proposed .... Some of these directly relate to the illegal status or contexts of cannabis itself.
>
> *Fischer et al., 2021: 63–64*

There are reasonable concerns that the regular use of significant amounts of cannabis by youth (under 18) represents a danger to physical and mental health. It should come as no surprise that these potential dangers increase as the age of the person consuming cannabis decreases. However, prohibition causes more damage than it deters. The commitment to prohibitionist notions complicates evidence-based policymaking.

Existing regulatory frameworks will need to confront the growing political unacceptability of criminal sanctions for cannabis use. However, persistent concerns remain around the potential for cannabis addiction (Ritter, 2021). While such extraordinary claims cannot be supported by rigorous contemporary research, police are likely to use the potential for the dangers associated with cannabis to justify stops, investigations, and possible arrests.

The connections between cannabis and crime amount to a "zombie theory." This association continues to shuffle through the pages of academic journals, refusing to die and feasting on the brains of naïve researchers and mercurial academics.[7] The poor research of the past connecting cannabis and crime has fallen apart as more examples, and better designs have emerged. Research on cannabis and crime continues. Of specific interest is to what extent police will use the potential for nonlegal cannabis possession to justify stops, investigations, and possible arrests. Will police require people possessing cannabis to *prove* their cannabis is legal? How consistently and rigorously will this be enforced? Will it lead to the creation of criminal records for otherwise law-abiding citizens?

## Notes

1 Research suggests that those with mental issues who can manage their conditions effectively are not at increased risk of reoffending (Pozzulo et al., 2021). In addition, studies on violence and severe mental illness suggest that most people with mental illness are not violent. Some believe that the correlation between mental illness and violence may be spurious or at least very misleading because there are many other factors present in the lives of those with mental health issues (e.g., poverty, substance use, unemployment, and homelessness) that are more important to understanding why some of these people behave violently (Serin et al., 2011).

2 See https://addictionresearch.nih.gov/abcd-study [accessed September 1, 2021].

3 See www150.statcan.gc.ca/n1/pub/82-003-x/2021004/article/00001-eng.htm [accessed June 5, 2022].
4 See www.thenmi.org/wp-content/uploads/2020/10/RMHIDTA-Marijuana-Report-2020-2.pdf [accessed June 5, 2022].
5 Personal communication, October 23, 2021.
6 See www.drivechangemc.org.au/ [accessed June 5, 2022].
7 The idea of zombie theories in criminology was first applied by John Roman to the crime decline. See https://johnkroman.substack.com/p/vanquishing-zombie-theories-of-the [accessed June 5, 2022].

# 7

# CANNABIS CRIMINOLOGY

## Back to the Future

### Introduction

In this book, we presented a novel approach to studying cannabis in criminology by linking numerous issues in the field with the history of cannabis prohibition and justice policy. As we documented, these issues have long been of interest to some criminologists. However, as the legal status of cannabis is updated, so too must criminology's approach. Based on our analysis, key findings emerged. These include how stigma around cannabis remains relevant and how persistent inequalities associated with policing cannabis continue to harm Black and Brown people. In addition, we have noted research that suggests that coercive care and control within diversion programs amounts to incomplete reform and reifies, rather than challenging, the underlying assumptions of prohibition. Finally, we complicated past research on cannabis use and crime and began the process of uncovering how economic theories in criminology can assist jurisdictions seeking to disrupt illicit cannabis markets.

In this chapter, we argue that many of these challenges can be traced to the success of the New Prohibitionists and the associated failure(s) of public criminology. More work is needed to properly frame the results of research that highlight the costs of cannabis prohibition and the limited benefits associated with its criminalization. We believe that the future of cannabis criminology involves exploring new ways to engage audiences on these questions. However, as we point out below, the future cannot be divorced from the past. The impulse toward public criminology must contend with a paradox. Previous research, studies, and government-funded reports have time and again concluded that cannabis reform is needed. These recommendations have been ignored for decades.

Whatever the challenges, robust research must continue and do more to engage people who use cannabis as key "insiders." This chapter includes a research program

DOI: 10.4324/9781003232292-7

based on the five thematic areas that have organized this book. These include law, society, and social control; police and policing cannabis; race, ethnicity, and criminalization; the economics of cannabis; and cannabis and crime. Together these themes suggest the potential for recasting stigma as a predatory feature of prohibition, documenting the limited value of policing cannabis, and considering the potential for cannabis liberalization to apply restorative approaches to combat racial injustices.

In addition, we propose research specifically designed to compare regulatory regimes and outline lessons learned that could assist in expanding legal cannabis and addressing illicit markets and their related harms. Economic theories may be especially useful. Although "law-based" paradigms (Fischer et al., 2021) are likely to remain a focus for some researchers, we have uncovered only limited evidence that cannabis and crime are connected. We predict that concerns about impaired driving will grow. In jurisdictions where cannabis is legal, lawmakers will need to carefully consider what to do about unregulated cannabis. Will policing the illicit use of cannabis shift to a focus on regulatory enforcement of legal cannabis?

Cannabis research, no matter how credible, detailed, or sound, will rarely be enough on its own to initiate or sustain cannabis policy reform. More dynamic approaches to public criminology are needed. We offer some suggestions, but more work is needed. Future researchers might consider a research "duty of care" given the racial history of cannabis and the harms that result from persistent myths around cannabis and crime. Engaging prohibitionist ideas and those perpetrating them is not for the faint of heart. The days of the quiet scholar slowly documenting knowledge, fully ensconced in the proverbial ivory tower while the world burns around them, are long gone. Perhaps, combating the nonsense of cannabis policy requires engaging the ironic impulse associated with social media.

## Three Persistent Problems in Cannabis Criminology

The analysis in this book has uncovered three broad problems at the intersection of criminological theory and practice. First, stigma remains around cannabis use and is fed by the prohibitionist tendencies of the past. Both can harm people who use cannabis, their families, and their communities. As Ritter (2021) notes, drug policy has historically been shaped by the questions of morality, ideology, and assumptive virtue. The underlying normative and ethical positions about drugs shaped and continue to influence policy in subtle ways, such as resisting legalization, pathologizing cannabis use, and maintaining moralistic judgments that all cannabis use is problematic.

This is not to say there are no risks to consuming cannabis (Wang, 2022). However, the adverse outcomes associated with cannabis use have been historically exaggerated. These positions are nurtured by groups within societies whose values and preferences align with those in government (Heidt & Wheeldon, 2022). Cannabis policy is perhaps the best, if still incomplete, example of how shifting norms influence governance policy. Based on the research reviewed in this book, we believe that cannabis liberalization must consider the obstinate influence of prohibition if it is to confront the harms associated with entanglements with the criminal justice system.

The second problem relates to the persistent inequalities resulting from policing cannabis. The policing of cannabis has led to racially unequal outcomes and increasingly deadly encounters (Baum, 1996; Tonry, 1994). Black and Brown people are arrested at higher rates than White people even after controlling for incidence and other sociodemographic variables (Koch et al., 2016; Owusu-Bempah & Luscombe, 2021). Understanding police discretion with people who use drugs (PWUD) is of increasing interest. Policing drug use allocates limited resources to policies that often erode public trust, further ethnic divisions, and alienate communities (del Pozo et al., 2021; Fagan et al., 2010). It is hard to see this issue as disconnected from the recent high-profile police killings of Black men and boys and how a police culture rooted in "warrior culture" results in aggressive law enforcement tactics (Kraska, 2001). It is unconscionable and morally injurious that police remain empowered to strip-search Black children on the mere suspicion that they possess cannabis. It must stop.

Third, and final, is the problem of diversion. Diversion is likely to remain a crucial part of decriminalization. Some view mandatory treatment programs in lieu of a criminal record as progressive drug reform. However, accepting this approach obscures the essential contradictions and hypocrisies at the heart of prohibition. It results in acquiescing to outdated ideas about addiction, crime, and the false promise of prohibition based on the idea that people who use cannabis are "sick" and need to be "treated" (Szalavitz, 2015b; Taylor et al., 2016). Replacing the harms of incarceration with the coercion found in many diversion programs is hardly an unalloyed good.

In criminology, the medical model has been part of the expanding carceral state (Drake, 2012) and is being extended through community-based treatment programs that can rely upon the criminal justice for a steady stream of clients. However, new approaches require that longstanding and harmful ideas around drug use must first be "undone" (Szalavitz, 2021). Linking cannabis and criminal justice demands that we contend with the punitive character of the justice system. We maintain that this allows the underlying assumptions of the war on drugs to go unchallenged. Addressing these assumptions requires expanding our understanding of cannabis, prohibition, and social control. It also means engaging in an analysis of sharing criminological research, acknowledging the long reach of the New Prohibitionists (Heidt & Wheeldon, 2022), and revisiting older ideas about the difference between meaningful and illusory reform (Cohen, 1979, 1985).

## The New Prohibitionists and Public Criminology

Historically, the failure of the criminal justice system to learn from its past is difficult to doubt (Walker, 1997). A history of punitive justice policies can be linked to the Puritanical approach to moral legislation, the rise of the modern penitentiary, and the continuing desire to use the prohibition of certain substances as a proxy for the social control of various "undesirable" behaviors and ethnicities. The prohibition of cannabis has intersected with many aspects of criminology and led to criminal justice policies that have had adverse consequences on the poor, the powerless, and people of color. The assumptions, language, and laws maintaining prohibition continue to inform the study of deviance and crime, even as the harms inflicted by past penal modalities are rarely acknowledged. The notion that good research will lead to good practice is belied by decades of criminological experience. Combating prohibition requires considering how to improve efforts to share criminological research. To solve any problem, we first need to define it.

## *The New Prohibitionists*

As introduced in Chapter 1 and revisited throughout the book, a new wave of prohibitionists has emerged against the normalization of cannabis in social and cultural terms. By weaponizing social anxieties built on nearly a century of the demonization of drugs, the New Prohibitionists seek to limit the use of cannabis by misrepresenting past research (Heidt & Wheeldon, 2022). Since these individuals and groups often espouse a firm commitment to drug treatment and mental health, rather than prison, the New Prohibitionists are often taken more seriously by modern media outlets. As we argued, the New Prohibitionists now seem like cautious progressive treatment advocates, indistinguishable from other drug policy reformers who suggest that cannabis use leads to addiction (Ritter, 2021). These views are based on a specific idea of drug use and on a deliberate and selected misreading of scientific research.

Howard Becker, whose work on cannabis we explored in Chapter 6, identified the increasing influence from the field of psychiatry decades ago:

> The moral crusader, however, is more concerned with ends rather than the means. When it comes to drawing up specific rules (typically in the form of legislation to be proposed to a state legislature of the Federal Congress) he frequently relies on the advice of experts. Lawyers, expert in the drawing of acceptable legislation, often play this role. Government bureaus in whose jurisdiction the problem falls may also have the necessary expertise as did the Federal Bureau of Narcotics in the case of the marihuana problem.
>
> As psychiatric ideology, however, becomes increasing acceptable, a new expert has appeared—the psychiatrist .... The influence of the psychiatrist in other realms of the criminal law has increased in recent years.
>
> In any case, what is important about this example is not that psychiatrists are becoming increasingly influential, ... at some point in the development of his crusade, often requires the services of a professional who can draw up the appropriate rules in the appropriate form. *The crusader himself is often not*

> *concerned with such details. Enough for him that the main point has been won; he leaves the implementation to others.*
>
> *1963: 151–152, italics added*

The notion that this is a competition belies the racial history of cannabis prohibition and the associated harms that remain (Solomon, 2020). Recently, researchers once cited to justify continuing cannabis prohibition have taken great pains to clarify that their findings suggest cannabis does not *cause* psychosis (D'Souza et al., 2022). However, the damage has been done.

There are challenges beyond prohibitionist ideals being embedded in many poor-quality cannabis studies. Others are seeking funding from an infrastructure that explicitly focuses on efforts to prove the adverse consequences of cannabis use. It is notable that research designed to explore benefits has consistently been "… delayed or blocked" (Newhart & Dolphin, 2019: 26). For early career researchers who are trying to establish themselves in an emerging area of scholarship, there is pressure to uncover politically useful correlations that are likely to get published and generate media attention. Unfortunately, the precarity of academia can inspire the dark side of careerism. It may lead to two kinds of adaptations. The first is "salami-slicing," where scholars split up findings from datasets to publish discrete works that are essentially the same.[1] This led to a well-known criminologist publishing two nearly identical papers in the journals *Criminology* and *Social Problems* (Wheeldon et al., 2014).

The second is p-hacking or data dredging. This occurs when the patient process of testing relevant propositions from credible theories by defining and operationalizing specific variables is replaced by data mining practices. Designed to uncover all possible correlative connections within a large dataset, these associations can allow for bizarre conclusions like "cannabis use predicts subsequent violent offending, suggesting a *possible causal effect*" (Schoeler et al., 2016: 1663, italics added). As any introductory stats student knows, there either is or is not a causal relationship between two variables. A "possible causal effect" is not a scientific term.

The challenge in cannabis research is that such claims can find a home in a media environment where the more outlandish the claim, the more likely it is to get published. Today

> [c]ommercial pressures lead media organizations to feature incendiary stories that receive the most attention. Further, while platforms proliferate, similar content is dispersed widely as media power is concentrated in a small number of old and new media corporations …. Search engines direct users to a limited selection of heavily trafficked and well-financed sites.
>
> *Owen, 2019: 8*

Combining opportunist researchers with a media culture that cares more about clicks than accuracy represents a serious problem for evidence-based cannabis policy. One option is rethinking public criminology.

## *Public Criminology*

Public criminology was first made as a call for criminologists to get more involved in debates about crime, criminals, and society's formal and informal responses beyond the hallowed halls of the academy (Carrabine, Lee, & South, 2000). This view has been expanded to emphasize work that informs public understanding of crime, punishment, criminal law, and criminal justice (Uggen & Inderbitzin, 2010). Inderbitzin (2011) further specified that the value of public approaches to criminology allows

> those with the interests and skills to carry criminological theories and research into the public debate offer an important service. Among other tasks, they may debunk myths and help to reframe the cultural image of the criminal, they may offer social facts on crime and punishment and bring context to highly sensationalized cases, they may work with communities to compile data and answer pressing questions, and they may bring the best available evidence to conversations and debate on issues of criminal justice public policy.[2]

This work is partly motivated by the belief that there is a wide gap between criminological research and public opinion and that future generations of criminologists can be inspired to address the consequences. This means confronting and attempting to explain why the findings from different government commissions, committees, and inquiries around the world have failed to influence policy. Almost without exception, the resultant recommendations to adopt more tolerant approaches to cannabis use were rejected (Bewley-Taylor et al., 2014). One challenge has been the role of newspapers, magazines, and other media that have long supported antidrug campaigns. Levine notes (2003: 148):

> Since the 1920s, top editors in the news media have clearly recognized, as an economic fact of their business, that an alarming anti-drug story can increase sales of magazines and newspapers. This is especially so when the story is about drugs that threaten middle-class teenagers and their families. News editors and TV producers understand that a front page or "top of the news" story about a tempting, dangerous, illegal drug can attract readers and TV viewers. There is no doubt that many publishers, editors and broadcasters have believed deeply in fighting drugs. But few of the causes that people in the media believe in can so easily be turned into stories that are simultaneously good for business and for public relations.

Cannabis prohibition is based on a profoundly antiscience orientation that has undermined drug policy for decades (Stevens, 2007). Research alone cannot overcome this legacy. For example, while one study found that cannabis liberalization was responsible for increased cannabis use among youth (Shi et al., 2015), a subsequent replication refuted the main findings (Stevens, 2019). Future cannabis-informed research programs must involve efforts to replicate early research in this area to correct the record, where appropriate, and ensure our troubling history of racialization, prohibition, criminalization, and incarceration is not repeated.

Perhaps the most crucial area of research related to cannabis and crime is exploring why punitive approaches persisted despite more than a century of reports warning against criminal sanctions for cannabis. Reports repeatedly concluded that cannabis need not be treated like other drugs, and criminalizing its use would do more harm than good. This might be seen as an ethical issue worthy of consideration by criminologists and others working at the intersection of drugs, research, and policy. In addition, as we have argued in this book, contemporary regulation schemes would benefit by understanding past international efforts to study cannabis and its use.

An early example of note comes from the 1893 Indian Hemp Drugs Commission (IHDC). The IHDC had a mandate to investigate the cultivation and trade of cannabis, the effect of their consumption upon the "social and moral condition" of the people, and the desirability of prohibition (Mills, 2003). The report concluded that the moderate use of cannabis was not a cause of physical harm or insanity. Among people who used cannabis, only 5% were estimated to be using it excessively, despite its widespread availability. There were few negative social consequences. Consuming cannabis was unlikely to induce criminal behavior, and even those who used it regularly were "hardly likely to threaten public order except in the rarest of circumstances." Because of these conclusions, the IHDC could not recommend prohibition and recognized that the uncontrolled and natural growth of cannabis would render such a measure almost pointless (Rushton, 2008).[3]

Emily Dufton (2017: 14) points to the Panama Canal Zone report (1925) as one of the first influential reports on cannabis in the US. The committee agreed that

> there is no evidence that marijuana is a "habit-forming" drug in the sense in which the term is applied to alcohol, opium, cocaine, etc., or that it has any appreciably deleterious influence on the individual using it.

Another example of note was released in 1944. The New York Academy of Medicine issued an extensively researched report known as *The La Guardia Report*. The report concluded that cannabis was less dangerous than other drugs. It increased feelings of relaxation, disinhibition, and self-confidence. It also warned that cannabis use could decrease physical activity and increase anxiety. Contrary to earlier research and popular belief, the report concludes that consuming cannabis did not induce violence, insanity, or sex crimes, nor led to addiction or other drug use. Harry Anslinger derided the report as "… giddy sociology and medical mumbo-jumbo" (Booth, 2003: 240), and his campaign against cannabis continued undeterred by insights provided by scientific studies.

In 1969, the UK *Wootton Report on Cannabis* was prepared by the Hallucinogens Subcommittee of the Advisory Committee on Drug Dependence. The report did not recommend legalization. It did, however, conclude that the UK should drastically reduce penalties for cannabis. The report stated:

> There is no evidence that this activity is causing violent crime or aggression, anti-social behaviour, or is producing in otherwise normal people conditions of dependence or psychosis, requiring medical treatment …
>
> … we think it is also clear that, in terms of physical harmfulness, cannabis is very much less dangerous than the opiates, amphetamines and barbiturates, and also less dangerous than alcohol …
>
> … our objective is clear: to bring about a situation in which it is extremely unlikely that anyone will go to prison for an offence involving only possession for personal use or for supply on a very limited scale.[4]

Two reports in the 1970s also challenged cannabis prohibition. A report by the National Commission on Marihuana and Drug Abuse (1972) summarized their findings by stating: "The Commission feels that the criminalization of possession of marihuana for personal use is socially self-defeating as a means of achieving this objective."[5] In Canada, a similar report went even further. Seen as a counterpart to the *Wootton Report* and the *La Guardia Report*, the Le Dain Commission's final report (1974) suggested decriminalizing cannabis and a fine of just $100 for the possession of any drug, including "hard drugs" like cocaine and heroin.[6]

An essential question for criminologists is why government-commissioned reports that considered use in India, Panama, the UK, the US, and Canada were insufficient to protect people from punitive cannabis policies. Why does methodologically problematic research continue to be published, and how can criminologists better present findings at odds with the moral–legal nexus of the times? An updated approach to public criminology could present cannabis prohibition as a profound example of how racist and immoral religious assumptions have shaped societal attitudes, national laws, and international conventions. Such an effort could build on past research, highlight the profound moralistic attitudes that persist around drug use, and explore new ways to distribute credible contemporary research. Of course, step one is engaging in this research. Below we outline some areas of interest based on our analysis in this book.

## New Directions in Cannabis Criminology

In Chapter 1, we defined five foci for cannabis criminology. Next, in sequential chapters, we presented criminological theories, key concepts, relevant research, and new directions associated with each area. Below we offer a summary of this work and outline a future research agenda.

### *Law, Society, and Social Control*

Theoretical starting points include demonology, labeling theory, and conflict theory. While demonology is not a criminological theory in any meaningful sense, it can be a means to understand how moral judgments about right and wrong get connected to good and evil. As we have noted, it is remarkably persistent within criminology, although increasingly hidden by assumptions about human nature (Heidt & Wheeldon, 2015). Labeling theory can provide some insights into how the legal status of cannabis impacts people who use it (Lemert, 1951). For example, people who use cannabis and other drugs may be labeled as criminals, and this label may be internalized by otherwise law-abiding citizens. Young (1971) and Cohen (1972) have argued that this type of labeling could eventually lead to the phenomenon known as the deviancy amplification spiral.

Conflict theory, based on the perspective of those caught up in the justice system, can uncover how criminal law, legal codes, punishment, and other forms of social control harm those with the least power within societies (Chambliss & Seidman, 1971). As we have demonstrated, cannabis policies both justified and increased the overpolicing of Black and Brown people. This observation can be connected to Sellin's (1938) earlier work on culture conflict and how the subsequent confluence of stigma, prohibition, and culture led to efforts to prohibit cannabis. These theories explain the shift from demonizing cannabis and those who used it to understand the role of criminal law in creating expectations about who is defined as deviant and criminal. As criminologists began to consider crime through a more critical lens, some questioned older assumptions. Three key concepts inform this area. They include stigma, normalization, and medicalization.

Specific questions might include: How can the history of cannabis moral panics be confronted, understood, and overcome? How did cannabis prohibition intersect with the culture of control? Have cannabis laws based on demonizing people who use cannabis undermined public trust in government? Do cannabis stigmas differ for people based on their frequency of use? What might this mean for legalization? Do different levels of stigma around cannabis use interact or intersect? What role can street art play by repurposing other messages? Figure 7.1 presents an "updated" poster with a new message. Table 7.1 provides the outline of a research program in this area.

### *Police and Policing Cannabis*

There is little doubt that the prohibition of cannabis has impacted policing, and decades of research documented the adverse outcomes of many enforcement strategies. Three theories from criminology and criminal justice studies are of immediate interest. First, strain theories consider how strains and stressors may produce negative emotions, such as frustration and anger, resulting in impulsive crimes (Agnew, 2006). This might include the indignities of race-based policing, which might serve as another strain that leads to increased criminal behavior (Unnever et al., 2009). As

**FIGURE 7.1** Let's grow. Street art with added pro-cannabis messaging that alters a Brooklyn Botanical Garden advertisement in NYC subway station. "War of Drugs by Poster Boy NYC" is licensed under CC BY 2.0

we have documented, people of color are more likely to be targeted with cannabis enforcement, less likely to be diverted, and consistently receive harsher penalties at higher rates for the same drug offenses.

Social control theories are also relevant. These theories focus on how proper socialization keeps people in line and how misbehavior can be controlled (Nye, 1958). Police represent the formal means by which society can maintain order. Based on a consensus view of society, some see the police as coming from and working on behalf of the community that they police. This is based on the assumed general agreement in the community about law and order. As we argued in Chapter 3, framing police as the best means to enforce social order and emphasizing nuisance crimes leads to overpolicing and has shaped enforcement patterns related to cannabis. This focus also allows for an ever-growing system of policing. If order is expected, and laws tend to criminalize an activity many refuse to view as problematic, justice systems will expand and grow to enforce the law (Kraska, 2006; Vitale, 2018).

If these theories help explain why the prohibition of cannabis profoundly changed policing, three key concepts can help explain how. These concepts include the war on drugs, police militarization, and predatory policing. This view of an ever-expanding system of control has been described using stark terms. The suggestion that the US criminal justice system has become "predatory" (Page & Soss, 2021) is hard to deny. Cannabis prohibition is a key part of this larger story. Used to validate police snooping, stalking, and interference, prohibition has justified a range of intrusions on people who use cannabis. Some questions of immediate interest include: Did the US Department of Defense 1208 or 1033 program impact police militarization? Do perceptions of the "war on drugs" goals among law enforcement influence police tactics? Will decreasing police contacts for cannabis possession influence community views of police legitimacy? In what ways? The diagram in

**TABLE 7.1** Cannabis criminology research program: Law, society, and social control

| *Theory* | *Concept and question(s)* | *Research of interest* | *Method(s)* |
|---|---|---|---|
| Demonology | Stigma—Have laws that demonize people who use cannabis undermined public trust in government? | Brewster, 2017<br>Newhart and Dolphin, 2019 Seddon and Floodgate, 2020 | Qualitative |
| Demonology | Stigma—Do different levels of stigma around cannabis use (macro/meso/micro) interact? | Hathaway, 2004<br>Reid, 2020 | Qualitative |
| Demonology | Stigma—Do cannabis stigmas differ based on the frequency of use, and what might this mean for legalization? | Hathaway et al., 2011<br>Reid, 2020 | Qualitative |
| Labeling | Normalization—How has cannabis normalization varied by country/region and demographics? | Parker, 2005 | Quantitative |
| Labeling | Normalization—How can the history of cannabis moral panics be confronted, understood, and overcome? | Cody, 2006<br>Young, 1971 | Qualitative |
| Labeling | Normalization—How do shifting media environments influence the construction of moral panics? | Bennett, 2018<br>Klocke and Muschert, 2010 | Qualitative |
| Conflict | Medicalization—How did cannabis prohibition intersect with the culture of control? | Black, 1976<br>Garland, 2001<br>Sellin, 1938 | Qualitative |
| Conflict | Medicalization—How do people who use cannabis and are diverted to "education" or "treatment" programs describe their experience? | Ashton, 2008<br>Price et al., 2021<br>Spivakovsky et al., 2018 | Qualitative |
| Conflict | Medicalization—How have the "New Prohibitionists" risen to prominence despite poor research? | Heidt and Wheeldon, 2022 | Qualitative |

FIGURE 7.2 Operation intrusion. "Operation Intrusive—Birmingham" by West Midlands Police is licensed under CC BY-SA 2.0

Figure 7.2 was shared by the West Midlands Police to suggest a positive view of cannabis intrusions. Table 7.2 provides additional considerations as part of a critical and criminologically-informed research program.

## Race, Ethnicity, and Criminalization

It is now widely accepted that the criminal justice system perpetuates systemic biases against people of color. This is especially true of cannabis prohibition. This research area is based on the work of Alexander (2010), Bell (1994), Capers (2014), Delgado and Stefancic (2017), Fornili (2018), Mejía and Csete (2016), Nyika and Murray-Orr, (2017), and Western and Pettit (2010). Three theories are relevant to our analysis in this book. First, biological and psychological positivist theories focused on physical traits and inherited genetic predispositions allowed for the association between race-based conclusions about crime and criminal behavior and the inability to balance competing stimuli and urges (Heidt & Wheeldon, 2015). The association between race and crime became accepted wisdom and justified policies based on presumed racial inferiority.

Critical race theory (CRT) emerged from this context. Its application in criminology is connected to the construction of cultural and psychosocial meanings and the view that the law exists to penalize and order social relations. As demonstrated in Chapter 4, the role of race and cannabis prohibition is clear, and the war on drugs and cannabis has "disproportionately affected disadvantaged black Americans"

**TABLE 7.2** Cannabis criminology research program: Police and policing cannabis

| *Theory* | *Concept and question(s)* | *Research of interest* | *Method(s)* |
|---|---|---|---|
| Strain | The war on drugs—Do perceptions of the "war on drugs" goals among police officers influence their tactics? | Dandurand, 2021<br>Owusu-Bempah and Luscombe, 2021<br>Stohr et al., 2020 | Qualitative |
| Strain | The war on drugs—Do decreases in police contacts for cannabis prohibition influence community views of police legitimacy? In what ways? | Berger and Luckmann, 1966<br>Gelman et al., 2007<br>Testa et al., 2021<br>Tyler et al., 2014<br>Zinberg and Robertson, 1972 | Qualitative/ quantitative |
| Strain | The war on drugs—How are new developments (i.e., cuckooing) framed in ways designed to engender public/political support? | Spicer et al., 2020<br>Spicer et al., 2021 | Qualitative/ quantitative |
| Social control | Police militarization—Does research indicating increased vulnerability for certain groups shape policing tactics such as "no-knock" warrants? | Balko, 2014<br>Blau and Blau, 1982<br>Murch, 2015 | Qualitative |
| Social control | Police militarization—Did the US Department of Defense programs impact police militarization? How? | Kraska, 2001 | Qualitative/ quantitative |
| Social control | Police militarization—How can models of expanded police discretion with PWUD be shared? | Dandurand, 2021<br>del Pozo et al., 2021<br>Mastrofski, 2004 | Qualitative/ quantitative |
| CJ growth | Predatory policing—Can cannabis liberalization lead to other kinds of police reform? | Brown, 2022<br>O'Guinn, 2022<br>Vitale, 2018 | Qualitative/ quantitative |
| CJ growth | Predatory policing—How do police view their role in jurisdictions with shifting cannabis laws? | Dandurand, 2021<br>Stohr et al., 2020 | Qualitative/ quantitative |
| CJ growth | Predatory policing—How can jurisdictions deemphasize cannabis enforcement, given its history as a lucrative means to support departmental budgets? | Brown, 2022<br>Kraska, 2006<br>Page and Soss, 2021 | Qualitative/ quantitative |

(Tonry, 1994: 27). Recognizing this past and acknowledging the harms are essential features of restorative justice that can provide a vital shift for thinking about crime and expand ideas about addressing past injuries (Pepinsky & Quinney, 1991). This must include thinking about state crime, including harms perpetrated by the criminal justice system. Restorative justice offers a means to think about cannabis and the damage done under prohibition.

**FIGURE 7.3** Race and injustice. "Salt City 24.jpg" by US Marshals Service is licensed under CC BY 2.0

Key concepts include how race has been used as a social construct. A recent analysis has linked the operations of the American criminal justice system with the exploitation of the poor, Black, and politically unconnected populations (Page & Soss, 2021). To make sense of how race-based predatory systems of injustice persist, we argued that the social construction of race has perpetrated the long shadow of slavery. We are not the first to demonstrate that unconscious racism remains a feature of the American criminal justice system. In Europe, this can be connected to how drug policies were used to cement colonial rule and exploit people, land, and resources, and ingrain racialized hierarchies (Daniels et al., 2021).

Questions of interest might include: How many people would have been spared from criminal justice system contact had cannabis not been a focus of the war on drugs? How many tax dollars would have been saved? What have been the tangible and intangible costs to those in contact with the criminal justice system, and what are the intergenerational consequences for the families of those in contact with the criminal justice system? If Figure 7.3 provides suggests a positive portrayal of policing cannabis, Table 7.3 outlines a more critical research program.

## *The Economics of Cannabis*

Economic theories in criminology all adhere to the basic logic of the classical school. In short, people tend to be selfish and act to maximize pleasure and minimize pain. These theories assume that people are rational decision-makers who

**TABLE 7.3** Cannabis criminology research program: Race, ethnicity, and criminalization

| *Theory* | *Concept and question(s)* | *Research of interest* | *Method(s)* |
|---|---|---|---|
| Biological and psychological positivism | Social construct—Does linking slavery and colonialism shift public attitudes about race-based cannabis enforcement? | Daniels et al., 2021<br>Paris, 2000 | Qualitative/ quantitative |
| Biological and psychological positivism | Social construct—How does the social construction of Black boys as older and less innocent impact cannabis enforcement? | Goff et al., 2014<br>Owusu-Bempah and Luscombe, 2021 | Qualitative/ quantitative |
| Biological and psychological positivism | Social construct—Can research suggesting cannabis laws sought to protect White people rather than punish non-White people assist public understanding? | Fisher, 2021 | Qualitative/ quantitative |
| Critical race theory | Predation—Can analysis to assess costs to society of cannabis prohibition impact policy reform? | Mejía and Csete, 2016<br>Western and Pettit, 2010 | Quantitative |
| Critical race theory | Predation—Can research demonstrating disparate racial outcomes influence cannabis policy? | Sanchez et al., 2020<br>Sewell, 2020<br>Sewell et al., 2021<br>Sheehan et al., 2021 | Qualitative/ quantitative |
| Critical race theory | Predation—How much public cannabis revenue is directed to police versus social equity programs? | Mize, 2020 | Quantitative |
| Restorative justice | Reconciliation—Can reports of assaultive and dehumanizing race-based police tactics shape public views on race and justice? | N/A | N/A |
| Restorative justice | Reconciliation—How can policies designed to implement social and racial justice models of cannabis reform be successfully implemented? | N/A | N/A |
| Restorative justice | Reconciliation—To what extent do new policies provide redress for a century of prohibition and 50 years of the war against drugs? | N/A | N/A |

exercise control over their behavior and apply logic to criminal decision-making. There are three theoretical starting points of immediate interest. There are three theoretical starting points of immediate interest. These include deterrence theory, routine activities theory (RAT), and rational choice theory. Gary Becker's (1976) economic deterrence theory of crime uses the expected utility principle from economics to understand crime. This theory suggests that offenders will maximize their interests based on rational calculation. Deterrence theories attempt to assess optimal punishment in multiple contexts to specify how offenders respond to the costs of crime imposed by the criminal justice system.

Another theory of interest in this book is RAT (Cohen & Felson, 1979). Connected to environmental criminology in which the question of the "place" of criminal events is central, this approach builds on the idea that criminal events occur where opportunities for crime exist. This may be especially relevant as criminology turns toward assessing decision-making with legal cannabis regimes. The potential for RAT as a framework to understand cannabis markets is connected to its flexibility. Clarke and Cornish's (1985) rational choice theory is another formulation in this tradition. This theory emphasizes the similarities between offenders and nonoffenders and suggests that other criminological theories tend to "overpathologize" crime. Essentially, this is a criticism of the medical model or the idea that criminality is something that needs treatment to be cured. It is also a critique of the sociological theories that attribute crime to poor social conditions and poverty.

Like the other theories in this area, economic decision-making models provide the basis for some formulations (Clarke & Cornish,1985). While some are critical of the applicability of rational choice to drug use, this view may need qualification when considering jurisdictions in which cannabis is legal. For example, various incarnations of rational choice theory may provide a basis to consider decision-making around cannabis based on its status as a consumer good. Developing responsible regulation regimes requires a clear understanding of typical behavior patterns among people who use cannabis and how these patterns relate to the overall cannabis economy.

If the above theories can help explain the underlying logic of the economics of cannabis, three concepts help explain cannabis as a commercial product. First, the Alchian - Allen theorem suggests that there is a tendency for drugs to become more potent and more dangerous when they are prohibited. The second concept relates to the complexity of cannabis markets (Sandberg, 2012a) and requires rethinking if or how cannabis businesses can operate without the routine financial arrangements, infrastructure, and police protection. Third, and final, is how cost/benefit analyses are linked through criminological considerations when cannabis is viewed as a consumer good. An open question is whether cannabis cafés will emerge and how they can be sustained. Figure 7.4 provides one example, but others certainly exist.

Questions of interest include: How do the heavy regulations, limited access, high cost, and low-quality cannabis affect the behavior of illicit market dealers

**FIGURE 7.4** Oregon cannabis café. "Oregon Cannabis Café" by Christine Jump is licensed under CC BY 2.0

and decisions made by cannabis consumers? How do vital elements of production, distribution, potency, and price compare between legal and illegal markets? Is the potency of cannabis related to laws or regulations? Why do people who use cannabis choose legal cannabis markets over illegal cannabis markets? Do potency and price impact the success of legal cannabis versus its illicit counterparts? How can those who rely upon illicit markets be enticed into the legal cannabis marketplace? Table 7.4 provides an outline.

## *Cannabis Use and Crime*

As we have demonstrated throughout this book, of all the research areas that should be of interest to criminologists who study cannabis, the question of cannabis and crime is perhaps the least interesting in some ways. With the exception of cannabis and impaired driving, most associations between cannabis and crime are spurious, inconclusive, or a function of dubious research designs, limited data, and differing definitions. Despite this fact, law-based approaches to cannabis research are likely to remain popular (Fischer et al., 2021). Unfortunately, this focus may overwhelm other efforts and be used to serve punitive ends and administrative criminological interests. As we argued in Chapter 6, the best way to understand the problems with such pronouncements is to look to jurisdictions where cannabis legalization and regulation have existed for years. In Canada, Washington, Colorado, California, and elsewhere, few credible reports suggest that there is significantly more crime, more adverse mental health diagnoses, or more violence.

Prohibition continues to cast its shadow over contemporary analysis. The intersection of biosocial and psychological theories and fears that cannabis serves as a gateway into dangerous subcultures has led to popular myths surrounding addiction, cannabis use disorder, and even cannabis-induced psychosis. It is deeply troubling that in 2022 a noted drug policy expert uncritically cites the claim that "... between

**TABLE 7.4** Cannabis criminology research program: The economics of cannabis use

| *Theory* | *Concept and question(s)* | *Research of interest* | *Method(s)* |
|---|---|---|---|
| Deterrence | Alchian–Allen theorem—Is the potency of cannabis related to cannabis laws or regulations? | Cowan, 1986<br>Thornton, 1998 | Quantitative/ qualitative |
| Deterrence | Alchian–Allen theorem—Does cannabis prohibition, decriminalization, or regulation increase the price of cannabis? | Cowan, 1986<br>Lawson and Nesbit, 2013<br>Mahamad et al., 2020 | Quantitative/ qualitative |
| Deterrence | Alchian–Allen theorem—Can legalization create markets for less potent cannabis? | Cowan, 1986<br>Thornton, 1998 | Quantitative/ qualitative |
| RAT | Cannabis markets—Why do people who use cannabis choose legal cannabis markets over illegal cannabis markets? | Heidt, 2021<br>Kjellberg and Olson, 2017<br>Sandberg, 2012 | Qualitative |
| RAT | Cannabis markets—Can disruption of illicit cannabis markets support legal cannabis marketplaces? | Coomber and Moyle, 2018<br>Dandurand, 2021<br>Moeller, 2016 | Quantitative/ qualitative |
| RAT | Cannabis markets—How do elements of production and distribution compare between legal and illegal markets? | Dayton and Adams, 2017<br>Robinson and Scherlen, 2014 | Quantitative/ qualitative |
| Rational choice theory | Cannabis as consumer good—How can existing consumers be enticed into the legal market? | Dayton and Adams, 2017<br>Dandurand, 2021<br>Wesley and Murray, 2021 | Quantitative/ qualitative |
| Rational choice theory | Cannabis as consumer good—How can access to legal cannabis become more convenient for consumers? | Heidt, 2021<br>Osborne and Fogel, 2017<br>Thies, 2012 | Qualitative |
| Rational choice theory | Cannabis as consumer good—How can regulation models balance ease of cannabis access with public health messaging? | Wesley and Murray, 2021 | Quantitative/ qualitative |

10% and 30% of people who consume cannabis will develop a cannabis use disorder" (Ritter, 2021: 21, 45). While extraordinary, this assertion cannot be supported by rigorous contemporary research. Nevertheless, this perpetuates a particular view of cannabis as dangerous and may justify the very policies we have shown to be costly, divisive, racist, and unethical. The criminological theories described above help frame existing justice policy based on criminalization, medicalization, and stigmatization. Three concepts suggest how these ideas operate in practice.

The persistent view that cannabis use can be associated with undesirable subcultures is old and is connected to our analysis in Chapter 2. While the use of biological and psychological theories to justify the Brain Disease Model of Addiction (BDMA), understanding their application to coerced care and mandated treatment through the justice system is in its infancy (Ashton, 2008; Price et al., 2021; Spivakovsky et al., 2018). Questions of immediate interest include: Does youth cannabis use predict future criminality? Do higher rates of youth cannabis use result in high rates of crime over the life course? Are individual- and population-level associations between cannabis and crime significant? Does access to products with higher levels of THC directly relate to increased violence, mental health diagnoses, or general harm among people who use them?

A crucial cross-cutting question is whether the myths of cannabis and crime can be confronted and what role, if any, criminologists should have to combat the adverse consequences of a century of cannabis prohibition. Education will be key. Figure 7.5 provides an example of sorts. Table 7.5 suggests how much research and engagement may be needed to reorient the study of cannabis in the post-prohibition era.

As we noted above, the most important immediate question for serious scholars related to cannabis and crime is impaired driving. In a recent review on driving and cannabis, Pearlson and colleagues (2021) advocate expanding public health campaigns and public service announcements emphasizing the risks of "stoned driving," such as those used in Australia, and argue that these should be applied elsewhere and possibly adapted to address the dangers associated with driving after mixing cannabis and alcohol. In addition, the effects of cannabis vary between individuals when compared to alcohol because of individual variation in tolerance level, smoking technique and devices, and differences in absorption levels of THC. Different substances present different types of risks for drivers (Sewell et al., 2009). Pearlson and associates (2021) also recommend that the National Institute on Drug Abuse (NIDA) devote more resources to studying the effects of these forms of

**FIGURE 7.5** Cannabis education. "Fresh Washington State Cannabis Education" by Uncleweed is licensed under CC BY-SA 2.0

**TABLE 7.5** Cannabis criminology research program: Cannabis use and crime

| *Theory* | *Concept and question(s)* | *Research of interest* | *Method(s)* |
|---|---|---|---|
| Social learning theories | Cannabis use as subculture—Does legalization influence cannabis "status" as a forbidden substance? | Akers and Cochran, 1985<br>Becker, 1963<br>Orcutt, 1987 | Quantitative/qualitative |
| Social learning theories | Cannabis use as subculture—Has cannabis liberalization led to increased youth cannabis use? | Gruczaet al., 2018<br>Johnson et al., 2019<br>Ta et al., 2019 | Quantitative/qualitative |
| Social learning theories | Cannabis research as subculture—Why does flawed research continue to be published and cited, even when it cannot be replicated? | Hart, 2017<br>Heidt and Wheeldon, 2022<br>Solomon, 2020<br>Szalavitz, 2021 | Quantitative/qualitative |
| Biosocial criminology | BDMA—If BDMA is correct, why is CUD treatment decreasing, even where cannabis is legalized? | Askari et al., 2021<br>Mennis et al., 2021<br>Philbin et al., 2019 | Quantitative/qualitative |
| Biosocial criminology | BDMA—If cannabis is addictive, why do the overwhelming majority who consume it never become addicted? | Hart, 2021<br>Heyman, 2013<br>Lewis, 2015 | Quantitative/qualitative |
| Biosocial criminology | BDMA—Why does society continue to define, demonstrate, and explain addiction in simplistic and unscientific ways? | Hart, 2021<br>Heidt and Wheeldon, 2022<br>Solomon, 2020<br>Szalavitz, 2015a | Quantitative/qualitative |
| Psychological theories | Cannabis psychosis—Are cannabis legalization and crime rates in general linked? | Chang and Jacobsen, 2017<br>Dragone et al., 2017<br>Lu et al., 2021 | Quantitative/qualitative |
| Psychological theories | Cannabis psychosis—Does consuming cannabis increase the propensity for committing violent crimes? | Berenson, 2019<br>Di Forti et al., 2019<br>Murray et al., 2017 | Quantitative/qualitative |
| Psychological theories | Cannabis psychosis—Why, despite evidence to the contrary, do experts continue to perpetuate myths about the dangers of cannabis? | Callahan et al., 2022<br>Lu et al., 2021<br>Ritter, 2021 | Quantitative/qualitative |

cannabis and to developing procedures for making them available to investigators for this purpose. Of immediate interest is assessing the value of current tests to determine blood THC levels and gauge impairment through roadside sobriety tests (Pearlson et al., 2021). The accuracy, replicability, and utility of these tests for law enforcement is an area that criminologists may wish to investigate in the future.

## Engaging Cannabis Prohibition

Embracing cannabis criminology includes a commitment to research that is theoretically informed, relies on credible research designs, and defines the concepts that are to be tested and explored in more defensible ways. The research questions we outlined above are a good starting point. We have no doubt other scholars will correct, refine, and improve both how we conceive of cannabis in criminology and the kinds of questions and research that ought to be undertaken. However, the potential for this emphasis to promote meaningful, rather than illusory, cannabis reform remains contested. The old approaches to research dissemination are unlikely to be successful unless they consider other concepts. These include the role of public criminology, the value of myth-busting, and the need to embrace the ironic impulse within contemporary social media spaces. Such efforts must also consider what we call a "duty of care" in cannabis research to ensure that people who use cannabis are treated with more respect by the systems that attempt to regulate their behavior.

While many are interested in how research can best be communicated to policymakers (Pesta et al., 2016), public criminologists consider how to inform the public about issues such as crime, punishment, criminal law, and criminal justice (Uggen & Inderbitzin, 2010). However, as we noted in Chapter 2, sharing research with policymakers and the public is inadequate to challenge myths and moral panics. As Currie (1999:13) put it more than 20 years ago:

> For too long, we've been accustomed to being in a one-down position, always lamenting the fact that politicians pay no attention to us and ignore what we know. I think that could change. But it will change only if, and when, we develop the organizational capacity to raise public consciousness on these issues to a level that neither politicians, nor anyone else, can ignore.

Another approach consistent with public criminology is *Weed Out Misinformation*. Led by Daniel Bear, Weed Out Misinformation was created by cannabis researchers and students at Humber College in Toronto. This followed a survey of 1,600 cannabis consumers in Canada about how they accessed information about cannabis, who they trusted to deliver cannabis information, and what topics they wanted to see in public education campaigns about cannabis.[7] One goal is:

> Instead of making alarmist claims or stigmatizing users, harm reduction education focuses on helping people understand how to be safer, reduce risk and minimize adverse results. The lack of understanding around safe substance use gave rise to myths, especially among young people.[8]

This sort of honest, scientifically based, and stigma-free discussion about cannabis has the potential to help people make informed decisions and maximize benefits when they consume cannabis. It is too rare.

A related effort involves exploring ways to combine efforts to explain criminological research with outreach and engagement through social media. A recent example has been outlined by McCormick (2022: 191). His use of a Facebook group to share research, engage in criminological critique, and provide a place for students curious about visual and cultural criminology is unique and potentially applicable to other areas of criminology, including the study of cannabis. Interested readers can find our "Cannabis, Criminology, and Culture" group on Facebook to participate in this nascent effort. The potential and challenges associated with building online communities to share information, note emergent research, and connect ideas and developments deserve more attention. Another idea is how to embrace the ironic impulse as part of online culture. The potential that satirical techniques to offer a mental shorthand to understand an issue and allow people to challenge cannabis prohibition with humor. An example may be helpful.

In Chapter 1, we recounted the reaction to a photograph of Snoop Dogg smoking cannabis before performing at the Super Bowl Half Time show in Los Angeles. Although the recreational use of cannabis has been legal in California for more than five years, the *New York Post* presented his consumption of cannabis as negative and using judgmental terms.[9] In the past, this coverage might have successfully been replicated in other media and even gained a foothold as an example of moral decay or a danger to youth. Instead, it was roundly mocked.[10]

Comedian John Fugelsang retweeted the article, writing: "NY Post: Black Male Does Something Completely Legal in the State of California." Some called out the *Post* itself. For example, another user tweeted: "I brushed my teeth when I got up this morning, where's my NY Post article," and "I would have been surprised if the story was Snoop did NOT smoke weed before the Half Time show … good reporting NY Post!!!"[11] Others noted the hypocrisy at the heart of this coverage. People tweeted: "Snoop Dogg Engages in Totally Legal Conduct at Event

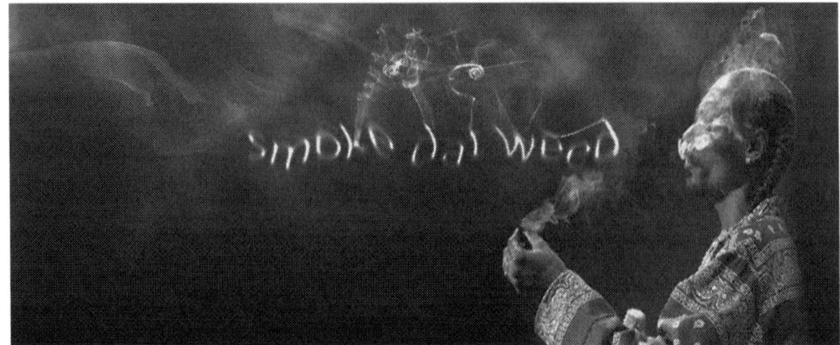


**FIGURE 7.6** Cannabis and prohibition culture jamming. "Smoke dat weed—Snoop Dogg" by Imilyas is licensed under CC BY 2.0.

Sponsored by Company That Sells Drugs," and "Scandal! Man does completely legal thing he is famous for before beer ad riddled live TV event!"[12] Figure 7.6 provides one response.

Embracing irony in this manner is not without risks. For some, scholars should be neutral observers and never comment on contemporary social issues or engage in politics. Indeed, challenging myths in online spaces cannot, on its own, lead to better policy. However, when combined with credible research and comparative evidence, such an online approach is perhaps worthy of more consideration. As we have documented, the enforcement of cannabis laws remains unequal in application and outcome. These persist even where cannabis has been legalized, and inequalities based on race and ethnicity undermine racial justice worldwide. In jurisdictions where cannabis possession has been decriminalized, racial and ethnic disparities exist for those who get diverted to cannabis diversion programs.

Given the damage of a century of prohibition, those interested in cannabis and crime have an obligation not to publish in this area merely to serve careerist concerns (Wheeldon et al., 2014). Challenging the persistence of coercive cannabis programs requires resetting the research agenda. As jurisdictions have begun to decriminalize and legalize cannabis, past research on the dire risks of cannabis appears farcical. Going forward, researchers should establish robust research designs, employ careful analytic strategies, and recognize that their research may be deliberately misconstrued. Remaining silent in the face of dangerous misinformation can no longer be seen as an acceptable strategy, even if one is rewarded with tenure as a result.

While adopting this sort of "duty of care" is not a legal obligation, it can be defined as a duty to look after vulnerable individuals and communities and protect them from harm that would likely result from poor research. This requires researchers to take personal responsibility for the damage their flawed research might do. At a minimum, this means acknowledging the problems with definitions, research designs, analytic strategies, and the generalizability of their conclusions on cannabis. Conceiving this as a duty is consistent with Solomon (2020: 5), who suggests that cannabis researchers need to ask themselves some tough questions about how cannabis research continues to perpetuate myths about cannabis without acknowledging the ongoing harm caused by its prohibition. Step one, of course, is to engage in research that focuses on critical questions relevant to understanding cannabis, criminology, and culture.

If cannabis criminology can rely on existing theories and approaches within the criminological canon, it must look to new kinds of data and double down on efforts to return qualitative research to a place of prominence within the field (Jacques, 2014). An emerging source of data on drug policy is people who use drugs (PWUD). There have been a variety of recent efforts to incorporate the insights of this population into criminological research (Copes et al., 2018; Copes et al., 2019; Copes et al., 2021; Greer & Ritter, 2019; Greer & Ritter, 2020; Wheeldon, 2021). Prioritizing those who use cannabis and other insiders requires rethinking the problematic and exclusionary methodologies of the past.

It explicitly demands that we revisit the importance of considering, including, and privileging the views of those who use cannabis. International studies from Poland (Wanke et al., 2022), Norway (Sandberg, 2008; Sandberg, 2013), Sweden (Feltmann et al., 2021), Nigeria (Nelson, 2021), and Mexico (Agoff et al., 2021) offer important insights regarding people who use cannabis. As we noted, many of the policy problems unfolding as Canada continues to adapt its model of legalization and regulation were predicted by cannabis insiders and others within the subculture (Heidt, 2021; Heidt et al., 2018). Incorporating other voices may be crucial to understanding the finer aspects of cannabis legalization and regulation. Prioritizing the experiences of people who use cannabis can provide needed nuance and result in suggestions that directly challenge the institutionally grounded ideas based on prohibitionist assumptions.

Drafting intelligent policies and regulations for cannabis requires understanding those who are involved in the cannabis trade. Moving forward means abandoning the abstracted, exclusionary, and irresponsible research designs of the past. One solution is for criminologists who engage in drug research to examine the experiences of PWUD and others through more participatory, inclusive, and creative research approaches. Some proposals for cannabis reform have been proposed by organizations like *Transform* based in the UK. These include guides that focus on comparative approaches to cannabis policy[13] and broader blueprints that connect cannabis regulation with other drug reforms.[14] In future work, we hope to assess these contributions and develop our own model of responsible regulation that attempts to reconcile tensions between commerce and control, liberty and safety, and justice and fairness. This will require realigning existing regulatory cannabis models to focus on access, equity, and tolerance; reconceiving public safety; and explicitly recommitting to consent as central to any cannabis diversion programs. Stay tuned.

## Conclusion

Cannabis prohibition remains a costly, foolish international endeavor that has done incalculable damage to individuals, families, and communities. As new research programs emerge and regulation schemes are advanced, there is a worry that the amount of commentary and opinion about the effect of cannabis regulation has created too much "white noise" within the field (Oldfield et al., 2021). We have attempted to boost the signal and cut through the clatter by focusing on how criminalizing cannabis has impacted discrete areas of criminology. Since various issues and divergent research agendas shape cannabis reform, we have prioritized a broad description incorporating multiple views. Understanding this process offers a means to expand the criminological imagination (Young, 2011) by rethinking the history of the discipline and reassessing cannabis use, drug policy, and contemporary research. In this book, we have uncovered four essential concerns.

The first is that policing cannabis is unequal in application and outcome. Disparities in enforcement occur when cannabis is decriminalized (Sheehan et al.,

2021). Historic disparities in cannabis arrests (Owusu-Bempah & Luscombe, 2021) appear to persist even where cannabis has been legalized.[15] Solving this problem means developing new models of policing PWUD and must confront the fact that unless police are specifically directed not to interfere with people who use cannabis but are not breaking any other law, racial disparities will continue. Introduced in Chapter 1 and described further in Chapter 3, much more work is needed to reorient police accountability and make more of Brown's (2022) conceptual contribution that liberalizing cannabis policy can open the door to other sorts of police reform. This will require engaging in theory, compiling and replicating research, and considering carefully how these policies operate in practice.

The second issue concerns the decriminalization of cannabis and the apparent shift away from the prison–industrial complex and toward the treatment–industrial complex and coercive care (Spivakovsky et al., 2018). As discussed in Chapter 2 and connected with medicalizing and pathologizing cannabis use, mandating treatment programs to avoid criminal sanctions is deeply problematic (Ashton, 2008; Price et al., 2021). While replacing criminal punishment with administrative sanctions may be a step in the right direction, the strategic submission to drug treatment to avoid a criminal record is not informed consent (Stevens, 2011). More work is needed to uncover how other models can connect people and resources by embracing destigmatization and creating relationships based on mutual respect and shared obligation (Fox, 2015).

The third issue concerns the difficulties within jurisdictions that have legalized cannabis and sought to dismantle and disrupt illicit markets. This early work has shown that emphasizing public health goals ahead of market conditions can complicate legal cannabis as a sustainable industry (Wesley & Murray, 2021). In Chapter 5, we demonstrated that economic theories have an underappreciated role in understanding the operation of legal cannabis markets. As Heidt (2021) has shown, cannabis insiders in British Columbia predicted many of the problems that have since emerged.

We have consistently argued that responsible regulation regimes require understanding the motivations of people who use cannabis, the complexity of cannabis markets, and the nature of the overall cannabis economy. As cannabis is increasingly viewed as a consumer good, the role of the police may change illicit markets in ways that are predictable in some ways and perhaps unknowable in others. These have international dimensions (Dandurand, 2021). More work is needed to assess how to attract cannabis consumers to the legal market while retaining reasonable, and not reactive, public health approaches.

In this book, we have developed our view of cannabis as a critical case study in moral–legal-cultural renegotiation (Wheeldon & Heidt, 2022). Our approach favors a pragmatic approach to research at the risk of sacrificing staid conceptual coherence to one dogmatic view or another (Wheeldon, 2015). Throughout this book, we have noted how the history of cannabis prohibition has left a legacy that is difficult to overcome (Ritter, 2021; Szalavitz, 2021). Since criminalizing cannabis has tainted every aspect of the criminal justice system, making sense of its repeal requires assessing the prohibition of cannabis by focusing on police, courts, and corrections. It also may demand something far more elusive.

Our focus on cannabis can provide a means to confront criminology's shadow, including our own moralistic, punitive, and judgmental natures (Maruna et al., 2004). People who use cannabis are not evil. In most cases, they are not sick or in need of help. It is past time that those who try to discipline or punish people who use cannabis ask themselves some tough questions about why such practices persist, even as the costs and consequences of cannabis prohibition are increasingly evident. The international liberalization of cannabis should be seen as an opportunity to understand how states adapt to the legalization of once illicit substances. While legalizing cannabis may be inevitable, responsible regulation may not be. Learning from cannabis may offer a means to understand how tolerance, harm reduction, and community support can be expanded. Cannabis criminology is one contribution to this worthy goal.

## Notes

1 See pages 5 and 6 here: https://asc41.com/wp-content/uploads/ASC-Criminologist-2019-03.pdf [accessed June 1, 2022].

2 See www.oxfordbibliographies.com/view/document/obo-9780195396607/obo-9780195396607-0137.xml [accessed September 1, 2021].

3 The story is complex. For example, Shamir and Hacker (2001: 440) state that two of the three Indian members of the commission were against the regulation of cannabis and attempted its prohibition by trying to prove that the commission's alleged respect to India's cultural traditions was but a construct. These members, Raja Soshi Sikhareswar Roy and Lala Nihal Chand, supported their argument by showing that neither of India's religions with the highest number of followers (Hinduism, Islam, and Sikhism) approved drug consumption for spiritual purposes, so it was likely that the British authorities and "ganja smokers" were actually making up these Indian customs (see Shamir & Hacker, 2001: 453). See "How Bad Ganja Be? The Indian Hemp Drugs Commission's Discourse on Cannabis." https://blogs.ed.ac.uk/digitalhumanities2020/research/the-indian-hemp-drugs-commissions-discourse-on-cannabis/ [accessed June 1, 2022].

4 See www.ukcia.org/research/wootton/sec6.php [accessed June 1, 2022].

5 See www.druglibrary.org/schaffer/library/studies/nc/ncrec1_17.htm [accessed June 2, 2022].

6 See www.cbc.ca/archives/entry/ledain-tables-final-report-recommending-decriminalization [accessed June 1, 2022].

7 For more see www.weedoutmisinformation.ca/ [accessed June 3, 2022].

8 See https://humber.ca/today/news/weed-out-misinformation [accessed June 5, 2022].

9 See www.thedailybeast.com/new-york-post-dragged-for-narcing-on-snoop-doggs-weed-smoking [accessed June 5, 2022].

10 See www.independent.co.uk/life-style/ny-post-snoop-dogg-weed-b2015838.html. [accessed June 4, 2022].

11 See https://twitter.com/JohnFugelsang/status/1493262750423859208, https://twitter.com/laurancewiese/status/1493259831670710281, and https://twitter.com/KarinAbcarians/status/1493259476383657987 [accessed June 5, 2022].

12 See https://sports.yahoo.com/twitter-users-mock-york-posts-212207732.html [accessed May 5, 2022].

13 See https://transformdrugs.org/publications/how-to-regulate-cannabis-3rd-ed#:~:text=Early%20experiences%20of%20cannabis%20legalisation,well%20as%20protecting%20public%20health [accessed June 5, 2022].

14 See https://transformdrugs.org/assets/files/PDFs/blueprint-for-regulation-fulltext-2009.pdf [accessed June 7, 2022].

15 See www.vice.com/en/article/akvpe4/race-drug-arrests-canada [Accessed July 25, 2022].

# REFERENCES


Abastillas, M., Michael, I., & Smith, T. (2020). Howard Becker: An intellectual appreciation. *Silicon Valley Sociological Review, 18*(8). Retrieved from https://scholarcommons.scu.edu/svsr/vol18/iss1/8

ACDD. (1968). *Report on cannabis by the Advisory Committee on Drug Dependence*. London: Home Office. Retrieved from www.ukcia.org/research/wootton/index.php

Ackerman, M. S., & Lutters, W. G. (1996). An introduction to the Chicago School of Sociology. *Interval Research Propriety,* 1–25. Retrieved from www.academia.edu/7042690/An_Introduction_to_the_Chicago_School_of_Sociology._Lutters_Ackerman

Adda, J., McConnell, B., & Rasul, I. (2014). Crime and the depenalization of cannabis possession: Evidence from a policing experiment. *Journal of Political Economy, 122*(5), 1130–1202. https://doi.org/10.1086/67693

Agnew, R. (2006). *Pressured into crime*. Boston, MA: Oxford University Press.

Agoff, C., Fondevila, G., & Sandberg, S. (2021). Cultural stigmatization and police corruption: Cannabis, gender, and legalization in Mexico. *Drugs: Education, Prevention and Policy*. https://doi.org/10.1080/09687637.2021.2004089

Akers, R. (1989). A social behaviorist's perspective on integration of theories of crime and deviance. In *Theoretical integration in the study of deviance and crime: Problems and prospects*, eds. S. Messner, M. Krohn, and A. Liska. Albany, NY: State University of New York Press (pp. 23–36).

Akers, R.L. (1998). *Social Structure and Social Learning*. Los Angeles: Roxbury.

Akers, R. L., & Cochran, J. K. (1985). Adolescent marijuana use: A test of three theories of deviant behavior. *Deviant Behavior, 6*(4), 323–346.

Alchian, A., & Allen, W. (1967). *Exchange and production* (2nd ed.). Belmont, CA: Wadsworth.

Alexander, M. (2010). *The new Jim Crow: Mass incarceration in the age of colorblindness*. New York: The New Press.

Anderson, D. M., Hansen, B., & Rees, D. I. (2013). Medical marijuana laws, traffic fatalities, and alcohol consumption. *Journal of Law and Economics, 56*(2), 333–369.

Andrews, D. A., & Bonta, J. (2003). *The psychology of criminal conduct* (3rd ed.). Cincinnati, OH: Anderson.

Anslinger, H. J. (1943). The psychiatric aspects of marihuana intoxication. *Journal of the American Medical Association, 121*(3), 212–213.

Anslinger, H., & Cooper, R. (1937). Marijuana, assassin of youth. *American Magazine, 124*(1), 19.

APA (2013). Diagnostic and Statistical Manual of Mental Disorders (DSM-V). Arlington, VA: American Psychiatric Association.

Ashton, M. (2008). The new abstentionists. *Drug Scope, 1*(1), 1–25.

Askari, M. S., Keyes, K. M., & Mauro, P. M. (2021). Cannabis use disorder treatment use and perceived treatment need in the United States: Time trends and age differences between 2002–2019. *Drug and Alcohol Dependence, 229*(1), 109154.

August, K. (2013). Women in the marijuana industry. *Humboldt Journal of Social Relations, 35*, 89–103.

Aydelotte, J. D., Brown, L. H., Luftman, K. M., Mardock, A. L., Teixeira, P., Coopwood, B., & Brown, C. (2017). Crash fatality rates after recreational marijuana legalization in Washington and Colorado. *American Journal of Public Health, 107*(8), 1329–1331. https://doi.org/10.2105/AJPH.2017.303848

Baker, J., & Goh, D. (2004). *The cannabis cautioning scheme three years on: An implementation and outcome evaluation*. Sydney: NSW Bureau of Crime Statistics and Research.

Balko, R. (2013). How did America's police become a military force on the streets? *ABA Journal*. Retrieved from www.abajournal.com/magazine/article/how_did_americas_police_become_a_military_force_on_the_streets/?utm_source=feedburner&utm_medium=feed&utm_campaign=ABA+Journal+Magazine+Stories

Balko, R. (2014). *Rise of the warrior cop: The militarization of America's police forces*. New York: Public Affairs.

Baum, D. (1996). *Smoke and mirrors: The war on drugs and the politics of failure*. New York: Little Brown.

Baum, D. (2016, April). Legalize it: How to win the war on drugs. *Harper's Magazine*. Retrieved from https://harpers.org/archive/2016/04/legalize-it-all/.

Bear, D. (2014). *Acting out, adapting, or standing firm? Drugs policing in a London borough*. PhD thesis. London: London School of Economics.

Becker, G.S. (1968) Crime and punishment: an economic approach. *Journal of Political Economy* 76: 169–217.

Becker, G.S. (1976). *The economic approach to human behavior*. Chicago: University of Chicago Press.

Becker, H. S. (1951). The professional dance musician and his audience. *American Journal of Sociology, 57*, 136–144.

Becker, H. S. (1953). Becoming a marihuana user. *American Journal of Sociology 59*(3), 235–242.

Becker, H. S. (1955). Marijuana use and the social context. *Social Problems, 3*(1), 354.

Becker, H. S. (1963). *Outsiders: Studies in the sociology of deviance*. New York: The Free Press.

Becker, H. S. (1999). The Chicago School, so-called. *Qualitative Sociology, 122*, 3–12.

Beckett, K., and Herbert, S. (2008, December 8). *The consequences and costs of marijuana prohibition*. Seattle, WA: ACLU. Retrieved from www. aclu-wa.org/docs/consequences-and-costs-marijuana-prohibition

Belackova, V., Ritter, A., Shanahan, M., & Hughes, C. E. (2017). Assessing the concordance between illicit drug laws on the books and drug law enforcement: Comparison of three states on the continuum from "decriminalised" to "punitive". *International Journal on Drug Policy, 41*, 148–157.

Beletsky, L., & Davis, C. S. (2017, August). Today's fentanyl crisis: Prohibition's iron law revisited. *International Journal of Drug Policy, 46*, 156–159.

Bell, D. (1992). *Faces at the bottom of the well: The permanence of racism*. New York: Basic Books.

Bell, D. (1995). Who's afraid of critical race theory? *University of Illinois Law Review, 4*, 893–910.

Bennett, C. (2018). Drugs, moral panics and the dispositive. *Journal of Sociology, 54*(4), 538–556.

Bennett, E. (2021). "Consumer Activism, Sustainable Supply Chains, and the Cannabis Market" in *The Routledge Handbook of Interdisciplinary Cannabis Research*, Eds. Dominic Corva and Joshua Meisel, (pp. 192–200). London: Routledge.

Bennett, J. S. (1974). Le Dain Commission of Inquiry into the Non-Medical Use of Drugs tables fourth and final report. *Canadian Medical Association Journal, 110*(1), 105–108.

Benson, M. (2019). Brexit and the classed politics of bordering: The British in France and European belongings. *Sociology*. https://doi.org/10.1177/0038038519885300

Bentham, M. (1998). *The politics of drug control.* London: Macmillan.

Berenson, A. (2019). *Tell your children: The truth about marijuana, mental illness, and violence.* New York: The Free Press.

Berger, P., & Luckmann, T. (1966). *The social construction of reality*. Garden City, NY: Doubleday.

Bernard, J. (1991). From fasting to abstinence: The origins of the American temperance movement. In S. Barrows & R. Room (Eds.), *Drinking: Behavior and belief in modem history* (pp. 337–353). Berkeley, CA: University of California Press.

Bernard, T. J., & Snipes, J. B. (1996). Theoretical integration in criminology. *Crime and Justice: A Review of Research, 20*, 301–348.

Bernard, T. J., Snipes, J. B., & Gerould, A. L. (2010). *Vold's theoretical criminology*. New York: Oxford University Press.

Best, J. (2001). *Damned Lies and Statistics: Untangling numbers from the media, politicians, and activists.* Berkeley, CA: University of California Press.

Beweley-Taylor, D. (2001). *The United States and international drug control, 1909–1997.* London: Continuum.

Beweley-Taylor, D., Blickman, T., & Jelsma, M. (2014). *The rise and decline of cannabis prohibition: The history of cannabis in the UN drug control system and options for reform.* Amsterdam: Global Drug Policy Observatory/Transnational Institute.

Black, D. J. (1976). *The behavior of law.* New York: Academic Press.

Black, D. J. (1984). *Towards a general theory of social control.* New York: Academic Press.

Blackman, S. J. (2004). *Chilling out: The cultural politics of substance consumption, youth and drug policy.* Maidenhead: Open University Press/McGraw-Hill.

Blau, J. R., & Blau, P. M. (1982). The cost of inequality: Metropolitan structure and violent crime. *American Sociological Review, 47*, 114–129.

Blocker, J. S. Jr. (1989). *American temperance movements: Cycles of reform.* Boston, MA: Twayne Publishers.

Blumer, H. (1969). *Symbolic interactionism: Perspective and method.* Englewood Cliffs, NJ: Prentice Hall.

Blumstein, A. (1982). On the racial disproportionality of United States' prison populations. *Journal of Criminal Law and Criminology, 73*(3), 1259–1281.

Blumstein, A., Cohen, J., & Farrington, D. P. (1988). Criminal career research: It's value for criminology. *Criminology, 26*, 1–35.

Blumstein, A., & Wallman, J. (2006). The crime drop and beyond. *Annual Review of Law and Social Science, 2*(1), 125–146.

Bonnie, R. J, & Whitebread, C. H. (1970). The forbidden fruit and the tree of knowledge: An inquiry into the legal history of American marijuana prohibition. *Virginia Law Review, 56*(6), 971–1203.

Bonnie, R. J., & Whitebread, C. H. (1999). *The marijuana conviction: A history of marijuana prohibition in the United States.* New York: Lindesmith Publishing.

Booth, M. (1999). *Opium: A history.* New York: St. Martin's Press.

Booth, M. (2003). *Cannabis: A history*. New York: St. Martin's Press.

Borodovsky, J. T., & Budney, A. J. (2018). Cannabis regulatory science: Risk–benefit considerations for mental disorders. *International Review of Psychiatry, 30*(3), 183–202. https://doi.org/10.1080/09540261.2018.1454406

Bourgois, P. (2003). *In search of respect: Selling crack in El Barrio*. Cambridge: Cambridge University Press.

Boyd, G. (2002). Collateral damage in the war on drugs. *Villanova Law Review, 47*, 839–845.

Boyd, S. C. (2007). *Hooked: Drug war films in Britain, Canada, and the United States*. Toronto: University of Toronto Press.

Boyd, S. C. (2010). Reefer madness and beyond. In M. Deflem (Ed.), *Popular culture, crime and social control* (pp. 3–24). Bingley: Emerald Insights.

Boyd, S. C. (2017). *Busted: An illustrated history of drug prohibition in Canada*. Halifax: Fernwood.

Braithwaite, J. (1989). *Crime, shame and reintegration*. Cambridge University Press.

Braithwaite, J. (2021). Glimmers of cosmopolitan criminology. *International Criminology, 1*, 5–12.

Brantingham, P. J., & Brantingham, P. L. (1981). *Environmental criminology*. Beverly Hills, CA: Sage.

Broom, D.H. & Woodward, R.V. (1996). Medicalisation reconsidered: toward a collaborative approach to care. *Sociology of Health & Illness*, 18: 357–378. https://doi.org/10.1111/1467-9566.ep10934730

Brecher, E. (1972). *Licit and illicit drugs: The Consumers Union report on narcotics, stimulants, depressants, inhalants, halluncinogens, and marijuana—Including caffeine, nicotine, and alcohol*. Boston, MA: Little, Brown.

Brewster D. (2017). Culture(s) of control: Political dynamics in cannabis policy in England & Wales and the Netherlands. *European Journal of Criminology, 14*(5), 566–585.

Brown, M. (2022). Decriminalization as police reform. *Ohio State Legal Studies Research Paper No. 683*, February 2022. http://dx.doi.org/10.2139/ssrn.4032811

Brown, M., & Carrabine, E. (2021). The critical foundations of visual criminology. In *Visual Criminology*, edited by J. Wheeldon. (pp. 170–189). London: Routledge.

Brubacher, J. R., Chan, H., Erdelyi, S., Macdonald, S., Asbridge, M., Mann, R.E., Eppler, J., Lund, A., MacPherson, A., Martz, W., Schreiber, W. E., Brant, R., & Purssell, R. A. (2019). Cannabis use as a risk factor for causing motor vehicle crashes: A prospective study. *Addiction, 114*(9), 1616–1626. https://doi.org/10.1111/add.14663.

Bullington, B., & Block, A. A. (1990). A trojan horse: Anti-communism and the war on drugs. *Contemporary Crisis, 14*(1), 39–55.

Burruss, G. W., & Lu, Y. (2022). The value of data visualization for translational criminology. In J. Wheeldon (Ed.), *Visual criminology: From history and methods to critique and policy translation* (pp. 251–279). London: Routledge.

Butler, P. (2017). Police in America: Ensuring accountability and mitigating racial bias. *Northwestern Journal of Law & Social Policy, 11*, 385–401.

Callaghan, R. C., Vander Heiden, J., Sanches, M., Asbridge, M., Hathaway, A., & Kish, S. J. (2021). Impacts of Canada's cannabis legalization on police-reported crime among youth: Early evidence. *Addiction, 116*, 3454–3462. https://doi.org/10.1111/add.15535

Callahan, S., Bruner, D. M., & Giguerre, C. (2021). *Smoke and fears: The effects of marijuana on prohibition and crime*. Boone, NC: Appalachian State University Working Papers.

Campos, I. (2018). Mexicans and the origins of marijuana prohibition in the United States: A reassessment. *Social History of Alcohol and Drugs, 32*, 6–37.

Capers, I. B. (2014). Critical race theory and criminal justice. *Ohio State Journal of Criminal Law, 12*(1), 1–5.

Carrabine, E., Lee, M., & South, N. (2000). Social wrongs and human rights in late modern Britain: Social exclusion, crime control, and prospects for a public criminology. *Social Justice, 27*(2), 193–211.

Chambliss, W. J., & Seidman, R. B. (1971). *Law, order, and power*. Reading, MA: Addison-Wesley.

Chang, T. Y., & Jacobson, M. (2017). Going to pot? The impact of dispensary closures on crime. *Journal of Urban Economics, 100*, 120–136.

Chasin, A. (2016). *Assassin of youth: A kaleidoscopic history of Harry J. Anslinger's war on drugs*. Chicago, IL: The University of Chicago Press.

Childs, A., Coomber, R., & Bull, M. (2020). Do online illicit drug market exchanges afford rationality? *Contemporary Drug Problems, 47*(4), 302–319.

Chiu, V., Hall, W., Chan, G., Hides, L., & Leung, J. (2022). A systematic review of trends in US attitudes toward cannabis legalization. *Substance Use & Misuse, 57*(7), 1052–1061.

Chohlas-Wood, A., Gerchick, M., Goel, S., Huq, A. Z., Shoemaker, A., Shroff, R., & Yao, K. (2022). Identifying and measuring excessive and discriminatory policing. *University of Chicago Law Review, 89*, 441–451.

Christie, N. (1986). Suitable enemies. In H. Bianchi & R. van Swaaningen (Eds.), *Abolitionism: Towards a non-repressive approach to crime* (pp. 42–54). Amsterdam: Free University Press.

Christie, N. (2000). *Crime Control as Industry: Towards Gulags, Western Style*. United Kingdom: Taylor & Francis.

Christie, N. (2013). *Crime control as industry*. London: Taylor & Francis.

Clarke, R. V., & Cornish, D. B. (1985). Modeling offenders' decisions: A framework for research and policy. *Crime and Justice, 6*, 147–185.

Clarke, R. V. G., & Cornish, D. (1986). *The reasoning criminal*. New York: Springer-Verlag.

Clarke, R. V. & Felson, M. (1993). Routine activity and rational choice. Vol. 5, advances in criminological theory. New Brunswick, NJ: Transaction Books.

Cloward, R. A., & Ohlin, L. (1960). *Delinquency and opportunity: A theory of delinquent gangs*. New York: The Free Press.

Cody, D. L. (2006). *Smoke signals: Cannabis moral panics in the United States, Australia & Britain*. Master's thesis. University of Tasmania.

Cohen, A. K. (1955). *Delinquent boys; The culture of the gang*. New York: Free Press.

Cohen, L. E., & Felson, M. (1979). Social change and crime rate trends: A routine activity approach. *American Sociology Review, 44*, 588–608.

Cohen, S. (1972). *Folk devils and moral panics: The creation of the mods and rockers*. London: MacGibbon and Kee.

Cohen, S. (1974). Criminology and the sociology of deviance in Britain: A recent history and a current report. In P. Rock & M. McIntosh (Eds.), *Deviance and social control* (pp. 1–40). London: Tavistock.

Cohen, S. (1979). The punitive city: Notes on the dispersal of social control. *Contemporary Crises, 3*, 339–363. https://doi.org/10.1007/BF00729115

Cohen, S. (1982). *Against criminology*. New York: Transaction Publishers.

Cohen, S. (1985). *Visions on social control*. London: Polity Press.

Cohen, L. E., & Felson, M. (1979). Social change and crime rate trends: A routine activity approach. *American Sociology Review, 44*, 588–608.

Collins, J. (2020). A brief history of cannabis and the drug conventions. Symposium on drug decriminalization, legalization, and international law. *AJIL Unbound, 114*, 279–284.

Collins, J. (2021). *Legalising the drug wars: A regulatory history of UN Drug Control*. Cambridge: Cambridge University Press. https://doi.org/10.1017/9781009058278

Compton, R. (2017). Marijuana-impaired driving: A report to Congress. DOT HS 812 440 Washington, DC: National Highway Traffic Safety Administration. www.nhtsa.gov/sites/nhtsa.dot.gov/files/documents/812440-marijuana-impaired-driving-report-to-congress.pdf

Connor, J. P., Stjepanović, D., Le Foll, B., Hoch, E, Budney, A. J., & Hall, W. D. (2021). Cannabis use and cannabis use disorder. *Nature Reviews Disease Primers, 7*, 16. https://doi.org/10.1038/s41572-021-00247-4

Conrad, P., Schneider, J. W., & Gusfleld, J. R. (1992). *Deviance and medicalization: From badness to sickness*. Philadelphia, PA: Temple University Press.

Contreras, C. (2016). A block-level analysis of medical marijuana dispensaries and crime in the city of Los Angeles. *Justice Quarterly, 34*(6), 1069–1095.

Contreras, C. (2017). A block-level analysis of medical marijuana dispensaries and crime in the city of Los Angeles. *Justice Quarterly* 34(6), 1069–1095.

Coomber, R., & Moyle, L. (2018). The changing shape of street-level heroin and crack supply in England: Commuting, holidaying and cuckooing drug dealers across 'county lines'. *British Journal of Criminology, 58*(6), 1323–1342.

Copes, H., Brookman, F., Ragland, J., & Beaton, B. (2021). Sex, drugs, and coercive control: Gendered narratives of methamphetamine use, relationships, and violence. *Criminology*, 1–32. https://doi.org/10.1111/1745-9125.12295

Copes, H., Tchoula, W., Kim, J., & Ragland, J. (2018). Symbolic perceptions of methamphetamine: Differentiating between ice and shake. *International Journal of Drug Policy, 51*, 87–94.

Copes, H., Tchoula, W., & Ragland, J. (2019). Ethically representing drug use: Photographs and ethnographic research with people who use methamphetamine. *Journal of Qualitative Criminal Justice & Criminology, 8*(1), 21–35.

Cornish, D. B., & Clarke, R. V. (2002). Analyzing organized crimes. *Rational choice and criminal behavior: Recent Research and Future Challenges, 32*, 41–63.

Cort, B. (2017). *Weed, inc.: The truth about the pot lobby, THC, and the commercial marijuana industry*. Boca Raton: Health Communications.

Corva, D., & Meisel, J. S. (2021). *The Routledge handbook of post-prohibition cannabis research*. London: Routledge.

Cousijn, J., Goudriaan, A. E., & Wiers, R. W. (2011). Reaching out towards cannabis: Approach-bias in heavy cannabis users predicts changes in cannabis use. *Addiction, 106*(9), 1667–1674.

Cousijn, J., Toenders, Y. J., van Velzen, L. S., & Kaag, A. M. (2021). The relation between cannabis use, dependence severity and white matter microstructure: A diffusion tensor imaging study. *Addiction Biology, 2021*, e13081. https://doi.org/10.1111/adb.13081

Cousijn, J., Wiers, R. W., Ridderinkhof, K. R., van den Brink, W., Veltman, D. J., & Goudriaan, A. E. (2012). Grey matter alterations associated with cannabis use: Results of a VBM study in heavy cannabis users and healthy controls. *NeuroImage, 59*(4), 3845–3851. https://doi.org/10.1016/J.NEUROIMAGE.2011.09.046

Cowan, R. (1986). How the narcs created crack: A war against ourselves. *National Review, 38*(23), 26–34.

Cracknell, M. (2021). The resettlement net: "Revolving door" imprisonment and carceral (re) circulation. *Punishment & Society*, August. https://doi.org/10.1177/14624745211035837

Currie, E. (1999). Reflections on crime and criminology at the millennium. *Western Criminology Review, 2*(1), 1–13.

D'Souza, D. C., DiForti, M., Ganesh, S., George, T. P., Hall, W., Hjorthøj, C., Howes, O., Keshavan, M., Murray, R. M., Nguyen, T. B., Pearlson, G. D., Ranganathan, M., Selloni, A., Solowij, N., & Spinazzola, E. (2022). Consensus paper of the WFSBP task force on cannabis, cannabinoids, and psychosis. *World Journal of Biological Psychiatry*. https://doi.org/10.1080/15622975.2022.2038797

Dandurand, Y. (2006). Effective technical assistance in crime prevention and criminal justice. In *Maximizing the effectiveness of the technical assistance provided in the fields of crime prevention and criminal justice*. Vienna: United Nations European Institute for Crime Prevention and Control, Paper No. 49: 1237–4741.

Dandurand, Y. (2021). Law enforcement strategies to disrupt illicit drug markets. *International Centre for Criminal Law Reform and Criminal Justice Policy*. Retrieved from https://icclr.org/publications/law-enforcement-strategies-to-disrupt-illicit-drug-markets/

Daniels, C., Aluso, A., Burke-Shyne, N., Koram, K., Rajagopalan, S., Robinson, I., Shelly, S., Shirley-Beavan, S., & Tandon, T. (2021). Decolonizing drug policy. *Harm Reduction Journal, 18*(120). https://doi.org/10.1186/s12954-021-00564-7

Davenport, C., McDermott, R., & Armstrong, D. (2018). Protest and police abuse: Racial limits on perceived accountability. In M. D. Bonner, G. Seri, M. Rose Kubal, & M. Kempa (Eds.), *Police abuse in contemporary democracies* (pp. 165–192). Cham: Palgrave Macmillan.

Davis, M. (2012). *Jews and booze: Becoming American in the age of prohibition*. New York: New York University Press.

Dayton, T. & Adams, T. (2017). The State of Legal Marijuana Markets 5th Edition: Executive Summary. Arcview Market Research Group. Retrieved from: www.cdfa.ca.gov/calcannabis/documents/V3_Combined_FINAL_Part6.pdf

Decorte, T. (2010). The case for small-scale domestic cannabis cultivation. *International Journal of Drug Policy, 21*(4), 271–275.

Decorte, T., Lenton, S., & Wilkins, C. (2020). *Legalizing cannabis: Experiences, lessons and scenarios*. New York: Routledge.

Decorte, T., & Potter, G. (2015). The globalisation of cannabis cultivation: A growing challenge. *International Journal of Drug Policy, 26*. https://doi.org/10.1016/j.drugpo.2014.12.011

Degenhardt, L., Hall, W., & Lynskey, M. (2003). Exploring the association between cannabis use and depression. *Addiction, 98*(11), 1493–1504.

del Pozo, B (2022). *The police and the state: security, social cooperation, and the common good*. Cambridge: Cambridge University Press.

del Pozo, B., Sightes, E., Goulka, J. et al. (2021). Police discretion in encounters with people who use drugs: operationalizing the theory of planned behavior. *Harm Reduction Journal, 18*, 132. https://doi.org/10.1186/s12954-021-00583-4

Delgado, R., & Stefanic, J. (2001). *Critical race theory: An introduction*. New York: New York University.

Di Forti, Marta, Diego Quattrone, Tom P. Freeman, Giada Tripoli, Charlotte Gayer-Anderson, Harriet Quig-ley, Victoria Rodriguez, Hannah E. gsma, Laura Ferraro, Caterina La Cascia, Daniele La Barbera, Ilaria Tarricone, Domenico Berardi, Andrei Szöke, Celso Arango, Andrea Tortelli, Eva Velthorst, Miguel Bernardo, Cristina Marta Del-Ben, Paulo Rossi Menezes, Jean-Paul Selten, Peter B. Jones, James B. Kirkbride, Bart P.F. Rutten, Lieuwe de Haan, Pak C. Sham, Jim van Os, Cathryn M. Lewis, Michael Lynskey, Craig Morgan, Robin M. Murray, and the EU-GEI WP2 Group. (2019). The contribution of cannabis use to variation in the incidence of psychotic disorder across Europe (EU-GEI): A multicentre case-control study. *Lancet Psychiatry, 6*(5), 427–436

DOJ (2013). Crime in the United States, 2012 U.S. Department of Justice—Federal Bureau of Investigation. Available at: https://ucr.fbi.gov/crime-in-the-u.s/2012/crime-in-the-u.s.-2012/persons-arrested/arrestmain.pdf

Donnelly, N., Hall, W., & Christie, P. (1995). The effects of partial decriminalisation on cannabis use in South Australia, 1985 to 1993. *Australian Journal of Public Health, 19*, 281–287.

Dragone, D., Prarolo, G., Vanin, P., & Zanella, G. (2017). Crime and the legalization of recreational marijuana. *Journal of Economic Behavior and Organization, 159*(C), 488–501.

Drake, D. (2012). *Prisons, punishment and the pursuit of security*. Basingstoke: Palgrave Macmillan.

Du Bois, W.E.B (1897). "The Conservation of Races" in Nahum Dimitri Chandler (ed.), *The Problem of the Color Line At the Turn of the Twentieth Century: The Essential Early Essays*, New York: Fordham University Press, 2015, pp. 51–65. Reprint of "The Conservation of Races," Washington, DC: American Negro Academy, 1897.

Dubois, S., Mullen, N., Weaver, B., & Bédard, M. (2015). The combined effects of alcohol and cannabis on driving: Impact on crash risk. *Forensic Science International, 248*, 94–100. https://doi.org/10.1016/j.forsciint.2014.12.018

Duff, C. (2003). Drugs and youth cultures: Is Australia experiencing the "normalization" of adolescent drug use? *Journal of Youth Studies, 6*(4), 433–446.

Duff, C., Asbridge, M., Brochu, S., Cousineau, M.-M., Hathaway, A. D., Marsh, D., & Erickson, P. G. (2012). A Canadian perspective on cannabis normalization among adults. *Addiction Research & Theory, 20*(4), 271–283.

Dufton, E. (2017b). *Grass roots: The fall and rise of marijuana in America*. New York: Basic Books.

Dufton, E. (2019). Puff, puff, puff, pass. Lessons from the defeat of marijuana decriminalization. *Perspectives on History*. Retrieved from www.historians.org/publications-and-directories/perspectives-on-history/april-2019/puff-puff-pass-lessons-from-the-defeat-of-marijuana-decriminalization

Duke, K., Gleeson, H., Dąbrowska, K., Herold, M., & Rolando, M. (2021). The engagement of young people in drug interventions in coercive contexts: Findings from a cross-national European study. *Drugs: Education, Prevention and Policy, 28*(1), 26–35.

Duke, S., & Gross, A. C. (1993). *America's longest war: Rethinking our tragic crusade against drugs*. New York: G.P. Putnam's Sons.

Durkheim, É. (1895/1982). *The rules of sociological method* (W. D. Halls, Trans.). New York, NY: The Free Press.

Durkheim, É. (1897/1951). *Suicide: A study in sociology* (J. A. Spaulding & G. Simpson, Trans.). New York, NY: The Free Press.

Duster, T. (1970). *The legislation of morality: Law, dugs and moral judgement*. New York: Free Press.

Earleywine, M. (2002). *Understanding marijuana: A new look at the scientific evidence*. Oxford: Oxford University Press.

Einstadter, W. J., & Henry, S. (1995). *Criminological theory*. Lanham, MD: Rowman and Littlefield.

Einstadter, W. J., & Henry, S. (2006). *Criminological theory*. Lanham, MD: Rowman and Littlefield.

Elliott, L. (2002). Con Game and restorative justice: Inventing the truth about Canada's prisons. *Canadian Journal of Criminology, 44*(4), 459–474.

Elliott, E. (2011). *Security, With Care: Restorative Justice and Healthy Societies*. Halifax, NS: Fernwood Publishing.

Elliott, J. C., Carey, K. B., & Vanable, P. A. (2014). A preliminary evaluation of a web-based intervention for college marijuana use. *Psychology of Addictive Behaviors, 28*(1), 288–293.

Elliott, M. L., Knodt,. A. R., Ireland, D., Morris, M. L., Poulton, R., Ramrakha, S., Sison, M. L., Moffitt, T. E., Caspi, A., & Hariri, A. R. (2020). What is the test-tetest reliability of common task-functional MRI measures? New empirical evidence and a meta-Analysis. *Psychological Science, 31*(7), 792–806.Ellis, L. (2005). Theoretically explaining biological correlates of criminal behavior. *European Journal of Criminology* 2: 287–315.

Ellis, L., & Hoffman, H. (Eds.). (1990). *Crime in biological, social, and moral contexts*. New York: Praeger.

Eysenck, H. J., & Gudjonsson, G. H. (1989). Crime and personality. In *The causes and cures of criminality* (pp. 43–89). Springer, Boston, MA.

Fagan, J. A., Geller, A., Davies, G., & West, V. (2010). Street stops and broken windows revisited. In *Race, ethnicity, and policing,* Edited by Stephen K. Rice Michael D. White (pp. 309–348). New York: New York University Press.

Farrington, D. P. (1992). Criminal career researh in the United Kingdom. *British Journal of Criminology, 32*(4), 521–536.

Featherstone, M., Lash, S., & Robertson, R. (1995). *Global modernities.* Thousand Oaks, CA: Sage Publications.

Felson, M. (2002). *Crime and everyday life.* Thousand Oaks, CA: Sage Publications.

Feltmann, K., Gripenberg, J., Strandberg, A. K., Elgán, T. H., & Kvillemo, P. (2021). Drug dealing and drug use prevention: A qualitative interview study of authorities' perspectives on two open drug scenes in Stockholm. *Substance Abuse Treatment Prevention Policy, 16,* 37. https://doi.org/10.1186/s13011-021-00375-w

Fischer, B., Daldegan-Bueno, D., & Reuter, P. (2021). Toward a "post-legalization" criminology for cannabis: A brief review and suggested agenda for research priorities. *Contemporary Drug Problems, 48*(1), 58–74.

Fischer, B., Lee, A., O'Keefe-Markman, C., & Hall, W. (2020). Initial indicators of the public health impacts of non-medical cannabis legalization in Canada. *EClinicalMedicine, 20,* 100294.

Fischer, B., Russell C., & Boyd N. (2020). A century of cannabis control in Canada: A brief overview of history, context and policy frameworks from prohibition to legalization. In T. Decorte, S. Lenton, & C. Wilkins (Eds.), *Legalizing cannabis: Experiences, lessons and scenarios* (pp. 89–115). London: Routledge.

Fishbein, D. (2001). *Biobehavioural perspectives in criminology.* Belmont, CA: Wadsworth.

Fisher, G. (2021). Racial myths of the cannabis war. *Boston University Law Review, 101,* 933–977.

Fornili, K. S. (2018). Racialized mass incarceration and the war on drugs: A critical race theory appraisal. *Journal of Addictions Nursing, 29*(1), 65–72. https://doi.org/10.1097/JAN.0000000000000215

Fox, K. J. (2012). Redeeming communities: Restorative offender reentry in a risk society. *Victims & Offenders,* 7(1), 97–120.

Fox, K. J. (2013). Restoring the social: Offender reintegration in a risky world. *International Journal of Comparative and Applied Criminology, 38*(3), 235–256.

Fox, K. J. (2015). Trying to restore justice: Bureaucracies, risk management and disciplinary boundaries in New Zealand criminal justice. *International Journal of Offender Therapy and Comparative Criminology, 59*(5), 519–538.

Freud, S. (1920). *Beyond the pleasure principle.* London: The International Psychoanalytic Press.

Freud, S. (1923) The ego and the Id. *TACD Journal, 17*(1), 5–22.

Frisher, M., Crome, I., Martino, O., Croft, P (2009). Assessing the impact of cannabis use on trends in diagnosed schizophrenia in the United Kingdom from 1996 to 2005. *Schizophrenia Research, 113*(2–3), 123–8.

Gabri. A.C., Galanti, M.R., Orsini, N., & Magnusson, C. (2022) Changes in cannabis policy and prevalence of recreational cannabis use among adolescents and young adults in Europe—An interrupted time-series analysis. *PLOS ONE 17*(1), e0261885. https://doi.org/10.1371/journal.pone.0261885

Gage, S. H., Hickman, M., & Zammit, S. (2016). Association between cannabis and psychosis: epidemiologic evidence. *Biological Psychiatry,* 79(7), 549–556.

Gage, S. H., Zammit, S., & Hickman, M. (2013). Stronger evidence is needed before accepting that cannabis plays an important role in the aetiology of schizophrenia in the population. *F1000 Medicine Reports, 5*(2). https://doi.org/10.3410/M5-2.

Gagnon, M., Gudiño, D., Guta, A., & Strike, C. (2020). What can we learn from the English-language media coverage of cannabis legalization in Canada? *Substance Use & Misuse, 55*(8), 1378–1381. https://doi.org/10.1080/10826084.2020.1741639

Garland, D. (1996). The limits of the sovereign state: Strategies of crime control in contemporary society. *British Journal of Criminology, 36*, 445–471.

Garland, D. (2001). *Culture of control: Crime and social order in contemporary society*. Chicago, IL: University of Chicago Press.

Garland, D. (2008). On the concept of moral panic. *Crime Media Culture, 4*(1), 9–30.

Geller, A., & Fagan, J. (2010). Pot as pretext: Marijuana, race, and the new disorder in New York City street policing. *Journal of Empirical Legal Studies, 7*, 591–633. https://doi.org/10.1111/j.1740-1461.2010.01190.x

Gelman, A., Fagan, J., & Kiss, A. (2007). An analysis of the New York City police department's "stop-and-frisk" policy in the context of claims of racial bias. *Journal of the American Statistical Association, 102*(479), 813–823.

Gerster, R., & Bassett, J. (1991). *Seizures of youth: the sixties and Australia*. Victoria: Hyland House.

Gibbons, D. C. (1994). *Talking about crime and criminals: Problems and issues in theory development in criminology*. Prentice Hall.

Gibson, J. L. (2004). Does truth lead to reconciliation? Testing the causal assumptions of the South African truth and reconciliation process. *American Journal of Political Science, 48*(2), 201–217.

Gieringer, D. H. (1999). The forgotten origins of cannabis prohibition in California. *Contemporary Drug Problems, 26*(2), 237–288.

Gladwell, M. (2019, January 14). Is marijuana as safe as we think? *New Yorker*. Retrieved from www.newyorker.com/magazine/2019/01/14/is-marij uana-as-safe-as-we-think

Glasser, I. (2000). American drug laws: The new Jim Crow, the 1999 Edward C. Sobota lecture. *Albany Law Review, 63*, 703–723.

Goff, P. A., Jackson, M. C., Di Leone, B. A., Culotta, C. M., & DiTomasso, N. A. (2014). The essence of innocence: Consequences of dehumanizing Black children. *Journal of Personality and Social Psychology, 106*(4), 526–545. https://doi.org/10.1037/a0035663.

Goffman, E. (1963). *Stigma: Notes on the management of spoiled identity*. New York: Simon and Schuster.

Goldstein, P. J. (1985). The drugs/violence nexus: A tripartite conceptual framework. *Journal of Drug Issues, 15*(4), 493–506.

Goode, E. (2005). *Drugs in American society*. New York: McGraw-Hill.

Goode, E., & Ben-Yehuda, N. (1994). Moral panics: Culture, politics, and social construction. *Annual Review of Sociology, 20*, 149–171.

Gopnik, A. (2015). The outside game. *New Yorker*. Retrieved from www.newyorker.com/magazine/2015/01/12/outside-game

Gracie, K., & Hancox, R. J. (2020). Cannabis use disorder and the lungs. *Addict (Abingdon, England), 116*(1), 182–190. https://doi.org/10.1111/add.15075

Gray, M. (1998). *Drug crazy: How we got into this mess and how we can get out*. New York: Random House.

Green, K. M., Doherty, E. E., & Ensminger, M. E. (2017). Long-term consequences of adolescent cannabis use: Examining intermediary processes. *American Journal of Drug and Alcohol Abuse, 43*(5), 567–575.

Green, K. M., Doherty, E. E., Stuart, E. A., & Ensminger, M. E. (2010). Does heavy adolescent marijuana use lead to criminal involvement in adulthood? Evidence from a multi-wave longitudinal study of urban African Americans. *Drug and Alcohol Dependence, 112*(1–2), 117–125.

Greer, A. M., & Ritter, A. (2019). "It's about bloody time": Perceptions of people who use drugs regarding drug law reform. *International Journal on Drug Policy, 64*, 40–46. https://doi.org/10.1016/j.drugpo.2018.12.006

Greer, A., & Ritter, A. (2020). The legal regulation of drugs and role of government: Perspectives from people who use drugs. *Drug and Alcohol Dependence, 206*, 107737. https://doi.org/10.1016/j.drugalcdep.2019.107737

Greer, A., Sorge, J., Selfridge, M., Benoit, C., Jansson, M., & Macdonald, S. (2020). Police discretion to charge young people who use drugs prior to cannabis legalization in British Columbia, Canada: A brief report of quantitative findings. *Drugs: Education, Prevention and Policy, 27*(6). https://doi.org/10.1080/09687637.2020.1745757

Grucza, R. A., Krueger, R. F., Agrawal, A., Plunk, A. D., Krauss, M. J., Bongu, J., ... & Bierut, L. J. (2018). Declines in prevalence of adolescent substance use disorders and delinquent behaviors in the USA: a unitary trend?. *Psychological Medicine, 48*(9), 1494–1503.

Grucza, R. A., Vuolo, M., Krauss, M. J., Plunk, A. D., Agrawal, A., Chaloupka, F. J., & Bierut, L. J. (2018). Cannabis decriminalization: A study of recent policy change in five U.S. states. *International Journal on Drug Policy, 59*, 67–75. https://doi.org/10.1016/j.drugpo.2018.06.016

Gullo MJ, Papinczak ZE, Feeney GFX, Young RMcd and Connor JP (2021) Precision mental health care for cannabis use disorder: Utility of a bioSocial Cognitive Theory to inform treatment. *Frontier Psychiatry* 12, 643107. doi: 10.3389/fpsyt.2021.643107

Haggerty, K. D. (2004). Displaced expertise: Three constraints on the policy relevance of criminological thought. *Theoretical Criminology, 8*(2), 211–231.

Haines-Saah, R. J., Johnson, J. L., Repta, R., Ostry, A., Young, M. L., Shoveller, J., Sawatzky, R., Greaves, L., & Ratner, P. A. (2014). The privileged normalization of marijuana use: An analysis of Canadian newspaper reporting, 1997–2007. *Critical Public Health, 24*(1), 47–61.

Hall, W. (2010). What are the policy lessons of national alcohol prohibition in the United States, 1920–1933? *Addiction, 105*, 1164–1173.

Hall, S. (2012). *Theorizing crime and deviance*. London: Sage Publications.

Hall, W. and Lynskey, M. (2020). Assessing the public health impacts of legalizing recreational cannabis use: the U.S. experience. *World Psychiatry, 19*(2), 179–186.

Hall, S., Critcher, C., Jefferson, T., & Roberts, B. (1978). *Policing the crisis: Mugging, the state and law and order*. London: Macmillan.

Halpern, A. (2018). Marijuana: Is it time to stop using a word with racist roots? *The Guardian*. Retrieved from www.theguardian.com/society/2018/jan/29/marijuana-name-cannabis-racism.

Hamilton, M. (2001). Drug policy in Australia: Our own? In J. Gerber & E. L. Jensen (Eds.), *Drug war American style: The internationalization of failed policy and its alternatives* (pp. 97–120). New York: Garland.

Hamilton, I. & Monaghan, M. (2019). Cannabis and psychosis: are we any closer to understanding the relationship? *Current Psychiatry Reports*, 21, 48. https://doi.org/10.1007/s11920-019-1044-x

Hamilton, I., Lloyd, C., Hewitt, C., & Godfrey, C. (2014). Effect of reclassification of cannabis on hospital admissions for cannabis psychosis: a time series analysis. *International Journal on Drug Policy, 25*(1), 151–156. https://doi.org/10.1016/j.drugpo.2013.05.016

Hamzeie, R., Savolainen, P. T., & Gates, T. J. (2017). Driver speed selection and crash risk: Insights from the naturalistic driving study. *Journal of Safety Research, 63*, 187–194.

Hanson, V. J. (2020). Cannabis policy reform: Jamaica's experience. In *Legalizing Cannabis* (pp. 375–389). London: Routledge.

Hart, C. (2017). Viewing addiction as a brain disease promotes social injustice. *Nat Human Behavior* 1, 0055.

Hart, C. L. (2021). *Drug use for grown-ups: Chasing liberty in the land of fear.* New York: Penguin Press.

Hartman R.L. & Huestis, M.A. (2013) Cannabis Effects on Driving Skills, *Clinical Chemistry, 59*(3), 478–492. https://doi.org/10.1373/clinchem.2012.194381

Hasin, D. S., Kerridge, B. T., Saha, T. D., Huang, B., Pickering, R, Smith, S. M., Jung, J., Zhang, H., & Grant, B. (2016). Prevalence and correlates of DSM-5 cannabis use disorder, 2012–2013: Findings from the National Epidemiologic Survey on Alcohol and Related Conditions-III. *American Journal of Psychiatry, 173*(6), 588–599.

Hasin, D. S., Saha, T. D., Kerridge, B. T., Goldstein, R. B., Chou, S. P., Zhang, H., ... & Grant, B. F. (2015). Prevalence of marijuana use disorders in the United States between 2001–2002 and 2012–2013. *JAMA Psychiatry, 72*(12), 1235–1242.

Hathaway, A. D. (2004). Cannabis users' informal rules for managing stigma and risk. *Deviant Behavior, 25*(6), 559–577.

Hathaway, A. D., Comeau, N. C., & Erickson, P. G. (2011). Cannabis normalization and stigma: Contemporary practices of moral regulation. *Criminology & Criminal Justice, 11*(5), 451–469.

Hathaway, A. D., & Erickson, P. G. (2003). Drug reform principles and policy debates: Harm reduction prospects for cannabis in Canada. *Journal of Drug Issues, 33*(2), 465–495.

Hawley, A. (1950). *Human ecology: a theory of community structure.* Ronald Press, New York.

Heidt, J. (2021). *Tangled up in green: Cannabis legalization in British Columbia after one year.* Abbottsford: Centre for Public Safety and Criminal Justice Research, University of the Fraser Valley.

Heidt, J. (2022). Criminological theory and criminal justice practice: A visual history. In J. Wheeldon (Ed.), *Visual criminology: From history and methods to critique and policy translation* (pp. 31–51). New York: Routledge.

Heidt, J., Dosanjh, A., & Roberts, D. (2018). *Great expectations: Perceptions of cannabis regulation in Abbottsford, BC.* Abbottsford: Centre for Public Safety and Criminal Justice Research, University of the Fraser Valley.

Heidt, J., & Wheeldon, J. (2015). *Introducing criminological thinking: Maps, theories, and understanding.* Thousand Oaks, CA: Sage Publications.

Heidt, J., & Wheeldon, J. (2022). Data, damn lies, and cannabis policy: Reefer madness and the methodological crimes of the new prohibitionists. *Critical Criminology, 30*, 403–419. https://doi.org/10.1007/s10612-020-09548-8

Henry, B., & Moffitt, T. E. (1997). Neuropsychological and neuro-imaging studies of juvenile delinquency and adult criminal behavior. In D. Stoff, J. Breiling, & J. D. Maser (Eds.), *Handbook of antisocial behavior* (pp. 280–288). New York: John Wiley.

Henry, S., & Milovanovic, D. (1996). *Constitutive criminology: Beyond postmodernism.* Thousand Oaks, CA: Sage Publications.

Heyman, G. M. (2013a). Addiction and choice: theory and new data. *Frontiers in Psychiatry, 4*, 31.

Heyman G. M. (2013b). Quitting drugs: quantitative and qualitative features. *Annual Review of Clinical Psychology*, 9: 29–59.

Hinton, E. (2017). *From the war on poverty to the war on crime: The making of mass incarceration in America.* Cambridge, MA: Harvard University Press.

Hinton, E., & Cook, D. (2021). The mass criminalization of Black Americans: A historical overview. *Annual Review of Criminology, 4*(1), 261–286.

Hirschi, T. (1969). *Causes of delinquency.* Berkeley, CA: University of California Press.

Hoffman, A. J. (2016). Reflections: Academia's emerging crisis of relevance and the consequent role of the engaged scholar, *Journal of Change Management, 16*(2), 77–96.

Horsley, M. (2017). Forget "moral panics". *Journal of Theoretical and Philosophical Criminology, 9*(2), 84–98.

Huber III, A., Newman, R., & LaFave, D. (2016). Cannabis control and crime: Medicinal use, depenalization and the war on drugs. *B.E. Journal of Economic Analysis & Policy, 16*(4), 1–35.

Hudak, J. (2020). *Marijuana: A short history*. Washington, DC: Brookings Institute.

Huestis, M. A., Mazzoni, I., & Rabin, O. (2011). Cannabis in sport: Anti-doping perspective. *Sports Medicine, 41*(11), 949–966.

Hughes, B., Matias, J., & Griffiths, P. (2018). Inconsistencies in the assumptions linking punitive sanctions and use of cannabis and new psychoactive substances in Europe. *Addiction, 113*, 2155–2157. https://doi.org/10.1111/add.14372.

Hughes, C., Shanahan, M., Ritter, A., McDonald, D. & Gray-Weale, F. (2014). *Evaluation of the ACT drug diversion programs. DPMP Monograph no. 25*. Sydney: National Drug and Alcohol Research Centre.

Hughes, C., Seear, K., Ritter, A., & Mazerolle, L. (2019). *Criminal justice responses relating to personal use and possession of illicit drugs: The reach of Australian drug diversion programs and barriers and facilitators to expansion*. Drug Policy Modelling Program Monograph 27. Sydney: National Drug and Alcohol Research Centre. Retrieved from https://ndarc.med.unsw.edu.au/resource/27-criminal-justice-responses-relating-personal-use-and-possession-illicit-drugs-reach

Hughes, C. E., & Stevens, A. (2007). *The effects of the decriminalization of drug use in Portugal. Discussion paper*. Oxford: The Beckley Foundation.

Hughes, C. E., & Stevens, A. (2010). What can we learn from the Portuguese decriminalization of illicit drugs? *British Journal of Criminology, 50*(6), 999–1022. https://doi.org/10.1093/bjc/azq038

Hughes, C. E., & Stevens, A. (2012). A resounding success or a disastrous failure: Re-examining the interpretation of evidence on the Portuguese decriminalisation of illicit drugs. *Drug and Alcohol Review, 31*(1), 101–113. https://doi.org/10.1111/j.1465-3362.2011.00383.x

Hughes, L., Schaible, L., & Jimmerson, K. (2019). Marijuana dispensaries and neighborhood crime and disorder in Denver, Colorado. *Justice Quarterly, 3*, 1–25. https://doi.org/10.1080/07418825.2019.1567807

Hunt, P., Pacula, R.L., & Weinberger, G. (2018). High on crime: Exploring the effects of dispensary laws on California counties. *Rand Corporation*. Retrieved from http://ftp.iza.org/dp11567.pdf

Jacobs, J. (1961). *Death and life of great American cities*. New York: Random House

Jacques, S. (2014). The quantitative-qualitative divide in criminology: A theory of ideas' importance, attractiveness, and publication. *Theoretical Criminology, 18*, 317–334.

Jacques, S., Rosenfeld, R., Wright, R., & Gemert, F. (2016). Effects of prohibition and decriminalization on drug market conflict: Comparing street dealers, coffeeshops, and cafés in Amsterdam. *Criminology & Public Policy, 15*. https://doi.org/10.1111/1745-9133.12218

Jenkins, D., & Leroy, J. (2021). *Histories of racial capitalism*. New York: Columbia University Press.

Jewkes, Y. (2004). *Media and crime*. London: Sage Publications.

Jiggens, J. L. (2001). *Marijuana Australiana: Cannabis use, popular culture, & the Americanization of drugs policy in Australia 1938–1988*. PhD thesis. Queensland University of Technology.

Jin, D., Henry, P., Shan, J., & Chen, J. (2021). Classification of cannabis strains in the Canadian market with discriminant analysis of principal components using genome-wide single nucleotide polymorphisms. *PLoS One, 16*(6), e0253387. https://doi.org/10.1371/journal.pone.0253387

Johns, A. (2001). Psychiatric effects of cannabis. *British Journal of Psychiatry, 178*, 116–122.

Johnson, B. (2021). *From harm to hope: A 10-year drugs plan to cut crime and save lives*. London: Ministry of Justice. Retrieved from www.gov.uk/government/publications/from-harm-to-hope-a-10-year-drugs-plan-to-cut-crime-and-save-lives/from-harm-to-hope-a-10-year-drugs-plan-to-cut-crime-and-save-lives

Johnson, R. M., Fleming, C. B., Cambron, C., Dean, L.T., Brighthaupt, S. C., & Guttmannova, K. (2019). Race/ethnicity differences in trends of marijuana, cigarette, and alcohol use among 8th, 10th, and 12th graders in Washington State, 2004–2016. *Prevention Science, 20*(2), 194–204. https://doi.org/10.1007/s11121-018-0899-0

Johnson, V. (1988). Adolescent alcohol and marijuana use: A longitudinal assessment of a social learning perspective. *American Journal of Drug and Alcohol Abuse, 14*(3), 419–439. https://doi.org/10.3109/00952998809001561

Jones, S. (2021). Christopher Rufo and the critical-race theory moral panic. *New York Magazine*. Retrieved from https://nymag.com/intelligencer/2021/07/christopher-rufo-and-the-critical-race-theory-moral-panic.html

Jonnes, J. (1996). *Hep-Catsy narcsy and pipe dreams: A history of America's romance with illegal drugs*. New York: Scribner.

Jutras-Aswad, D., Le Foll, B., Bruneau, J., Wild, T. C., Wood, E., & Fischer, B. (2019). Thinking beyond legalization: The case for expanding evidence-based options for cannabis use disorder treatment in Canada. *Canadian Journal of Psychiatry, 64*(2), 82–87. https://doi.org/10.1177/0706743718790955

Kaplan, J. (1970). *Marijuana: The new prohibition*. Cleveland, OH: World Publishing.

Kelly, J. F., Dow, S. J., & Westerhoff, C. (2010). Does our choice of substance-related terms influence perceptions of treatment need? An empirical investigation with two commonly used terms. *Journal of Drug Issues, 40*, 805–818.

Kelly, J. F., & Westerhoff, C. (2010). Does it matter how we refer to individuals with substance-related problems? A randomized study with two commonly used terms. *International Journal of Drug Policy, 21*, 202–207.

Kelly, K. (2020). Prohibition was America's first war on drugs. Retrieved from www.teenvogue.com/story/prohibition-war-on-drugs

Kennedy, R. (1997), *Race, crime and law*. Cambridge, MA: Harvard University Press.

Kepple, N. J., & Freisthler, B. (2012). Exploring the ecological association between crime and medical marijuana dispensaries. *Journal of Studies on Alcohol and Drugs, 73*(4), 523–530.

Kerrison, E. M., & Sewell, A. A. (2020). Negative illness feedbacks: High-frisk policing reduces civilian reliance on ER services. *Health Services Research*. https://doi.org/10.1111/1475-6773.13554

King, R.S. & Mauer, M. (2006). The war on marijuana: The transformation of the war on drugs in the 1990s. *Harm Reduction Journal* 3(6): 1–17.

Kittrie, N. (1971). *The right to be different: Deviance and enforced therapy*. New York: New York Univerity Press.

Kjellberg, H., & Olson, D. (2017). Joint markets: How adjacent markets influence the formation of regulated markets. *Marketing Theory, 17*(1), 95–123.

Klag, S., O'Callaghan, F., & Creed, P. (2005). The use of legal coercion in the treatment of substance abusers: An overview and critical analysis of thirty years of research. *Substance Use & Misuse, 40*(12), 1777–1795. https://doi.org/10.1080/10826080500260891

Klocke, B.V., & Muschert, G. W. (2010). A hybrid model of moral panics: Synthesizing the theory and practice of moral panic research. *Sociology Compass, 4*, 295–309.

Koch, D. W., Lee, J., & Lee, K. (2016). Coloring the war on drugs: Arrest disparities in Black, Brown, and white. *Race Social Problems, 8*, 313–325. https://doi.org/10.1007/s12552-016-9185-6

Korf, D. J. (2020). Coffeeshops in the Netherlands: Regulating the front door and the back door. In T. Decorte, S., Lenton, & C. Wilkins (Eds.), *Legalizing cannabis: Experiences, lessons and scenarios* (pp. 285–306). London: Routledge.

Kraska, P. B. (2001). *Militarizing the American criminal justice system: The changing roles of the armed forces and the police*. Boston, MA: Northeastern University Press.

Kraska, P. B. (2006). Criminal justice theory: Toward legitimacy and an infrastructure. *Justice Quarterly, 23*(2), 167–185.

Krissman, F. (2016). America's largest cannabis labor market. *Humboldt State University Working Paper.*

Kroon, E., Kuhns, L., & Cousijn, J. (2021). The short-term and long-term effects of cannabis on cognition: Recent advances in the field. *Current Opinion in Psychology, 38*, 49–55.

Kroon, E., Kuhns, L., Hoch, E., & Cousijn, J. (2020). Heavy cannabis use, dependence and the brain: A clinical perspective. *Addiction, 115*(3), 559–572.

Ksir, C., & Hart, C. (2016). Cannabis and psychosis: A critical overview of the relationship. *Current Psychiatry Reports, 18*(2), 12–23.

Lake, S., Kerr, T., Werb, D., Haines-Saah, R., Fischer, B., & Thomas, G. (2019). Guidelines for public health and safety metrics to evaluate the potential harms and benefits of cannabis regulation in Canada. *Drug and Alcohol Review, 38*(6), 606–621.

Lammy, D. (2017). *The Lammy Review: An independent review into the treatment of, and outcomes for, Black, Asian and minority ethnic individuals in the criminal justice system*. London: Lammy Review.

Laub, J. H. (2004). The life course of criminology in the United States: The American Society of Criminology presidential address, 2003. *Criminology, 42*, 1–25.

Lawson, D. (2020). *Flowers from the devil: An American opiate crisis, the criminalization of marijuana, and the triumph of the prohibition state, 1840–1940*. Graduate student theses. Missoula, MT: University of Montana.

Lawson, R. A., & Nesbit, T. M. (2013). Alchian and Allen revisited: Law enforcement and the price of weed. *Atlantic Economic Journal, 41*, 363–370.

Lemert, E. (1951). *Social pathology*. New York, NY: McGraw-Hill.

Leshner, A. (1997). Addiction is a brain disease, and it matters. *Science, 278*(5335), 45–47.

Levengood, T. W., Yoon, G. H., Davoust, M. J., Ogden, S. N., Marshall, B. D., Cahill, S. R., & Bazzi, A. R. (2021). Supervised injection facilities as harm reduction: A systematic review. *American Journal of Preventive Medicine, 61*(5), 738–749.

Levine, H. G. (2003). Global drug prohibition: Its uses and crises. *International Journal of Drug Policy, 14*, 145–153.

Levine, H. G., & Small, D. P. (2008). *Marijuana arrest crusade: Racial bias and police policy in New York City, 1997–2007*. New York: New York Civil Liberties Union.

Levine, G. H., & Siegel, L. (2015). Marijuana madness: The scandal of New York City's racist marijuana possession arrests. In J. A. Eterno (Ed.), *The New York City police department: The impact of its policies and practices* (pp. 117–161). New York: CRC Press.

Levinson-King, R. (2019, December 19). Why Canada's cannabis bubble burst. *BBC News*. Retrieved from www.bbc.com/news/world-us-canada-50664578?fbclid=IwAR2DSg2tefAFmCSwYNaENWv4nlOkFob43xBFCd7MVd-zt_krwgf_1ke4ymU

Lewis, H. (2019). Brexit and the failure of journalism. *The Atlantic*. Retrieved from www.theatlantic.com/international/archive/2019/10/brexit-journalism-failure/600580/

Lewis, M. (2015). *The biology of desire: Why addiction is not a disease*. Toronto: Doubleday Canada.

Leyton M. (2019). Cannabis legalization: Did we make a mistake? Update 2019. *Journal of Psychiatry & Neuroscience, 44*(5), 291–293. https://doi.org/10.1503/jpn.190136

Ligaya, A. (2019, April 20). Six months after legalization, high prices and supply issues boost illicit pot market. *Global News*. Retrieved from www.thestar.com/ business/2019/04/20/ six-months-after-legalization-high-prices-and-supply-issues-boost-illicit-pot-market. html.

Lilly, R. J., Cullen, F.T., & Ball, R. A. (2015). *Criminological theory: Context and consequences* (6th ed.). Thousand Oaks, CA: Sage Publications.

Lindesmith, A. R. (1938a). A sociological theory of drug addiction. *American Journal of Sociology, 43*(4), 593–613.

Lindesmith, A. R. (1938b). Argot of the underworld drug addict. *Journal of Criminal Law & Criminology, 29*, 261–273.

Link, B.G. & Phelan, J.C. (2001). Conceptualizing stigma. *Annual Review of Sociology*, *27*(1), 363–385.

Lira, M. C., Heeren, T. C., Buczek, M., Blanchette, J. G., Smart, R., Pacula, R. L. & Naimi, T. S. (2021). Trends in cannabis involvement and risk of alcohol involvement in motor vehicle crash fatalities in the United States, 2000-2018. *American Journal of Public Health, 111*, 1976–1985. https://doi.org/10.2105/AJPH.2021.306466

Livingston, J., & Boyd, J. (2010). Correlates and consequences of internalized stigma for people living with mental illness: A systematic review and meta-analysis. *Social Science and Medicine, 71*, 2150–2161.

Logan, W.A. (2014). After the Cheering Stopped: Decriminalization and Legalism's Limits. *Cornell Journal of Law and Public Policy*, 24: 319–351.

Lu, R., Willits, D., Stohr, M. K., Makin, D., Snyder, J., Lovrich, N., Meize, M., Stanton, D., Wu, G., & Hemmens, C. (2021). The cannabis effect on crime: Time-series analysis of crime in Colorado and Washington State. *Justice Quarterly, 38*(4), 565–595.

Luciano, M., Sampogna, G., Del Vecchio, V., Pingani, L., Palumbo, C., De Rosa, C., Catapano, F., & Fiorillo, A. (2014). Use of coercive measures in mental health practice and its impact on outcome: A critical review. *Expert Review of Neurotherapeutics, 14*(2), 131–141. https://doi.org/10.1586/14737175.2014.874286

Lutters, W. G., & Ackerman, M. S. (1996). Social relations in complex environments: An introduction to the Chicago School of Sociology. *UCI-ICS Social Worlds Lab #96–1*. Retrieved from http://user pages.umbc.edu/~lutters/pubs/1996_SWLNote96–1_ Lutters,Ackerman.pdf

Luty, J. (2016). The beginning of the end of prohibition: The politics of drug addiction. *BJPsych Advances, 22*, 242–250.

Lynch, M. (2012). Theorizing the role of the "war on drugs" in US punishment. *Theoretical Criminology, 16*(2), 175–199.

Lynch, M. J., & Michalowski, R. (2010). *A primer in radical criminology*. New York: Harrow and Heston.

MacCoun, R., & Reuter, P. (2001). *Drug war heresies: Learning from other vices, times and places*. Cambridge: Cambridge University Press.

MacCoun, R., Pacula, R. L., Chriqui, J. F., Harris, K., & Reuter, P. (2009). Do citizens know whether their state has decriminalized marijuana? Assessing the perceptual component of deterrence theory. *Review of Law and Economics, 5*, 347–371.

MacCoun, R. J. (2011). What can we learn from the Dutch cannabis coffeeshop system? *Addiction, 106*, 1899–1910. https://doi.org/10.1111/j.1360-0443.2011.03572.x

Mahamad, S., Wadsworth, E., Rynard, V., Goodman, S., & Hammond, D. (2020). Availability, retail price and potency of legal and illegal cannabis in Canada after recreational cannabis legalisation. *Drug and Alcohol Review, 39*, 337–346. https://doi.org/10.1111/ dar.13069

Males, M., & Buchen, L. (2014). *Reforming marijuana laws: Which approach best reduces the harms of criminalization? A five-state analysis*. San Francisco, CA: Centre on Juvenile and Criminal Justice.

Manderson, D. (1993). *From mr sin to mr big: A history of Australian drug laws*. Melbourne: Oxford University Press.

Manderson, D. (1999). Symbolism and racism in drug history and policy. *Drug and Alcohol Review, 18*(2), 179–186.

Marks, R. F. (1970). Book review: *John Kaplan, Marijuana: The new prohibition. Valparaiso University Law Review, 5*(1), 192–195.

Marqusee, M. (2005). *Wicked messenger: Bob Dylan and the 1960s*. New York: Seven Stories Press.

Martins, M. (2021). News media representation on EU immigration before Brexit: The "Euro-Ripper" case. *Humanities & Social Sciences Communications, 8*, 11. https://doi.org/10.1057/s41599-020-00687-5

Maruna, S. (2001). *Making good: How ex-convicts reform and rebuild their lives*. Washington, DC: American Psychological Association.

Maruna, S., Matravers, A., & King, A. (2004). Disowning our shadow: A psychoanalytic approach to understanding punitive public attitudes. *Deviant Behavior, 25*, 277–299.

Mastrofski, S. D. (2004). Controlling street-level police discretion. *Annals of the American Academy of Political and Social Science, 593*, 100–118.

May, T., & Hough, M. (2001). Illegal dealings: The impact of low-level police enforcement on drug markets. *European Journal on Criminal Policy and Research, 9*(2), 137–162.

Mazerolle, L., Soole, D.W. and Rombouts, S. (2007). Street-level drug law enforcement: a meta-analytic review. *Campbell Systematic Reviews, 3*, 1–47.

McCormick, C. (2022). Use of a visual criminology Facebook group in blended instruction. In J. Wheeldon (Ed.), *Visual criminology: From history and methods to critique and policy translation* (pp. 190–210). London: Routledge.

McLuhan, M. (1964). *Understanding media: The extensions of man*. New York: McGraw-Hill.

McWilliams, J. C. (1990). *The protectors: Harry J. Anslinger and the Federal Bureau of Narcotics, 1930–1962*. Newark, CA: University of Delaware Press.

McWilliams, J. C. (1992). Through the past darkly: the politics and policies of America's drug war. In W. O. Walker, III (Ed.), *Drug control policy: essays in historical and comparative perspective* (pp. 5–41). University Park: Pennsylvania State University Press.

Mead, G. H. (1934). *Mind, self, and society*. Chicago, IL: University of Chicago Press.

Meeks, D. (2006). Police militarization in urban areas: The obscure war against the underclass. *Black Scholar, 35*(4), 33–41.

Meier, M. H. Caspi, A., Ambler, A. Harrington, H., Houts, R., Keefe, R. S. E., McDonald, K., Ward, A., Poulton, R., & Moffitt, T. E. (2012). Persistent cannabis users show neuropsychological decline from childhood to midlife. *Proceedings of the National Academy of Sciences, 109*(40), E2657–E2664. https://doi.org/10.1073/pnas.1206820109

Meier, R. S., Kennedy, L., & Sacco, V. (2001). *The process and structure of crime: Criminal events and crime analysis*. New Brunswick, NJ: Transaction.

Meija, A. (2020). How bad ganja be? The Indian Hemp Drugs Commission's discourse on cannabis. Retrieved from https://blogs.ed.ac.uk/digitalhumanities2020/research/the-indian-hemp-drugs-commissions-discourse-on-cannabis/

Mejía, A., & Csete, J. (2016). The economics of the drug war: Unaccounted costs, lost lives, and missed opportunities. Retrieved from www.unodc.org/documents/ungass2016/Contributions/Civil/OpenSociety/The_Economics_of_the_Drug_War_-_Unaccounted_Costs_Lost_Lives_Missed_Opportunities.pdf

Melamed, J. (2015). Racial capitalism. *Critical Ethnic Studies, 1*, 76–85.

Meneses, R. A., & Akers, R. L. (2011). A comparison of four general theories of crime and deviance: Marijuana use among American and Bolivian university students. *International Criminal Justice Review, 21*(4), 333–352. https://doi.org/10.1177/1057567711408302

Mennis, J. (2020). Trends in adolescent treatment admissions for marijuana in the United States, 2008–2017. *Preventing Chronic Disease, 17*, E145. https://doi.org/10.5888/pcd17.200156

Mennis, J., & Stahler, G. J. (2020). Adolescent treatment admissions for marijuana following recreational legalization in Colorado and Washington. *Drug and Alcohol Dependence, 210*, 107960. https://doi.org/10.1016/j.drugalcdep.2020.107960

Mennis, J., Stahler, G. J., & Mason, M. J. (2021). Treatment admissions for opioids, cocaine, and methamphetamines among adolescents and emerging adults after legalization of recreational marijuana. *Journal of Substance Abuse Treatment*. https://doi.org/10.1016/j.jsat.2020.108228.

Mennis, J., Stahler, G. J., & McKeon, T. P. (2021). Young adult cannabis use disorder treatment admissions declined as past month cannabis use increased in the US: An analysis of states by year, 2008–2017. *Addictive Behaviors, 123*, 107049.

Merton, R. K. (1938). Social structure and anomie. *American Sociological Review, 22*, 635–659.

Mikuriya, T. H. (1969). Marijuana in medicine: Past, present and future. *California Medicine, 110*(1), 34–40.

Mills, C. W. (1959). *The sociological imagination*. Oxford: Oxford University Press.

Mills, J. H. (2003). *Cannabis Britannica: Empire, trade, and prohibition 1800–1928*. New York: Oxford University Press.

Miron, J. (2017). "How to kill the marijuana black market." The Denver Post (August 11th). Retrieved from: www.denverpost.com/2017/08/11/how-to-kill-the-marijuana-blackmarket/

Miron, J. A., & Zwiebel, J. (1991). Alcohol consumption during prohibition. *American Economic Review, 81*(2), 242–247.

Miron, J. A., & Zwiebel, J. (1995). The economic case against drug prohibition. *Journal of Economic Perspectives, 9*(4), 175–192.

Mitchell, O., & Caudy, M. S. (2017). Race differences in drug offending and drug distribution arrests. *Crime & Delinquency, 63*(2), 91–112.

Mize, J. (2020). Reefer reparations. *Willamette Law Review, 3*(2), 1–35.

Moeller, K. (2016) Temporal transaction patterns in an open-air cannabis market. *Police Practice and Research, 17*(1), 37–50.

Moeller, K., & Hesse, M. (2013). Drug market disruption and systemic violence: Cannabis markets in Copenhagen. *European Journal of Criminology, 10*(2), 206–221.

Moffitt, T. E. (1993). Life-course-persistent and adolescent-limited anti-social behavior: A developmental taxonomy. *Psychological Review, 100*, 674–701.

Monaghan, M. (2014). Drug policy governance in the UK: Lessons from changes to and debates concerning the classification of cannabis under the 1971 Misuse of Drugs Act. *International Journal of Drug Policy, 25*(5), 1025–1030. http://doi.org/10.1016/j.drugpo.2014.02.001

Monaghan, M., Wincup, E., & Hamilton, I. (2021). Scandalous decisions: Explaining shifts in UK medicinal cannabis policy. *Addiction, 116*, 1925–1933. https://doi.org/10.1111/add.15350

Mooney, L. J., Zhu, Y., Yoo, C., Valdez, J., Moino, K., Liao, J. Y., & Hser, Y. I. (2018). Reduction in cannabis use and functional status in physical health, mental health, and cognition. *Journal of Neuroimmune Pharmacology, 13*(4), 479–487.

Moore, A. (2015). The arc of reform? What the era of prohibition may tell us about the future of immigration reform. *Georgetown Immigration Law Journal, 28*(3), 521–554.

Morris, J. (2018, September). Does legalizing marijuana reduce crime? *Reason Foundation*. Retrieved from https://reason.org/wp-content/uploads/does-legalizing -marijuana-reduce-crime.pdf

Morris, R. G., TenEyck, M., Barnes, J. C., & Kovandzic, T. V. (2014). The effect of medical marijuana laws on crime: Evidence from state panel data, 1990–2006. *PloS One, 9*(3), e92816.

Murch, D. (2015). Crack in Los Angeles: Crisis, militarization, and Black response to the late twentieth-century war on drugs. *Journal of American History, 102*(1), 162–173.

Murray, G. F. (1986). Marijuana use and social control: A sociological perspective on deviance. *International Journal of Addiction, 21*(6), 657–669.

Murray, R. M., Englund, A., Abi-Dargham, A., Lewis, D. A., Di Forti, M., Davies, C., Sherif, M., McGuire, P., & D'Souza. D. C. (2017). Cannabis-associated psychosis: Neural substrate and clinical impact. *Neuropharmacology, 124*(15), 89–104.

Myran, D. T., Tanuseputro, P., Auger, N., Konikoff, L., Talarico, R., & Finkelstein, Y. (2022). Edible cannabis legalization and unintentional poisonings in children. *New England Journal of Medicine, 387*(8), 757–759.

Nelson, E.-U. E. (2021). "I take it to relax … and chill": Perspectives on cannabis use from marginalized Nigerian young adults. *Addiction Research & Theory, 29*(6), 490–499. https://doi.org/10.1080/16066359.2021.1895125

Newhart, M., & Dolphin, W. (2019). *The medicalization of marijuana: Legitimacy, stigma, and the patient experience.* New York: Routledge.

Niveau G & Dang C. (2003) Cannabis and violent crime. *Medicine, Science and the Law*, 43(2), 115–121.

Nussbaum, A., Thurstone, C., McGarry, L., Walker, B., & Sabel, A. L. (2015). Use and diversion of medical marijuana among adults admitted to inpatient psychiatry. *American Journal of Drug and Alcohol Abuse, 41*(2), 166–172.

Nye, F. I. (1958). *Family relationships and delinquent behavior.* John Wiley.

Nyika, L., & Murray-Orr, A. (2017). Critical race theory–social constructivist bricolage: A health-promoting schools research methodology. *Health Education Journal, 76*(4), 432–441.

O'Guinn BJ. (2022). Police training and accountability: a remedy or an impediment for reducing unarmed police shootings? *Crime & Delinquency*. February 2022. doi:10.1177/00111287221074959

Oldfield, K., Evans, S., Braithwaite, I., & Newton-Howe, G. (2021). Don't make a hash of it! A thematic review of the literature relating to outcomes of cannabis regulatory change. *Drugs: Education, Prevention and Policy*. https://doi.org/10.1080/09687637.2021.1901855

Olmo, R. D. (1991). The hidden face of drugs. *Social Justice, 18*(4 (46), 10–48.

Orcutt, J. D. (1987). Differential association and marijuana use: A closer look at Sutherland (with a little help from Becker). *Criminology, 25*, 341–358.

Osborne, G. B., & Fogel, C. (2017). Perspectives on cannabis legalization among Canadian recreational users. *Contemporary Drug Problems, 44*(1), 12–31.

O'Shaughnessy, W. (1842). *The Bengal dispensatory and companion to pharmacopoeia.* London: Allen.

Owen, D. (2017). *The state of technology in global newsrooms.* Washington, DC: International Center for Journalists. Retrieved from www.icfj.org/sites/default/files/ICFJTechSurveyFINAL.pdf

Owen, D. (2019). The Past Decade and Future of Political Media: The Ascendance of Social Media. OpenMind, Georgetown. www.bbvaopenmind.com/en/multimedia/audios/the-past-decade-and-future-of-political-media-the-ascendance-of-social-media

Owusu-Bempah, A., & Luscombe, A. (2021). Race, cannabis and the Canadian war on drugs: An examination of cannabis arrest data by race in five cities. *International Journal of Drug Policy*, 91. https://doi.org/10.1016/j.drugpo.2020.102937

Pacula, R. L., Powell, D., Heaton, P., & Sevigny, E. L. (2015). Assessing the effects of medical marijuana laws on marijuana use: The devil is in the details. *Journal of Policy Analysis and Management*, *34*(1), 7–31.

Page, J., & Soss, J. (2021). The predatory dimensions of criminal justice. *Science*, *374*(6565), 291–294. https://doi.org/10.1126/science.abj7782

Papinczak, Z. E., Connor, J. P., Feeney, G., Harnett, P., Young, R. M., & Gullo, M. J. (2019). Testing the biosocial cognitive model of substance use in cannabis users referred to treatment. *Drug and Alcohol Dependence*, *194*, 216–224.

Pardal, M. (2022). *The cannabis social club*. London: Routledge.

Paris, E. (2000). *Long shadows: Truth, lies, and history*. Toronto: Vintage Canada.

Parker, H. (2005). Normalization as a barometer: Recreational drug use and the consumption of leisure by younger Britons. *Addiction Research and Theory*, *13*(3), 205–215.

Parker, H., Williams, L., & Aldridge, J. (2002). The normalization of sensible recreational drug use: Further evidence from the N.W. longitudinal study. *Sociology*, *36*(4), 941–964.

Parker, H. J., Aldridge, J., & Measham, F. (1998). *Illegal leisure: The normalization of adolescent recreational drug use*. London: Routledge.

Pearlson, G. D., Stevens, M. C., & D'Souza, D. C. (2021). Cannabis and driving. *Frontiers in Psychiatry*, *12*.

Pearson, N. T., & Berry, J. H. (2019). Cannabis and Psychosis Through the Lens of DSM-5. *International Journal of Environmental Research and Public Health*, *16*(21), 4149–4163.

Pedersen, W., & Skardhamar, T. (2010). Cannabis and crime: Findings from a longitudinal study. *Addiction*, *105*, 109–118.

Pembleton, M. R. (2017). *Containing addiction: The Federal Bureau of Narcotics and the origins of America's global drug war*. Amherst, MA: University of Massachusetts Press.

Pepinsky, H. (1991). The peacemaking choice. Peacemaking in criminology and criminal justice. In H. E. Pepinsky & R. Quinney (Eds.), *Criminology as peacemaking* (pp. 300–304). Chicago, IL: Illinois University Press.

Pepinsky, H. E., & Quinney, R. (Eds.). (1991). *Criminology as peacemaking*. Chicago, IL: Illinois University Press.

Pesta, G. B., Ramos, J., Ranson, J. A., Singer, A., & Blomberg, T. G. (2016). *Translational criminology, research and public policy: Final summary report*. Florida: College of Criminology and Criminal Justice, Florida State University.

Philbin, M. M., Mauro, P. M., Santaella-Tenorio, J., Mauro, C. M., Kinnard, E. N., Cerda, M., & Martins, S. S. (2019). Associations between state-level policy liberalism, cannabis use, and cannabis use disorder from 2004 to 2012: Looking beyond medical cannabis law status. *International Journal of Drug Policy*, *65*, 97–103. https://doi.org/10.1016/j.drugpo.2018.10.010

Pinard, M. (2010). Collateral consequences of criminal convictions: Confronting issues of race and dignity. *New York University Law Review*, *85*, 457–534.

Pope Jr., H., & Yurgelun-Todd, D. (1996). The residual cognitive effects of heavy marijuana use in college students. *JAMA*, *275*(7), 521–527.

Pozzulo, J., Bennell, C., & Forth, A. (2015). *Forensic psychology* (4th ed.). Toronto: Pearson.

Pozzulo, J., Bennell, C., & Forth, A. (2021). *Forensic psychology*. Psychology Press.

Price, T., Parkes, T., & Malloch, M. (2021). Discursive struggles' between criminal justice sanctions and health interventions for people who use drugs: A qualitative exploration of diversion policy and practice in Scotland. *Drugs: Education, Prevention and Policy*, 28(2), 118–126. https://doi.org/10.1080/09687637.2020.1775180

Puras, D., & Hannah, J. (2017). Reasons for drug policy reform: Prohibition enables systemic human rights abuses and undermines public health. *British Medical Journal, 356*, i6586.

Queirolo, R. (2020). The effects of recreational cannabis legalization might depend upon the policy model. *World Psychiatry, 19*, 195–196. https://doi.org/10.1002/wps.20742

Queirolo, R., Rossel, C., Álvarez, E., & Repetto, L. (2019). Why Uruguay legalized marijuana? The open window of public insecurity. *Addiction, 114*(7), 1313–1321. https://doi.org/10.1111/add.14523

Quinney, R. (1970). *The Social Reality of Crime*. United States: Transaction Publishers.

Rafter, N. H. (2008). *The criminal brain: Understanding biological theories of crime*. New York: New York University Press.

Raine, A. (1993). *The psychopathology of crime: Criminal behavior as a clinical disorder*. Academic Press.

Raine, A. et al. (1993). Features of borderline personality and violence. *Journal of Clinical Psychology, 49*(2), 277–281.

Raine, A. (2013). *The anatomy of violence: Biological roots of crime*. New York: Pantheon Books.

Raine, A., & Buschbaum, M. S. (1996). Violence, brain imaging, and neuropsychology. In D. M. Stoff & R. B. Cairns (Eds.), *Aggression and violence: Genetic, neurobiological, and biological perspectives* (pp. 195–218). New York: Psychology Press.

Ramaekers, J. G., Robbe, H. W. J., & O'Hanlon, J. (2000). Marijuana, alcohol and actual driving performance. *Human Psychopharmacology: Clinical and Experimental, 15*(7): 551–558.

Reid, M. (2020). A qualitative review of cannabis stigmas at the twilight of prohibition. *Journal of Cannabis Research, 2*(46). https://doi.org/10.1186/s42238-020-00056-8

Reinarman, C. (2009). Cannabis policies and user practices: Market separation, price, potency, and accessibility in Amsterdam and San Francisco. *International Journal of Drug Policy, 39*, 28–37.

Reinarman, C., Cohen, P. D., & Kaal, H. L. (2004). The limited relevance of drug policy: Cannabis in Amsterdam and in San Francisco. *American Journal of Public Health, 94*(5), 836–842. https://doi.org/10.2105/AJPH.94.5.836

Reinarman, C., & Levine, H. G. (1997). *Crack in America: Demon drugs and social justice*. Berkeley, CA: University of California Press.

Ritter, A. (2021). *Drug Policy*. Routledge: London.

Ritzer, G., & Stepnisky, J. (2017). *Sociological theory*. Thousand Oaks, CA: Sage.

Robinson, M. (2004). Why crime? An integrated systems theory of antisocial behavior. Upper Saddle River, NJ: Pearson Prentice Hall

Robinson, M. B., & Scherlen, R. (2014). *Lies, damned lies, and drug war statistics: A critical analysis of claims made by the Office of National Drug Control Policy*. Albany, NY: State University of New York Press.

Rodríguez-Gómez, D. & Bermeo, M. J. (2020). The educational nexus to the war on drugs: A systematic review. *Journal on Education in Emergencies, 6*(1), 18–56.

Sagar, K. A., & Gruber, S. A. (2018). Marijuana matters: Reviewing the impact of marijuana on cognition, brain structure and function, & exploring policy implications and barriers to research. *International Review of Psychiatry, 30*(3), 251–267.

Saitz, R., Miller, S. C., Fiellin, D. A., & Rosenthal, R. N. (2020). Recommended use of terminology in addiction medicine. *Journal of Addictive Medicine, 15*(1), 3–7. https://doi.org/10.1097/ADM.0000000000000673

Sampson, R., & Laub, J. H. (1993). Crime in the making*: Pathways and turning points through life*. Cambridge, MA: Harvard University Press.

Sanchez, H. F., Orr, M. F., Wang, A., Cano, M. Á., Vaughan, E. L., Harvey, L. M., Essa, S., Torbati, A., Clark, U. S., Fagundes, C. P., & de Dios, M. A. (2020). Racial and gender inequities in the implementation of a cannabis criminal justice diversion program in a large and diverse metropolitan county of the USA. *Drug Alcohol Dependence, 216*, 108316. https://doi.org/10.1016/j.drugalcdep.2020.108316

Sandberg, S. (2008). Black drug dealers in a white welfare state: Cannabis dealing and street capital in Norway. *British Journal of Criminology, 48*. https://doi.org/10.1093/bjc/azn041

Sandberg, S. (2012a). The importance of culture for cannabis markets: Towards an economic sociology of illegal drug markets. *British Journal of Criminology, 52*(6), 1133–1151. https://doi.org/10.1093/bjc/azs031

Sandberg, S. (2012b). Is cannabis use normalized, celebrated or neutralized? Analysing talk as action. *Addiction Research & Theory, 20*(5), 372–381. https://doi.org/10.3109/16066359.2011.638147

Sandberg, S. (2013). Cannabis culture: A stable subculture in a changing world. *Criminology & Criminal Justice, 13*(1), 63–79.

Sanders, C. (2013). Learning from experience: Recollections of working with Howard S. Becker. *Symbolic Interaction, 36*(2), 216–228.

Santaella-Tenorio, J., Mauro, C. M., Wall, M. M., Kim, J. H., Cerdá, M., Keyes, K. M., ... & Martins, S. S. (2017). US traffic fatalities, 1985–2014, and their relationship to medical marijuana laws. *American Journal of Public Health, 107*(2), 336–342.

Savitz, L., Turner, S.H., & Dickman, T. (1977). The Origins of Scientific Criminology: Franz Gall as the First Criminologist, in R.F. Meier (ed.) *Theory in Criminology* (pp. 41–56). Beverly Hills, CA: Sage.

Schirmann, K. (2016, August 2). What it's like to be a "trim bitch" on an illegal weed farm. *Broadly Vice*. www.vice.com/en/article/qkggyp/what-its-like-to-be-a-trim-bitch-on-an-illegal-weed-farm-women-in-cannabis

Schoeler, T., Theobald, D., Pingault, J., Farrington, D., Jennings, W., Piquero, A., ... Bhattacharyya, S. (2016). Continuity of cannabis use and violent offending over the life course. *Psychological Medicine, 46*(8), 1663–1677.

Schur, E. (1965). *Crimes without victims. Deviant behavior and public policy: Abortion, homosexuality, and drug addiction*. Englewood Cliffs, NJ: Prentice-Hall.

Schwabe, A. L., Hansen, C. J., Hyslop, R. M., & McGlaughlin, M. E. (2019, March 28). Research grade marijuana supplied by the National Institute on Drug Abuse is genetically divergent from commercially available cannabis. *BioRxiv*. https://doi.org/10.1101/592725

Schwabe, A. L., & McGlaughlin, M. E. (2019). Genetic tools weed out misconceptions of strain reliability in *Cannabis sativa*: Implications for a budding industry. *Journal of Cannabis Research, 1*(1), 3.

Scott, J. G., Matuschka, L., Niemelä, S., Miettunen, J., Emmerson, B., & Mustonen, A. (2018). Evidence of a causal relationship between smoking tobacco and schizophrenia spectrum disorders. *Frontiers in Psychiatry*, 607

Seddon, T. (2007). The regulation of heroin: Drug policy and social change in early twentieth-century Britain. *International Journal of Social Law, 35*, 143–156.

Seddon, T. (2020). Immoral in principle, unworkable in practice: Cannabis law reform, the Beatles and the Wootton report. *British Journal of Criminology, 60*(6), 1567–1584.

Seddon, T., & Floodgate, W. (2020). *Regulating cannabis: A global review and future directions*. London: Palgrave Macmillan.

Sellin, T. (1938). *Culture, conflict and crime*. New York: Social Science Research Council.

Serin, R., Forth, A., Brown, S., Nunes, K., Bennell, C., & Pozzulo, J. (2011). *Psychology of criminal behavior*. Toronto: Pearson.

Sewell, A. A. (2020). Policing the block: Pandemics, systemic racism, and the blood of America. *City and Community, 19*(3), 496–505. https://doi.org /10.1111/cico.12517

Sewell, A. A., Feldman, J. M., Ray, R., Gilbert, K. L., Jefferson, K. A., & Lee, H. (2021). Illness spillovers of lethal police violence: The significance of gendered marginalization. *Ethnic and Racial Studies, 44*(7), 1089–1114. https://doi.org/10.1080/01419870.2020.1781913

Sewell, A. A., & Jefferson, K. A. (2016). Collateral damage: The health effects of invasive police encounters in New York City. *Journal of Urban Health, 93*(1), 42–67.

Sewell, A. R., Poling, J., & Sofuoglu, M. (2009). The effects of cannabis compared with alcohol on driving. *American Journal of Addiction, 18*(3), 185–193.

Shamir, R., & Hacker, D. (2001). Colonialism's civilizing mission: The case of the Indian Hemp Drug Commission. *Law & Social Inquiry, 26*(2), 435–461.

Shanahan, M., Hughes, C., & McSweeney, T. (2017). Police diversion for cannabis offences: Assessing outcomes and cost-effectiveness. In *Trends & issues in crime and criminal justice No. 532.* (pp. 1-13). Canberra: Australian Institute of Criminology.

Sheehan, B. E., Grucza, R. A., & Plunk, A. D. (2021). Association of racial disparity of cannabis possession arrests among adults and youths with statewide cannabis decriminalization and legalization. *JAMA Health Forum, 2*(10), e213435. https://doi.org/10.1001/jamahealthforum.2021.3435

Sherman, L. W., & Strang, H. (2007). *Restorative justice: The evidence.* London: Smith Institute.

Shi, Y., Lenzi, M., and An, R. (2015). Cannabis liberalization and adolescent cannabis use: A cross-national study in 38 countries. *PLoS One, 10*(11), e0143562. https://doi.org/10.1371/journal.pone.0143562

Shiner, M. (2015). Drug policy reform and the reclassification of cannabis in England and Wales: A cautionary tale. *International Journal of Drug Policy, 26*(7), 696–704.

Shiner, M., Carre, Z., Delsol, R., & Eastwood, N. (2018). *The colour of injustice: "Race," drugs and law enforcement in England and Wales.* London: Release Press.

Small, S. (1994). *Racialised Barriers: The Black Experience in the United States and England in the 1980's.* London: Routledge.

Smart, A. (2019, October 7). Trend of low potency products expected in Canadian legal recreational market. *CBC News*. Retrieved from www.cbc.ca/news/canada/british-columbia/trend-of-low-potency-products-expected-in-legal-recreational-cannabis-market-1.4853981

Smart, R., Caulkins, J. P., Kilmer, B., Davenport, S., & Midgette, G. (2017). Variation in cannabis potency and prices in a newly legal market: Evidence from 30 million cannabis sales in Washington state. *Addiction, 112*(12), 2167–2177.

Smiley, E. (2016). Marijuana & other drugs: Legalize or decriminalize. *Arizona Journal of International and Comparative Law, 33*, 825.

Smith, D. E. (2011). The evolution of addiction medicine as a medical specialty. *Virtual Mentor, 13*(12), 900–905.

Smith, J., & Merolla, D. (2020). Puff, puff, pass: The effect of racial prejudice on white Americans' attitudes towards marijuana legalization. *Du Bois Review: Social Science Research on Race, 17*(1), 189–200.

Smith, R.F. (1917). *Report of investigation in the State of Texas, particularly along the Mexican border, of the traffic in, and consumption of the drug generally known as "Indian Hemp," or Cannabis indica, known in Mexico and states bordering on the Rio Grande River as "Marihuana"; sometimes also referred to as "Rosa Maria," or "Juanita."* Washington, DC: US Department of Agriculture.

Solomon, R. (2020). Racism and its effect on cannabis research. *Cannabis and Cannabinoid Research, 5*(1), 2–5.

Solomon, R., Single, E. W., & Erickson, P. G. (1983). Legal considerations in cannabis possession policy. *Canadian Public Policy, 9*, 419–433.

Spicer. J. (2018). "That's their brand, their business": How police officers are interpreting county lines. *Policing and Society, 29*(8), 873–886. https://doi.org/10.1080/10439463.2018.1445742

Spicer, J. (2021). The policing of cuckooing in "County Lines" drug dealing: An ethnographic study of an amplification spiral. *British Journal of Criminology, 61*(5), 1390–1406.

Spicer, J., Moyle, L., & Coomber, R. (2020). The variable and evolving nature of "cuckooing" as a form of criminal exploitation in street level drug markets. *Trends in Organized Crime, 23*, 301–323. https://doi.org/10.1007/s12117-019-09368-5

Spivakovsky, C., Seear, K., & Carter, A. (Eds.) (2018). *Critical perspectives on coercive interventions: Law, medicine and society*. Abingdon: Routledge.

Spriggs, B. C. (2018, July 27). Missing big opportunity in "craft cannabis," say critics. *The Tyee*. Retrieved from https://thetyee.ca/News/2018/07/27/B.C.-Missing-Cannabis-Opportunity/

Stampp, K. (1956). *The Peculiar Institution: Slavery in the Ante-Bellum South*. New York: Alfred A. Knopf.

Stevens, A. (2007). When two dark figures collide: Evidence and discourse on drug-related crime. *Critical Social Policy, 27*(1), 77–99. https://doi.org/10.1177/0261018307072208

Stevens, A. (2011). *Drugs, crime and public health: The political economy of drug policy*. London: Routledge.

Stevens, A. (2012). The ethics and effectiveness of coerced treatment of people who use drugs. *Human Rights and Drugs, 2*(1), 7–16.

Stevens, A. (2019). Is policy "liberalization" associated with higher odds of adolescent cannabis use? A re-analysis of data from 38 countries. *International Journal on Drug Policy, 66*(3), 94–99.

Stevens, A., Hughes, C. E., Hulme, S., & Cassidy, R. (2021). Classifying alternative approaches for simple drug possession: A two-level taxonomy. *Northern Kentucky Law Review, 48*(2), 337–353.

Stevens, A., Hughes, C. E., Hulme, S., & Cassidy, R. (2019). Depenalisation, diversion and decriminalisation: A realist review and programme theory of alternatives to criminalisation for simple drug possession. *European Journal of Criminology*. https://doi.org/10.1177/1477370819887514

Stevens, A., & Zampini, G. F. (2018). Drug policy constellations: A Habermasian approach for understanding English drug policy. *International Journal of Drug Policy, 57*, 61–71.

Stohr, M., Makin, D., Stanton, D., Hemmens, C., Willits, D., Lovrich, N., … & Wu, G. (2020). An evolution rather than a revolution: Cannabis legalization implementation from the perspective of the police in Washington state. *Justice Evaluation Journal, 3*(2), 267–293.

Strang, H., Sherman, L. W., Mayo-Wilson, E., Woods, D., & Ariel, B. (2013). *Restorative justice conferencing (RJC) using face-to-face meetings of offenders and victims: Effects on offender recidivism and victim satisfaction: A systematic review*. Oslo: The Campbell Collaboration.

Subica, A. M., Douglas, J. A., Kepple, N. J., Villanueva, S., & Grills, C. T. (2018). The geography of crime and violence surrounding tobacco shops, medical marijuana dispensaries, and off-sale alcohol outlets in a large, urban low-income community of color. *Preventive Medicine, 108*, 8–16. https://doi.org/10.1016/j.ypmed.2017.12.020

Sullum, J. (2015a, August 21). Is cannabis causing more car crashes in Washington? *Reason Magazine Online*. Retrieved from https://reason.com/blog/2015/08/21/is-marijuana-causing-more-car-crashes-in

Sullum, J. (2015b, September 17). Supposedly neutral federal report stacks deck against marijuana legalization. *Forbes Online*. Retrieved from www.forbes.com/sites/jacobsullum/2015/09/17/supposedly-neutral-federal-report-stacks-the-deck-against-marijuana-legalization/

Sullum, J. (2015c). Too much public health. *Reason, 46*(9), 10–11.

Sullum, J. (2016). As fear and intolerance of marijuana declined, so did adolescent use. *Forbes.*

Szalavitz, M. (2015a). Genetics: No more addictive personality. *Nature, 522*, S48–S49. https://doi.org/10.1038/522S48a

Szalavitz, M. (2015b) *Unbroken brain: A revolutionary new way of understanding addiction.* New York: St. Martin's Press.

Szalavitz, M. (2021). *Undoing drugs: The untold story of harm reduction and the future of addiction.* New York: Hachette.

Szalavitz, M., &. Rigg, K. K. (2017). The curious (dis)connection between the opioid epidemic and crime. *Substance Use & Misuse, 52*(14), 1927–1931. https://doi.org/10.1080/10826084.2017.1376685

Ta, M., Greto, L., & Bolt, K. (2019). Trends and Characteristics in Marijuana Use Among Public School Students - King County, Washington, 2004-2016. *MMWR. Morbidity and Mortality Weekly Report, 68*(39), 845–850.

Taylor, A. H. (1967). American confrontation with opium traffic in the Philippines. *Pacific Historical Review, 36*(3), 307–324.

Taylor, S., Buchanan, J., & Ayres, T. (2016). Prohibition, privilege and the drug apartheid: The failure of drug policy reform to address the underlying fallacies of drug prohibition. *Criminology & Criminal Justice, 16*(4), 452–469.

Taylor, I., Walton, P., & Young, J. (1973). *The new criminology: For a social theory of deviance.* Boston, MA: Routledge & Kegan Paul.

Testa, A., Turney, K., Jackson, D. B., & Jaynes, C. M. (2021). Police contact and future orientation from adolescence to young adulthood: Findings from the pathways to desistance study. *Criminology*, 1–28. https://doi.org/10.1111/1745-9125.12297

Thies, C. F. (2012). The relationship between enforcement and the price of marijuana. *Journal of Private Enterprise, 28*(1), 79–90.

Thornberry, T. (1989). Toward and interactional theory of delinquency. *Criminology, 25*, 863–892.

Thornton, M. (1998). The potency of illegal drugs. *Journal of Drug Issues, 28*(3), 525–540.

Thornton, S. (1994). Moral panic, the media and British rave culture. In A. Ross & T. Rose (Eds.), *Microphone fiends: Youth music, youth culture* (pp. 176–192). London: Routledge.

Tonry, M. (1994). Race and the war on drugs. *University of Chicago Legal Forum*, 25–81.

Tonry, M. (2007). Determinants of penal policies. *Crime and Justice, 36*, 1–48.

Tonry, M. (2011). *Punishing race: A continuing American dilemma.* New York: Oxford University Press.

Tonry, M., & Melewski, M. (2008). The malign effects of drug and crime control policies on Black Americans. *Crime and Justice, 37*, 1–44.

Tyler, T. R., & Boeckmann, R. J. (1997). Three strikes and you are out, but why? The psychology of public support for punishing rule breakers. *Law & Society Review, 31*(2), 237–265. https://doi.org/10.2307/3053926

Tyler, T.R., Fagan, J. and Geller, A. (2014). Street Stops and Police Legitimacy. *Journal of Empirical Legal Studies, 11*, 751–785.

Uggen, C., & Inderbitzin, M. (2010). Public criminologies. *Criminology & Public Policy, 9*, 725–749.

United Nations Office on Drugs and Crime. (2019). *World drug report 2019.* Vienna: UNODC.

Unnever, J. D., Cullen, F. T., Mathers, S. A., McClure, T. E., & Allison, M. C. (2009). Racial discrimination and Hirschi's criminological classic: A chapter in the sociology of knowledge. *Justice Quarterly, 26*(3), 377–409.

van Boekel LC, Brouwers EP, van Weeghel J, Garretsen HF. (2013). Stigma among health professionals towards patients with substance use disorders and its consequences for healthcare delivery: systematic review. *Drug and Alcohol Dependence* 131(1–2):23–35.

Vitale, A. (2018). *The end of policing*. New York: Verso Books.

Vitiello, M. (2019). Marijuana legalization, racial disparity, and the hope for reform. *Lewis and Clark Law Review, 23*, 789–821.

Vitiello, M. (2021). The war on drugs: Moral panic and excessive sentences. *Cleveland State Law Review, 69*, 441–485.

Wacquant, L. (2009). *Prisons of poverty*. Minneapolis, MN: University of Minnesota Press.

Wagner, F. A., & Anthony, J. C. (2002). From first drug use to drug dependence: Developmental periods of risk for dependence upon marijuana, cocaine, and alcohol. *Neuropsychopharmacology, 26*(4), 479–488. https://doi.org/10.1016/s0893-133x(01)00367-0

Walker, S. (1980). *Popular justice: A history of American criminal justice*. Oxford: Oxford University Press.

Walsh, A., & Beaver, K. M. (2009). Biosocial criminology. In *Handbook on crime and deviance* (pp. 79–101). Springer, New York, NY.

Walter, B. (2022). *How civil wars start: And how to stop them*. New York: Random House.

Wang, G. S. (2022). Cannabis (marijuana): Acute intoxication. *UpToDate*. www.uptodate.com/contents/cannabis-marijuana-acute-intoxication?search=acute%20cannabis&source=search_result&selectedTitle=1~150&usage_type=default&display_rank=1

Wanke, M., Piejko-Płonka, M., & Deutschmann, M. (2022). Social worlds and symbolic boundaries of cannabis users in Poland. *Drugs: Education, Prevention and Policy*, 1–11. https://doi.org/10.1080/09687637.2022.2046706

Weisburd, D. L., & Piquero, A. (2008). How well do criminologists explain crime? Statistical modeling in published studies. *Crime and Justice, 37*, 453–502.

Wesley, J. J., & Murray, K. (2021). To market or demarket? Public-sector branding of cannabis in Canada. *Administration & Society, 53*(7), 1078–1105. https://doi.org/10.1177/0095399721991129

Western, B. (2006). *Punishment and inequality in America*. New York: Russell Sage Foundation.

Western B. & Pettit B. (2010). Incarceration and social inequality. *Daedalus, 139*(3), 8–19. Available at: www.amacad.org/sites/default/files/daedalus/downloads/Su2010_On-Mass-Incarceration.

Wheeldon, J. (2009). Finding common ground: Restorative justice and its theoretical construction (s). *Contemporary Justice Review, 12*(1), 91–100.

Wheeldon, J. (2015). Ontology, epistemology, and irony: Richard Rorty and re-imagining pragmatic criminology. *Theoretical Criminology, 19*(3), 396–415.

Wheeldon, J. (Ed.). (2021). *Visual criminology: From history and methods to critique and policy translation*. London: Routledge.

Wheeldon, J., & Heidt, J. (2007). Bridging the gap: A pragmatic approach to understanding critical criminologies and policy influence. *Critical Criminology, 15*(4), 313–325.

Wheeldon, J., & Heidt, J. (2012). Contesting evidence through a comparative research program (or understanding and implementing criminal justice reform in an era of dumb on crime). *International Journal of Criminology and Sociological Theory, 5*(2), 922–935.

Wheeldon, J., & Heidt, J. (2022). Cannabis criminology: Inequality, coercion, and illusions of reform. *Drugs: Education, Prevention and Policy*. https://doi.org/10.1080/09687637.2022.2081531

Wheeldon, J., Heidt, J., & Dooley, B. (2014). The troubles with unification: Debating assumptions, methods, and expertise in criminology. *Journal of Theoretical and Philosophical Criminology, 6*(2), 111–128.

White, M.A. & Burns, N.R. (2022). How to read a paper on the short-term impairing effects of cannabis: A selective and critical review of the literature. *Drug Science, Policy and Law*. doi:10.1177/20503245221119046

Williams III, F. P., & McShane, M. D. (2010). *Criminological theory* (5th ed.). Upper Saddle River, NJ: Prentice Hall.

Williams, J., & Bretteville-Jensen, A. L. (2014). Does liberalizing cannabis laws increase cannabis use? *Journal of Health Economics, 36*, 20–32.

Williams, S. (2019a, November 10). Amid shortages, black-market marijuana is thriving in Canada. *The Motley Fool*. Retrieved from www.fool.com/investing/2018/11/10/amid-shortages-black-market-marijuana-is-thriving.aspx

Williams, S. (2019b, February 9). Canada's black market to control 71% of marijuana sales in 2019. *The Motley Fool*. Retrieved from www.fool.com/investing/2019/02/09/canadas-black-market-to-control-71-of-marijuana-sa.aspx

Wilson, J.Q. (1975). *Thinking about crime*. New York: Basic Books.

Wilson, J. Q., & Herrnstein, R. J. (1985). *Crime and human nature*. New York: Simon & Schuster.

Wogen, J., & Restrepo, M. T. (2020). Human rights, stigma, and substance use. *Health and Human Rights, 22*(1), 51–60.

Young, J. (2011). *The criminological imagination*. Malden, MA: Polity Press.

Young, J. (1971). *The drugtakers*. London: Paladin.

Yücel, M., Solowij, N., Respondek, C., Whittle, S., Fornito, A., Pantelis, C., & Lubman, D. I. (2008). Regional brain abnormalities associated with long-term heavy cannabis use. *Arch Gen Psychiatry*, 65(6), 694–701.

Zakrzewski, W., Wheeler, A. P., & Thompson, A. J. (2020). Cannabis in the capital: Exploring the spatial association between medical marijuana dispensaries and crime. *Journal of Crime and Justice, 43*(1), 1–15. https://doi.org/10.1080/0735648X.2019.1582351

Zimring, F. (2007). *The great American crime decline*. New York: Oxford University Press.

Zimmer, L., & Morgan, J. P. (1997). *Marijuana myths, marijuana facts: A review of the scientific evidence*. New York: Lindesmith Center.

Zinberg, N., & Robertson, J. (1972). *Drugs and the public*. New York: Simon and Shuster.

# INDEX

*Note*: Page numbers in *italics* indicate figures and in **bold** indicate tables on the corresponding pages.

Made in the USA
Middletown, DE
28 August 2024

59947345R00102